BIG GAME HUNTING IN THE HIMALAYAS AND TIBET

BIG GAME HUNTING IN THE HIMALAYAS AND TIBET

MAJOR G. BURRARD

GYAN

Published by

Gyan Publishing House
5, Ansari Road
Daryaganj, New Delhi-110002
Phone: 011-47034999, 9811692060
E-mail: books@gyanbooks.com

Distribution Network
gyanbooks.com
India, USA, Canada, UK, Australia

ISBN: 978-93-6780-118-5 (PB)

First Published, 1925

2nd Impression 2024

Printed at: Gyan Press, Delhi.

BIG GAME HUNTING IN THE HIMALAYAS AND TIBET
Author: MAJOR G. BURRARD

A HUGE MASSIF IN THE GREAT HIMALAYAN RANGE.

The peak in the centre is Sri Kanta, 20,120 feet, and the river bed lies at an altitude of 8,000 feet. Thus the photograph shows 12,000 feet of cliff and slope.

BIG GAME HUNTING IN THE HIMALAYAS AND TIBET

BY

MAJOR G. BURRARD, D.S.O., R.F.A. (RETIRED)

AUTHOR OF "NOTES ON SPORTING RIFLES"

WITH SECTIONS BY

COL. A. G. ARBUTHNOT, C.M.G., D.S.O., R.A.;
W. B. COTTON, I.C.S.; COL. G. H. EVANS, C.B.E., C.I.E.;
SIR OTWAY WHEELER-CUFFE, BART., AND F. C. LOWIS

HERBERT JENKINS LIMITED
3 YORK STREET ST. JAMES'S
LONDON S.W.1 ✠ MCMXXV

To

P. N.

INTRODUCTION

SO many books dealing with the hunting of Big Game have been published in recent years that an addition to their number may seem to be superfluous. My reason for making such an addition is twofold. First, because relatively few books have appeared during the last twenty years which are solely devoted to the Himalayas and Tibet; secondly, because none of these, to my knowledge, contains any precise information which is likely to help the sportsman in his desire to find game by striking off the beaten track. For years past Kashmir has been regarded as the only possible hunting ground by at least eighty per cent. of those who wished to shoot in the Himalayas. A few venturesome spirits yearly wandered into the ranges immediately behind the principal hill stations, but still fewer ever penetrated far. As a rule they hardly hoped for anything more than an odd gooral or two, an occasional barking deer, and if they were very lucky a thar or serow. Black bear and panther have always been easily obtained. At the present time the cost of a shooting trip in Kashmir can become so excessive as to debar the ordinary government official, soldier or civilian, from attempting any but the shortest expeditions. It is undoubtedly true that the old hand will be able to keep his expenses within reasonable limits, but such ability is only to be acquired after experience, and experience may be too dear to buy. The result is that many sportsmen who feel the call of the hills are unable to respond. To all such in particular I would dedicate this book, for I sincerely feel that it may help them and give them confidence to try new ground where they will obtain excellent sport at a comparatively moderate cost. Once they have gained knowledge and experience elsewhere they can visit the shooting grounds of Kashmir and will then find that they will be better able to cope with the problem of costs and prices.

I believe that the geographical distributions of Himalayan and Tibetan game which I have suggested in this book strike a new note, and I also believe that such distributions are accurate. All the maps were drawn before the first Everest Expedition, and the reports brought back by the members of the Expedition completely confirmed the boundaries which I had fixed for the Tibetan Antelope and Gazelle and the *Ovis Ammon Hodgsoni*.

I would like to express my very real gratitude to Colonel A. G. Arbuthnot, C.M.G., D.S.O., R.A., for his ready and spontaneous help in contributing his excellent chapters on Ibex, Markhor, Oorial and Kashmir Stag. There is no greater authority or more experienced or successful shikari.

Mr. W. B. Cotton's chapter on the Leopard was really intended to deal with that animal from the point of view of the sportsman of the Plains of India. But the leopard, or panther, is so ubiquitous throughout the

Himalayas that I have been glad of an excuse for including Mr. Cotton's contribution, which in my opinion is the most able and brilliant exposition on the art of shooting leopard by sitting up which has ever been written. Sitting up is an art. This fact is appreciated by few and understood by still fewer. All who may wish to obtain information as to the best means of circumventing these cunning beasts, no matter whether they are thinking of the Plains of India, the Himalayas or even Africa, will be able to read Mr. Cotton's chapter with profit; and I feel convinced that they will then stand a better chance of obtaining success than they did before, no matter how great their experience or knowledge.

I am also most deeply indebted to Sir Otway Wheeler-Cuffe, Bt., Colonel G. H. Evans, C.B.E., C.I.E., and Mr. F. C. Lowis for their interesting and valuable contributions on the Burmese Serow, Burmese Gooral and Takin. All these animals are comparatively little known and few specimens have been obtained by sportsmen. These additions must add very largely to whatever utility this book may have.

Any knowledge which I have acquired of the geography of the Himalayas I owe entirely to many years' intimate association with my father, who served in the Survey of India for nearly forty years, during the last ten of which he held the post of Surveyor-General.

The Himalayas and Tibet probably provide the best stalking ground in the world, and Stalking is the method of hunting almost invariably employed when after Himalayan game. At the same time Still Hunting can be practised usefully and successfully in the thick jungles of the outer and middle ranges when such animals as black bear, sambhur or kakur may form the quarry. To my mind there are few more fascinating forms of sport than Still Hunting, but it is an art which is not often studied in India as carefully as it might be. I have, accordingly, included two chapters on Stalking and Still Hunting which I hope may prove of interest and even help to the novice. The old hunter can skip them without a qualm unless he be of a nature which delights in criticism.

I have purposely refrained from giving many measurements of animals or their heads. Measurements of heads are not of much interest unless the lists are complete, and it would be ridiculous to give a few abbreviated lists when the whole question has been dealt with so thoroughly in Rowland Ward's *Records of Big Game*. I would advise all sportsmen to include a copy of this work in their libraries: it is full of information and interest which never seems to pall.

One final word. If sport in the Himalayas, or anywhere else in the world, is to be enjoyed to its full, the sportsman must be able to converse with his followers and the local inhabitants. If he is tied to an interpreter he will find his trip is neither so interesting nor so successful. Every endeavour, therefore, should be made to learn the language of the country, while even smatterings of some local dialects will at times prove of the greatest possible help and may make just the whole difference in obtaining the most valuable information as to the whereabouts of game or of being left in ignorance.

For many of the native names of animals which I have given I am indebted to that excellent and invaluable publication, *The Indian Field Shikar Book.*

Throughout this book I have emphasised the importance of geography and maps. Excellent maps of the Himalayas may be obtained on payment by application to the Office of the Surveyor-General of India, 13, Wood Street, Calcutta. I would recommend the purchase of two types. The first on a scale of 1/M (1/1,000,000) or 16 miles to an inch, and the second the old Indian Atlas Sheets or the modern Degree Sheets which give every nullah with the greatest accuracy on a scale of 4 miles to the inch.

I cannot end this Introduction without expressing my most cordial and sincerest thanks to my friend Mr. H. T. Sheringham, the Angling Editor of the *Field*, to whose encouragement this book in the first place owes its inception and whose kindly criticism and generous help have ever been most ungrudgingly given throughout the past four years.

G. BURRARD.

WILLOW LODGE,
HUNGERFORD,
BERKS.
January, 1925.

CONTENTS

LIST OF ILLUSTRATIONS

MAPS

BIG GAME HUNTING IN THE HIMALAYAS AND TIBET

CHAPTER I

THE GEOGRAPHY OF THE HIMALAYAS

IN planning any expedition after big game which is to be a success, a knowledge of the general geography of the future hunting grounds is essential. And it will be all to the good if to this general knowledge can be added a thorough understanding of the local topography and the different areas in which the various species of game are to be found. I believe that this applies even more to the Himalayas than to any other part of the world. In more or less virgin country game is bound to be fairly plentiful, but in a country which has been shot over regularly for seventy years men cannot expect the best possible sport if they follow in each other's footsteps year after year. In spite of game laws, nullahs which were once excellent become shot out, and so people complain that there is no game left. The truth of the matter is that the majority of sportsmen either will not or cannot look for hunting grounds slightly off the beaten track. Plenty of such ground still exists. I do not for a moment maintain that nullahs will be found in which no white man has ever shot before; but there are plenty which but few white men have entered for very many years, and these are the places which should be sought.

The reasons for what is undoubtedly a general tendency to keep to the beaten track are two. First, an insufficient knowledge of the geography of the Himalayas and the distribution of the fauna; and second, the almost invariable custom of engaging a shikari at whatever hill station forms the point of departure and of being guided by him.

Let us consider the second of these two reasons first. A hillman from some distant village in Kumaon comes into Almora to make his fortune as a jhampani or coolie. He hears tales of sahibs who pay high wages to men who show them sport, and being more intelligent than the majority of his kind he begins to think. The slopes above his own village abound with gooral, and do not those accursed bears yearly eat up most of his corn? And surely are there not thar on those precipices at the head of the valley but a short march beyond his home? No sahib has been there in his lifetime: if he can but persuade one to come with him now, without doubt his fortune will be made. He haunts the hotels and club and at last obtains a hearing from some sahib who is anxious to try new ground. They set out and the expedition is a great success; delighted with his sport the sahib gives our worthy friend a much coveted suit and an excellent chit. Thus armed he soon gets taken on the next season and again brings his patron to his own home. The sport is still good, and he gets another first-class chit. And so he goes on, varying his beat by taking in some of the neighbouring valleys, until he gets the reputation of a really good shikari. Sahibs are then content to leave the planning of the expedition to him, and frequently make no effort even to follow it out on the map. But as years go by and sahib after sahib is taken to the same ground sport begins to deteriorate, and then the shikari falls back on the well-known routes which are familiar to every hillman in Kumaon and Garhwal, the pilgrim roads to the holy shrines of Jumnotri, Gangotri, Kedarnath and Badrinath. He now trades entirely on his reputation, dismissing with a wave of his hand any suggestions as to striking out a new line, and assuring his patron that he can guarantee good sport. And sport of a kind will probably be had, but the heads will be woefully small. This, however, does not worry the now famous shikari in the least. He declares that they are very big ones.

Such is the typical story of the majority of ordinary Himalayan shikaris. I myself have known quite a few to whom it would apply in almost every detail. Can it be wondered that sport is not what it used to be or what it should be? But without knowledge of geography the sportsman is in the hands of his shikari. That authority really only knows the country round his own village and the principal routes in his province, and there are many others of his kind who share that knowledge with him.

It is only fair to say, however, that the best Kashmir shikaris are different. Their knowledge and experience are far wider and more varied. Without realising it they have acquired a thorough understanding of the geography of their country. At the same time, be it said, they have also mastered very completely the art of running up a bill.

Let us now return to the first reason I gave for failure to leave the beaten track—an insufficient knowledge of the geography of the Himalayas and the distribution of the fauna. If this knowledge is once obtained the sportsman will no longer be dependent on his shikari. He will be able to plan his own expedition away from the beaten track and he will undoubtedly derive infinitely more pleasure from his trip as well as enjoy better sport. Let him take a shikari with him by all means. The man will be very useful in looking after the coolies and generally helping things to go with a swing if that energetic simile can be permitted in regard to dealings with a crowd of Himalayan villagers; but he will be no longer directing the operations; he will be following the superior knowledge and understanding of the white man.

When the hunting-grounds are reached some local goatherd should be engaged to show the best paths and haunts of game. Perfect familiarity with any particular neighbourhood can only be acquired by those whose life is spent in tending herds in the local nullahs. Such men are indispensable, but their sphere of utility does not begin until the goal is almost reached. The selection of the goal should rest with the sportsman, and by studying the geography of the Himalayas a good choice of locality can almost be assured. A certain number of men without doubt do act on the lines I have indicated, and not only are they almost invariably successful, but their trips do not cost them so much as they would if organised by some professional shikari. But the percentage of such independent sportsmen is very,

very small. The remainder hesitate to break out on a line of their own. They may perhaps, and very naturally, declare that their leave is short and their funds limited: they do not want to run the risk of throwing away both on some unprofitable wild-goose chase, and prefer to go to places which are known to harbour game. To such arguments I would answer that they will stand a better chance of getting good heads if they go to places which are not continually harassed by sportsmen; that the joys of hunting are so much keener in grounds of one's own selection than when following what is almost a tourist route; that the natural anxiety as to coming sport will be more than outweighed by the excitement of the explorer. Not that any really virgin ground remains to be discovered in the Himalayas proper—all exploring in that sense of the word has been done many years ago—but there are plenty of good nullahs which have not seen a white man's tent for many a long year.

I have frequently been asked how it is that, if these nullahs are so good, they have not been shot in regularly. There are, I think, two reasons. It may be that many years ago they were shot in regularly and all the good heads in them were killed off, since when they have been deserted and so by happy accident have become practically sanctuaries for game. For the second reason, there is the disinclination of sportsmen to go against the old proverb of the bird in the hand: they will not risk a disappointment. But the risk is well worth while. So I would say: Be bold. Refuse to follow tamely in the footsteps of a generation of predecessors.

I am sure that the risk will be imaginary and the joy very real, and I hope that the following pages may help to convince others. I make no apology for giving this outline of the geographical features of the Himalayas, because, as I have already said, an understanding of the subject will not only help very materially in the actual matter of obtaining sport, but will add very greatly to the interest and pleasure to be derived from any trip. The survey will also make clear the actual distribution of the different species of animals which are to be found in the country.

The accompanying sketch map shows the main mountain systems which go to make up the Himalayas, and some ranges in Tibet. In order to avoid confusion all minor ranges have been omitted, but a dotted line indicates the foot of the Himalayas, and so it can be assumed that the whole area between this dotted line and the plateau of Tibet is entirely composed of mountains of sorts.

The first range to consider is the main axis of the Himalayas or the Great Himalayan Range. This mighty chain runs from the Tsangpo or Brahmaputra in the east, where it culminates in the peak of Namcha Barwa (25,443 feet), in Tibet, to the Indus, in Kashmir, where it ends in the peak of Nanga Parbat (26,620 feet), and is the snowy range of which such a splendid view is obtained from the hill stations of Darjeeling, Naini Tal, Almora, Lansdowne, Mussoorie and Chakrata. The Great Himalayan Range bifurcates in a good many places to throw off minor ranges, and these ranges form the frame for the middle and lower hills which lie

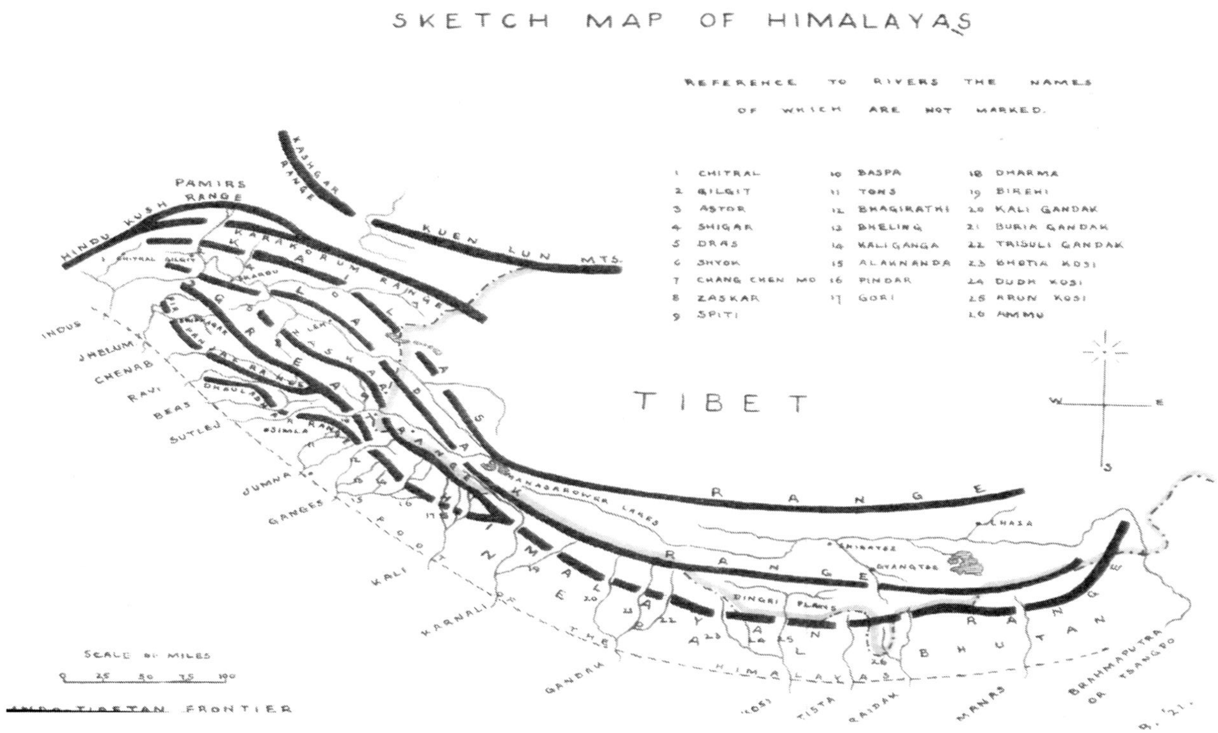
SKETCH MAP OF HIMALAYAS
REFERENCE TO RIVERS THE NAMES OF WHICH ARE NOT MARKED.
1 CHITRAL
2 GILGIT
3 ASTOR
4 SHIGAR
5 DRAS
6 SHYOK
7 CHANG CHEN MO
8 ZASKAR
9 SPITI
10 BASPA
11 TONS
12 BHAGIRATHI
13 BHELING
14 KALIGANGA
15 ALAKNANDA
16 PINDAR
17 GORI
18 DHARMA
19 BIREHI
20 KALI GANDAK
21 BURIA GANDAK
22 TRISULI GANDAK
23 BHOTIA KOSI
24 DUDH KOSI
25 ARUN KOSI
26 AMMU
TIBET
HINDU KUSH RANGE
PAMIRS RANGE
KASHGAR RANGE
KUEN LUN MTS.
KARAKORUM RANGE
INDUS
JHELUM
CHENAB
RAVI
BEAS
SUTLEJ
JUMNA
GANGES
KALI
KARNALI
GANDAK
TISTA
RAIDAK
MANAS
BRAHMAPUTRA OR TSANGPO
MANASAROWER LAKES
LHASA
GYANGTSE
DINGRI PLAINS
SIMLA
BHUTAN
R A N G E
THE HIMALAYAS
W E S
SCALE OF MILES
0 25 50 75 100
INDO-TIBETAN FRONTIER
9. '21.

between the snowy range and the foot of the Himalayas. For our special purposes most of these secondary ranges can be ignored, but there are three bifurcations of the Great Range which are of primary importance to the sportsman.

The first of these occurs near the peak of Nampa in Nepal, and here the Great Himalayan Range throws off a system to the north which forms a range running parallel to the main axis until it ends at the Indus river in Ladak. This range is known as the Zaskar Range, and is marked on the map.

The second tributary range is thrown off to the south side of the main axis near the peak of Bunder Poonch in Tehri-Garhwal and is called the Dhauladhar Range. The third bifurcation of the Great Himalayan Range occurs just north and west of the River Sutlej, and this secondary range also runs south of the main axis and is called the Pir Panjal Range. The map explains the courses of both these ranges. The Pir Panjal is the higher of the two and it carries many snow peaks. The Dhauladhar Range only carries snow peaks at its eastern end, and west of the Sutlej it rapidly decreases in height. The Pir Panjal Range also decreases in height as it goes westwards, but not so rapidly as the Dhauladhar Range. The snows seen from Simla are mostly those of the Dhauladhar and Pir Panjal Ranges, though of course some high peaks on the Great Himalayan and Zaskar Ranges can be seen as well. From Dharmsala it is chiefly the snows of the Pir Panjal that are in evidence, while from Dalhousie only the right of the snowy panorama is composed of Pir Panjal peaks, on the left being the Great Himalayan heights which can be seen over the top of the diminishing Pir Panjal Range.

Beyond the Great Himalayan and Zaskar Ranges and approximately parallel to them runs the Ladak Range, and beyond this again is the Kailas Range. Both these systems lie in Tibet for the greater parts of their lengths.

The Hindu Kush and Karakorum Ranges form the extreme northern boundaries of Indian territory and lie to the north of the western portion of the Kailas Range.

All the different ranges mentioned above are very clearly marked on the latest 1/2M (32 miles to the inch) and 1/4M (64 miles to the inch) maps published by the Survey of India. The old Indian Atlas Sheets and modern Degree Sheets which are on a much larger scale, namely 4 miles to the inch, give too much detail for an easy study of main geographical features, but they are invaluable for planning routes, etc. The main snowy ranges can, however, be followed on them roughly by studying the general lines of the glaciers, which are marked white. East of the Dhauladhar Range there is no system which carries any glaciers to the south of the main axis, and so when a glacier is reached (as one travels from the foothills to the snows) anywhere in this region, one knows at once that it belongs to the Great Himalayan Range.

All these various mountain systems hold different kinds of game, and consequently it is obvious that if we want to hunt some species which lives on the Zaskar Range, for instance, we must first cross the Great Hima-

The Southern Approach to a Pass over the Zaskar Range.
Photographed from an altitude of 15,000 feet.

layan Range in order to get to it; while if we want to search for some animal which inhabits the Ladak Range to the west of Nepal we shall have first to cross both the Great Himalayan and Zaskar Ranges, while if we are starting on this particular trip from somewhere in the Punjab we may have to cross the Dhauladhar and Pir Panjal Ranges as well.

Now ranges may be crossed in two ways: either by climbing over them, in which case the lowest col, or pass, in any particular locality is selected, or else by following up the bed of some river which rises beyond the range we want to cross, and which has cut a gorge through the mountains all ready for us. A high pass is always a serious obstacle to any shooting expedition, particularly early in the season when the snow may be so deep that it will be impossible for loaded coolies to cross it. By following up river gorges all high passes are avoided, and generally speaking this is much the best plan to adopt, although if the river winds about a lot the distance may be doubled, or even trebled. In such a case it frequently pays to leave the river and make a short cut over some intervening spur, provided the pass is not too high or difficult. In the foothills where the altitudes are low this is the usual course adopted, but when it comes to crossing the Great Himalayan Range it will invariably be better, if possible, to select a route by some river which rises beyond it. This may not always be practicable. In Kashmir, for instance, no river rises north of the main axis, and consequently a crossing must be made by the Zoji La (11,300 feet), which is the lowest point in the Great

Himalayan Range (with the exception of river gorges), and is really the only easy pass across it.

The same principle applies to the crossing of the Zaskar and Ladak Ranges, but there are fewer rivers rising to the north of these systems than to the north of the Great Himalayan Range, and consequently the selection of such routes is strictly limited. Fortunately the passes across the Zaskar and Ladak Ranges are very much easier than those across the main axis. This is because the Great Himalayan Range is composed of granite, the hardest of all rocks, which withstands the ravages of the elements and consequently is not worn away into slopes, but retains almost for ever its original formations of steep cliffs. The Zaskar and Ladak Ranges, on the other hand, consist of various kinds of tumbled shales, and so here steep cliffs are the exception and gentle slopes the rule.

Another reason for the different nature of the passes is the snowfall. The Great Himalayan Range bears the main brunt of the monsoon which comes up from the south and west, and comparatively few of the snow-laden clouds are left to pass over to deposit their burden on the Zaskar and Ladak systems. The result is that the snowfall on the main axis is infinitely heavier than on those mountains which lie behind it, and consequently while the average snow line on the Great Himalayan Range is about 15,000 feet, it is as high as 19,000 feet in the Zaskar and Ladak Ranges. The majority of passes over the two latter systems are about 17,000 feet. On the Great Himalayan Range this would be well above the limit of perpetual snow, which would add greatly to the travellers' difficulties, but on the Zaskar and Ladak Ranges it would be clear of snow except early in the season.

Rivers which Rise North of the Ladak Range

Let us now examine the various courses of the rivers of the Himalayas and see how they can help us to get to the shooting grounds. Three rivers rise beyond the Ladak Range, and cut through or round all mountains to the south of this system. They are the Indus, Sutlej and Tsangpo or Brahmaputra. The last can be dismissed at once on account of the extreme length of its course, quite apart from the fact that the difficulties of passing through various savage tribes would be insuperable for an ordinary sporting expedition. There are, in fact, at present only two white men who have ever accomplished the journey: Colonel Bailey and Major Morshead. The Indus is almost equally useless through all the lower part of its course for identical reasons. Indeed, in this case no white man has as yet succeeded in following the river right up from the plains of India. In its upper course both it and several of its tributaries provide most useful routes in various districts. But for the purpose of crossing any great mountain system it is really of little help.

The Sutlej, on the other hand, is a most useful river and its bed makes an ideal route right through the Dhauladhar, Great Himalayan, Zaskar and Ladak Ranges. Many years ago the Government of India realised its utility and built the Hindustan-Tibet road along it from Simla to the Tibetan frontier. This road is the greatest boon to any sportsman who wishes to shoot in the surrounding districts, more especially as bungalows and rest-houses have been built at every stage.

The River Karnali, rising between the Zaskar and Ladak Ranges

The Karnali rises on the southern slopes of the Ladak Range behind the Zaskar Range. Its course is then parallel to the latter mountain system and it cuts through the main axis of the Himalayas just east of the Zaskar Range bifurcation. Consequently it will be seen that although the Karnali actually rises to the north of the Zaskar Range it does not create a passage through it but only through the Great Himalayan Range. The country between the Zaskar and Ladak Ranges near the upper course of the Karnali consists of the open flat plains which are the usual feature of Western Tibet, and the river has cut a small canyon through these plains. The Karnali enters Nepal near the shrine of Kojarnath and nothing is known of its course until it emerges from Nepal into the plains of India, where it is named the Gogra.

Rivers which Rise North of the Great Himalayan Range

Let us now consider those rivers which rise north of the main axis of the Himalayas, and whose gorges provide a passage through the Great Range. In addition to those which have already been mentioned there are fourteen. Taking them in order from west to east, they are as follows :

1. *Bhagirathi.* This is one of the main feeders of the Ganges. It rises in the Zaskar Range (where it is known as the Jadhganga) in Tehri Garhwal, and cuts right through the main axis below Gangotri between the peaks of Bunder Poonch and Sri Kanta. There is a good pilgrim road along it as far as Gangotri, and there are three passes across the Zaskar Range at its head. The Thaga La (nearly 18,000 feet): Jelukhaga or Tsang Tsok La (17,500 feet): a high and difficult pass beyond the camping ground of Jadhaphu on the way to the Mana Glacier which is well over 18,000 feet.

N.B.—It should be noted that " La " is the Tibetan word meaning a pass, and that " Khaga " is the Hindi word.

2. *Alaknanda.* This is the other main feeder of the Hardwar Ganges. It cuts through the main range below the village of Josimath. Above this place it consists of two branches, the Vishnu Ganga and the Dhauli Ganga. The former passes the shrine of Badrinath, and the pass across the Zaskar Range at its head is the Mana La (17,890 feet). The Dhauli Ganga rises above the village of Niti at the foot of the famous Niti Pass (16,500 feet), which is one of the easiest routes across the Zaskar Range. East of the Niti La there is the Chor Hoti Pass, which leads to the more difficult Chota Hoti and Bara Hoti Passes, both nearly 18,000 feet.

There is a good pilgrim and trade road along the Alaknanda as far as Josimath; and it continues up both the Vishnu and Dhauli branches, but it is not quite so good beyond the bifurcation.

3. *Gori*. One of the three rivers which make up the Kali or Sarju. It rises in the Zaskar Range in Kumaon above the village of Milam and cuts through the Great Himalayan Range east of Nanda Devi (25,645 feet), the highest peak in actual British territory. There is a good road as far as Milam, and beyond this village there is a regular trade route across the Zaskar Range into Tibet. It is difficult to understand why this route is such a favourite, as it entails the crossing of three high passes. The first of these after leaving Milam is the Untadhura Pass (17,500 feet). After this comes the Kangri Pass, which is nearly 18,000 feet, and then the Kangri Bingri (18,300 feet) must be crossed before the Zaskar Range has finally been left behind.

4. *Dharma*. The middle of the three Kali affluents. It rises in the Zaskar Range at the foot of the Dharma La (18,000 feet), which is not a difficult pass by any means. The road up the Dharma is not quite so good as those up the more popular pilgrim routes, but it is quite fair.

5. *Kali*. The eastern affluent and the main stream. It rises in the Zaskar Range at the Lipu Lek La (16,750 feet), which is the easiest of all passes across this range. There is a good pilgrim and trade route the whole way up the course of the river, and the obstacles are so slight that pilgrims frequently cross the Lipu Lek Pass in mid-winter on their way to the Holy Lakes of Manasarowar and the sacred peak of Kailas.

6. *Birehi*. The great tributary of the Karnali. Its entire course lies in Nepal and the sole geographical information about it is derived from the report of an

A halt on the Summit of a Pass over the Zaskar Range, 17,500 feet.

Indian explorer who travelled up it in 1873. There is certain to be at least one pass across the Ladak Range at its head.

7. *Kali Gandak.* There are three Gandaks, all of which cut through the main axis and which then unite and emerge from Nepal as one river. Very little is known of their courses as they all lie wholly within Nepal. The Kali Gandak rises at the Photu Pass (15,080 feet), which is an exceptionally low pass across the Ladak Range.

8. *Buria Gandak.* This branch of the Gandak rises near the No Pass (16,600 feet), which is a pass across the Ladak Range.

9. *Trisuli Gandak.* Even less is known of this branch than of the other two. In 1865 an Indian explorer followed it up nearly to its source and did not find the road difficult. There is undoubtedly a pass across the Ladak Range at its head.

10. *Bhotia Kosi.* Like the Gandak, the Kosi has three main branches, but the middle one, the Dudh Kosi, does not cut through the Great Himalayan Range, although it rises slightly in rear of the main crest line. The pass at its head is the Pangula La (20,000 feet) which is probably the highest pass in the Himalayas, and one of the most difficult. This is a pass across a spur of the main range, and not across the Ladak Range. In the same way the Bhotia Kosi does not rise in the Ladak Range proper, although its source is situated 35 miles north of the actual crest-zone of the main axis. The Bhotia Kosi is of importance because east of this river basin the country between the Ladak and Great

Himalayan Ranges changes its nature. From the basin of the Karnali to that of the Bhotia Kosi it is entirely mountainous, but directly the Bhotia Kosi basin is left the country opens out into flat plains.

Accordingly the pass at the head of the Bhotia Kosi, although not actually across the Ladak Range, is across a mountain system beyond which lies country similar in features to that which is found only to the north of the Ladak Range farther west. This pass is the Thanglang Pass and its height is 18,460 feet.

We are indebted for our knowledge of the course of the Bhotia Kosi to another Indian explorer who travelled up it in 1871. The gorge is very precipitous and the road very difficult.

11. *Arun Kosi.* This great river rises in the open plains between the Ladak and Great Himalayan Ranges which have been described before and which are called the Tingri Maidan (or plain). It cuts through the main axis just east of Mount Everest. The average height of the Tingri Maidan is about 15,000 feet, and there are undoubtedly many passes from it across the Ladak Range. But, as has already been pointed out, here the features of the country are identical on both sides of the Ladak Range.

12. *Tista.* The basin of this river is Sikkim. It probably has the heaviest annual rainfall of all the Himalayan rivers, because it is situated at the head of the Bay of Bengal and so gets the full benefit of the monsoon. Further, there are here no lesser Himalayan ranges of any prominence to break its force. The Tista rises in the rear of the Himalayan crest-zone, but not

in the trough behind the Great Range. But here again the country between the main axis and the Ladak Range consists of open plains, and the upper basin of the Tista is *comparatively* flat. The river rises at Lake Tso Lhama, and there are several passes across to the basins of the Arun Kosi and Tsangpo.

13. *Raidak.* This river lies entirely in Bhutan and nothing is known of its course.

14. *Manas.* Little, if any, more is known of the Manas. In 1838 Captain Pemberton traversed Bhutan from west to east and discovered that there were several passes leading from Tibet into the basin of the Manas.

Rivers which Rise on the Southern Side of the Great Himalayan Range and cut through the Pir Panjal Range

1. *Jhelum.* This, the Hydaspes of the Greeks, is one of the most important rivers in the Himalayas from the sportsman's point of view, for the basin of the Jhelum is Kashmir. The valleys of the various tributaries of the Jhelum provide routes through Kashmir towards many different shooting grounds. At the head of the Jhelum's tributary, the Sind river, is the Zoji La, the easiest pass across the main axis of the Great Himalayan Range. The height of this pass is only 11,300 feet, but since it is on the main axis the snowfall is heavy; it is, however, generally open for coolies in March, and can be crossed by ponies from May to December.

At the head of the Kishenganga tributary of the Jhelum is another pass over the main axis, the Burzil Pass (13,500 feet). Although not high, this pass should be treated seriously, as it has a bad name for avalanches. It is seldom clear of snow for more than two months in the year, but there are rest-houses along the route. North of the Burzil Pass the country between the Great Himalayan and Ladak Ranges is not mountainous as in other parts but consists of an elevated plateau, the Plains of Deosai, the average height of which is about 13,000 feet. In the summer there is a route across these plains and the Ladak Range down to Skardo, the chief town of Baltistan, which is situated on the River Indus.

2. *Chenab.* The Acesines of the Greeks. This river has two chief upper streams, the Chandra and the Bhaga, which rise on opposite sides of the road to the Baralacha Pass (16,047 feet), which is a pass over the Great Himalayan Range. The ascent on both sides of this pass is comparatively gradual, and consequently the chief difficulty is the snowfall, which is usually very heavy. The Chenab cuts through the Pir Panjal Range in Kishtwar.

Rivers which Rise on the Southern Side of the Pir Panjal Range and cut through the Dhauladhar Range

1. *Ravi.* This is the smallest of the five rivers of the Punjab, and was known to the Greeks as the Hyaraotes. It has its source in a remarkable mountain basin formed by a bend in the Dhauladhar Range towards the Pir Panjal Range. This basin is sixty miles in circumference and makes the little state of Bara Bangahal. The gorge by which the Ravi leaves Bara

Bangahal may, without exaggeration, be described as almost inaccessible: it appears to have been scooped out of the solid rock, and its sides are perpendicular. The passes into this extraordinary basin are easy over the Dhauladhar Range, but those over the Pir Panjal Range are difficult.

On leaving Bara Bangahal the Ravi flows through the valley and state of Chamba.

2. *Beas.* The Thyphasis of the Greeks, the basin of this river is Kulu. It rises at the foot of the Rohtang Pass (13,500 feet), which is a pass across the Pir Panjal Range, and it cuts through the Dhauladhar Range at Largi by a precipitous defile, up which there is no road. There are two passes across the Dhauladhar Range west of the Beas, the Bubu Pass (10,000 feet) and the Dulchi Pass (6,000 feet). The former is the favourite as it is very easy, and there is a saving of two marches, but as a rule it is only open from May to November on account of snow. East of the Beas there are two passes over the Dhauladhar Range from the Sutlej valley, the best of which is the Jaloari Pass (10,000 feet).

Rivers which Rise on the Southern Side of the Great Himalayan Range east of the Dhauladhar Bifurcation

1. *Jumna.* This river is too well known to need much description. It rises above the shrine of Jumnotri at the peak of Bunder Poonch just at the place where the Dhauladhar Range breaks off from the main axis, and it leaves the Himalayas west of Mussoorie.

2. *Bheling.* A tributary of the Bhagirathi which rises south of the peak of Jaonli above the village of Gunge. It joins the Bhagirathi at Tehri.

3. *Kaliganga or Mandakini.* An important tributary of the Alaknanda which joins its parent river on the right bank at Rudrprayag. The Mandakini drains the southern slopes of the peaks of Kedarnath and Badrinath, and its source is situated near the shrine of Kedarnath. There is a good pilgrim road up to the shrine of Kedarnath.

4. *Pindar.* Another tributary of the Alaknanda which joins it on the left bank at Karnprayag. There is a good road right along this river to its source at the Pindari Glacier, with forest bungalows at every stage out from Almora. The trip to the Pindari Glacier is almost a tourist route.

5. *Ammu.* This is a tributary of the Raidak which drains the Chumbi Valley just east of Sikkim. The Chumbi Valley is the only place where the Tibetan frontier crosses to the south of the Great Himalayan Range.

The rivers tabulated above are only a few of many which rise on the southern slopes of the main Himalayan axis. All the larger rivers, such as the Alaknanda, have many small tributaries which frequently unite one with another before joining the main stream: but each one of these small tributaries has created a valley or nullah of its own, and consequently all are worth the consideration of the sportsman who is anxious to leave the beaten track. I have only given a few in order to indicate the type of river which should be sought for on the map. It may be safely assumed that all rivers which rise anywhere on the main Himalayan axis have their origin in glaciers.

Some other Himalayan Rivers which are of Peculiar Interest to Sportsmen (arranged in Alphabetical Order)

Astor. A tributary of the Indus which joins that river on its left bank below Bunji. The Astor rises on the north side of the Burzil Pass which was described in the summary of the Jhelum, and flows along the northern side of the Great Himalayan Range. Its valley forms the route to Gilgit and other excellent shooting grounds.

Baspa. This is a tributary of the Sutlej. It rises in the bifurcation of the Great Himalayan and Dhauladhar Ranges and its valley separates these two systems for the whole of its length until the river joins the Sutlej at Kilba, where there is an excellent forest bungalow. At the head of the Baspa Valley there is the Nela Pass into the Bhagirathi Valley. The altitude of this pass is nearly 17,000 feet, and it is not usually open before the end of May. The valley of the Baspa is mostly broad and flat with steep cliffs on either side, and it has been described as the most beautiful valley in the Himalayas outside Kashmir.

Chitral. This river is a branch of the Kabul River, which in its turn is a tributary of the Indus. The fort of Chitral is situated on the Chitral River which rises in the Hindu Kush Range.

Dras. Another tributary of the Indus which rises on the north side of the Great Himalayan Range near the Zoji La, and it forms the route to Ladak and also to Baltistan before the shorter route to that province over the Deosai Plains is open.

Gilgit. This is an important tributary of the Indus which joins it on the right bank above Bunji. The town of Gilgit is situated on this river near the junction of its two principal feeders, the Hunza and the Yasin. The Hunza rises on the south face of the Hindu Kush-Karakorum system, and there are two passes across this range at its head which lead to the Pamirs. These passes are the Kilik and the Mintaka, both about 15,600 feet, and they are seldom, if ever, clear of snow, owing to the lower level of the snow-line on account of the comparatively high altitude. The Hunza River cuts through the Kailas Range just at its beginning.

The Yasin branch of the Gilgit River rises in the Hindu Kush Range near Darkot, where Lieutenant Hayward was murdered in 1870. There is a track to Chitral up the valley of the Yasin.

Shigar. There are two Shigar Rivers, and both are tributaries of the Indus. The South Shigar is an affluent of the Dras, which has been mentioned above. The North Shigar joins the Indus on its right bank near Skardo, the capital of Baltistan. It rises on the southern slopes of the Karakorum Range and cuts through the Kailas Range. Askole, the most northerly village in Baltistan, and the favourite starting-point for mountaineering expeditions into the Karakorum, is situated on the Shigar River.

The Northern Approach to a Pass over the Zaskar Range.
Photographed from 15,500 feet.

Shyok. Yet another tributary of the Indus which rises in the Karakorum Range, and, cutting through the Kailas Range, joins the Indus on its right bank some way above Skardo. The famous Karakorum Pass (18,550 feet) is situated at the head of the Shyok. This is a pass across the Karakorum Range and is the regular caravan route to Yarkand. The slopes are easy, the only difficulty being the altitude. The snowfall is here light, because this country is so protected from the monsoon by all the different mountain systems to the south and east. The Shyok receives one feeder which is of great importance to sportsmen, the Chang Chen Mo, which flows between the Karakorum and Kailas Ranges.

Spiti. This river, which drains a large area behind the Great Himalayan Range, is the principal tributary of the Sutlej. It has two main troughs which are separated by a spur of the Zaskar Range. The basin of the Spiti, which gives its name to that province, is surrounded by mountains, and except for the channel of the river can only be entered by passes across these mountains.

Tons. A tributary of the Jumna which has a longer course than the parent stream. It has two main feeders, the Tons and the Pabur, both of which rise on the southern slopes of the Dhauladhar Range near the Borasu and Borendo Passes respectively. These are passes across the Dhauladhar Range into the valley of the Baspa. There are several other passes across this part of the Dhauladhar which lie at the heads of other feeders of the Tons. None of these passes are easy on account of the heavy winter snowfall.

Zaskar. This river rises on the northern slopes of the Great Himalayan Range near the Baralacha Pass and joins the Indus on its left bank near Leh. Its valley forms the route from the valley of the Chenab to Ladak.

I have now finished my sketch of the geography of the Himalayas. I expect the majority of my readers will skip it, at any rate at first, but let me again urge the importance of studying this long chapter closely. The trouble will be amply repaid, and, once the geographical distribution of the various species of game is thoroughly understood, much time will be saved, and shooting trips can be planned with greater confidence of success.

It will have been noticed that I have made no allusion to any political boundaries and restrictions otherwise than mentioning the fact that the courses of rivers in Nepal and Bhutan have not been properly explored. It is to be hoped that in future years Tibet will be thrown open to the sportsman, at any rate to a greater degree than it is at present. The political boundary between India and Tibet is clearly marked on the sketch map, but in the description of the country I have only dealt with geographical boundaries and ignored any political difficulties which may lie in the way at the present time.

CHAPTER II

STALKING

STALKING is the art of: (*a*) sighting an animal from a considerable distance; and (*b*) then getting so close to it without being observed that a shot can be obtained. Almost all wild game which are hunted by stalking are provided by Nature with three senses which are exceptionally developed and acute, as their very existence depends on the exercise of these faculties, namely: eyesight, hearing, smell. In stalking an animal it is accordingly necessary to avoid (1) being seen, (2) being heard, and (3) being smelt.

The sight of all antelope, gazelle, deer, sheep and goats, which are the species of game most commonly stalked, is wonderfully good, but it is not backed up by education and training as is that of human beings. They are frequently unable to distinguish a human at a glance unless he betrays himself. This is not surprising. Wild animals have no illustrated books with pictures which show the various cuts and colours of clothes worn by different men: nor have they any Anthropological Gardens which they can visit in order to study all sorts and conditions of humans at their leisure. In fact, wild animals are handicapped by lack of knowledge, and they have to rely more on instinct. It is a common thing for a deer to walk up to within a few yards of a man in wooded country, when the man is in no way hidden behind anything. The man need take but two precautions: he must not emphasise his outline in any way, but take every care to let it merge into some background, and *above all he must keep absolutely still.* The slightest movement will betray him at once. In all forms of hunting this is the most important of all factors which make for success: it is so obvious that every sportsman will agree as to its importance without hesitation. Yet I know of no rule in hunting which is broken more universally and consistently.

Go out into any English country field on a summer evening and scan the parts near the edge of some thick hedge or wood for rabbits. You know well the colour and size and shape of a rabbit, so you start well equipped, yet it is astonishing how you fail to see them. At last you are sure you have made out one: there can be no doubt about it: and then suddenly a distant shot causes a momentary alarm. Immediately the ground becomes covered with scurrying bunnies, and where you at first saw but one you now see fifty. Their movement has betrayed them. And then you wonder why the one you really did make out has not joined in the stampede, and a closer inspection shows that it was not a rabbit at all but a lump of earth.

I remember how once, when I was strolling through an English wood, rifle in hand, I suddenly came on a clearing but twenty yards across, at the far end of which was the trunk of a fallen tree. On this trunk was a brownish lump. I raised the rifle thinking it was a rabbit, but there was no sign of a twitch or move and I began to doubt. Then I realised that it was nothing but a large fungus with some earth on it, and I laughed at the thought of putting a bullet into an old fungus. What a fool I should have looked! I stared again at the inanimate mass. Of course it was a fungus—fancy ever mistaking it for anything else. I turned my head to look round and out of the corner of my eye I saw the fungus jump off the trunk and run away. It was a rabbit after all!

Now here was I on the search for rabbits. I knew exactly what they looked like and was expecting one at every turn. I had had considerable experience of hunting and knew the little habit wild creatures have of keeping absolutely still when they think they are observed. I knew all this and was trained and experienced, and yet that rabbit completely took me in. Is it altogether surprising, therefore, that wild animals which are not expecting men, which do not know exactly in what guise a man will appear, and which have not been trained and educated, fail sometimes to distinguish a hunter who in no way advertises his presence by sudden movements or by silhouetting himself against a different-coloured background?

Here we have the whole secret of how to avoid being seen by game. Make no sudden movements and no pronounced silhouettes.

Naturally the easiest way of carrying out these two great principles is to keep under cover of some natural feature which hides you from your quarry. This is ever the safest way and the best, and it is far preferable to make a long round under cover than to risk a few yards in the open. Sometimes the round under cover is impossible, but when such a way is open it should invariably be selected. Now what constitutes cover? Bushes, a tree trunk, a depression in the ground, a mountain spur, a ridge, the dry (or perhaps wet) bed of a stream, a hillock, a boulder. In short, any natural object sufficiently large and opaque to prevent your being seen. And the larger it is the better, as then your movements need not be so cramped. You should adapt your manner and rate of advance according to the nature of the cover behind which you are hiding. Where you are entirely hidden from view walk upright, as there is no necessity for you to cramp yourself in any way. Also remember that you may be delayed for a long time later waiting for the game to change its position slightly so as to give you a chance of crossing some open space without being observed.

Have you known the long day's patience belly down on frozen drift,
While the head of heads is feeding out of range?

Further, there is always the chance that the game may suddenly move away altogether. Accordingly never waste time, but move quickly when you can do so without undue exertion or risk of detection. If you are walking upright behind some ridge, for example, you can make good time. There is no need to run, as you do not want to get more out of breath than necessary; but step out, since it is far more fatiguing to run or walk fast when advancing in the crouching position which you may have to adopt later on. In other words, when conditions are easy make the most of them;

walk in a natural attitude and do not delay a moment.

When the cover becomes lower you will have to stoop, or even crawl on your hands and knees. Again do not delay, but at the same time do not try and rush matters so as to get hopelessly out of breath, for then you will be unable to hold your rifle steady.

Finally, there may come a time when you will have to cross a bare open space in full view. If the quarry is grazing or moving it may possibly place some natural object between itself and the open space. Watch carefully for such a possibility. If there is none you will have to crawl in the open. This is the very last resource, but you must ever be prepared. The only way is to crawl absolutely flat on your front, and in doing so do not forget that there is a part of your body contained (rather than concealed) in the seat of your trousers. If, however, you are crawling down hill, it is better to move feet first lying on your back, as it will then be far easier to come up at once to a sitting position ready to fire.

I have already emphasised the manner in which movement, especially sudden movement, betrays you to an animal. This maxim must now be more than ever borne in mind. Your progress should be so slow as to be almost imperceptible. Watch a wild beast of prey stalking its quarry and see how slowly it moves : watch a cat stalking a bird. A leopard, perhaps the best stalker of all, will frequently take half an hour to cross a space which the average human hunter would pass in a couple of minutes—and, to his own thinking, slowly at that. If the animal stares in your direction keep perfectly still and try to avoid moving a single muscle. Remember my story of the rabbit. The patience of wild animals is wonderful—they have no ideas of time like men—and it may take ten or fifteen minutes to satisfy one that all is well. During the whole of this time it will probably be subjecting the hunter to a most careful scrutiny, and if he makes a single betraying movement the game is lost. All beginners make the mistake of trying to crawl too fast, and far more game is lost and frightened by this fault than by any other. Of course I am assuming that we have now got to the final stage of our stalk. It is unnecessary to crawl when at a considerable distance, say over a mile, but even then with many species of game no liberties can be taken, and a very slow advance is still of paramount importance, but as soon as cover has once again been reached a spurt can be put on.

We seem, however, to have left our final crawl. Let us continue it. When the quarry has been approached sufficiently close to warrant a shot the utmost precautions should still be taken. Many men scare their game at the last moment through carelessness in getting into a shooting position. Very slow and deliberate movements are now more than ever essential, as one good shot at a stationary animal is worth half a dozen galloping snaps. You will probably be out of breath after your crawl: if so, wait until you are steady once more. Never dawdle, but never try to hurry matters by making quick, sudden movements: there is an infinity of difference between slow, cautious movement and dawdling.

As regards the distance from which the shot should be taken there is no fixed rule. So much depends on the general type of country, the peculiar nature of that particular bit of ground, the accuracy of the rifle used, the size of the animal hunted and the skill of the hunter as a rifle shot. It should, however, be the immutable aim of the sportsman to get as near as he possibly can, and at any rate sufficiently near to make a hit in a vital part a fairly certain proposition. After all, the real skill in stalking is exhibited in the final approach. If rifles could be used with accuracy at 800 yards no skill would be required: the last advance is the most difficult part, and to shirk this last advance by risking a long shot is to admit defeat, for the art of stalking is to approach to within 100 or 150 yards, and this should always be your goal. Sometimes the nature of the ground renders such a close approach quite impossible, but you should never be contented with a shot at 200 yards if it is humanly possible to get within 150.

Do not, however, try to get much nearer than 100 yards. At or beyond this distance an animal will stand for a moment and stare at you, should you betray yourself, in order to make out exactly what you are, just as I stood and stared at that rabbit which I concluded was a fungus. But if they see any sort of movement within about 30 yards of them they will bound away at once and, perhaps, look afterwards. The reason for this is that beasts of prey, such as leopards, both snow and ordinary, spring on their victims from close quarters, and consequently animals are much more suspicious of any kind of movement at fairly close range. But at 100 yards it is different: they know that no leopard could dash on them from such a long way off, and they stop to see what it was that caught their eye.

Such are the precautions which the hunter must take against being seen by the game during the actual stalk, but there are other precautions which should be practised before the stalk is begun or even before the game is sighted. The two main principles are the same: avoid all sudden movements and pronounced silhouettes.

It must always be your endeavour to see the game before it sees you. All wild animals are wonderfully protected by Nature in the matter of pronounced silhouettes. True, they sometimes make the mistake of crossing a sky-line, but when lying down in the open they merge most wonderfully into the surrounding landscape. Of course you will see them at once if they become alarmed and betray their presence by moving away, but after all if you only see them when they start to move away you will not gain very much. Remember that, just as it is difficult for you to spot the animals when they are lying down motionless, so is it equally hard for them to spot you when you are sitting down spying, even when in the open. Consequently, it should be your endeavour to move about as little as possible directly you have reached ground where you think you may see game. Never be in too much of a hurry. Beginners always make this mistake and try to cover large tracks of country in the shortest possible time: doubtless they get splendid exercise, but they see little game. Every minute with your glasses is worth while. Having once reached some vantage spot, sit down and make yourself comfortable and carefully examine every bit of ground with either your field-glasses, or, if the quarry is very small and some of the ground at a considerable distance, with your telescope. Having once really satisfied yourself that there really is no game on the ground before you, move on to the next vantage spot with the comfort that there is no chance of alarming any game on your way thither, and once it is reached repeat the same careful scrutiny of the country.

And your silhouette. First of all never show yourself on the sky-line, as this renders the most pronounced silhouette of all. If you have to cross the crest of a ridge select some spot where there is a mound, stone, bush, boulder or what not, and slowly crawl over, keeping as close to the projection as possible, not forgetting to examine the ground ahead of you carefully after every six inches' advance. There is always a chance of finding an animal just the other side of a ridge, so again let me remind you, move slowly.

But you will frequently be spying from the open, and here let me remark that it is better to cross a ridge and spy from below the sky-line on the further side than to stay with your head appearing over the crest. Having taken up your position in the open you will, of course, be still—at least I hope I have persuaded you to try—but there is still the risk of your showing a pronounced silhouette against the background. In order to avoid this you must have clothes whose colour merges as nearly as possible into the surrounding landscape, the colour depending on the country in which you intend to hunt. I do not believe in having both coat and breeches of the same colour, in fact I think the latter should be somewhat lighter than the coat, while the coat itself might be patched with different shades to advantage, if you are not too particular about your appearance. The whole secret is to avoid anything in the nature of blatant contrast either in colour or shade, and the way to achieve this end is to break up a surface as much as possible after the manner of camouflage artists. Not that I think you need emulate Joseph in his coat of many colours. But I do believe, as said, that it is better to have breeches of a different shade from the coat, and the more variations that can be brought in in the way of shirt, hat, puttees or stockings the better. A white handkerchief should never be used, and do not forget the glint of the sun on your rifle barrel.

I have now tried to tell how you can best elude the eyesight of a wild animal both before and during the stalk, so let us now turn to its next protective sense, hearing.

Wild animals can be classed in three main groups: first, those that live chiefly on the flesh of other species; secondly, those species which provide food for the first class; and thirdly, those that are sufficiently strong to look after themselves, neither preying nor being preyed upon. The first class includes tigers and leopards, in fact all the *felidæ* and beasts of prey. The second class includes all deer, antelope, gazelle, sheep and goats. The third includes elephant, buffalo, rhinoceros and bear. There are exceptions to each of these main classifications, I know, but generally speaking they can be taken as correct. The second class is the one which provides sport for the stalker, and is so well represented in the Himalayas. Now all the animals in both the first two classes live either by killing or by avoiding being killed. It is not surprising, therefore, that their sense of hearing is abnormally acute: the existence of each class is largely dependent upon this sense. In fact the hearing of all wild animals of these two classes is of quite a different type from any human capabilities, being more on a par, as Mr. Cotton emphasises in his chapter on the leopard, with microphones than any ears of men. It is, indeed, well-nigh impossible to move so quietly, that no noise which a wild animal can detect is made. There are, however, certain little weaknesses which all game exhibit, and by studying these weaknesses it is possible to circumvent their miraculous hearing.

First of all, as with movements, animals are far more frightened of sounds which are near by than of those which are some considerable distance away, and for the same reasons. Consequently they will frequently not take much notice of some noise you may happen to make when yet a long way off, although they have heard it clearly. Why is this? Because some kinds of noise can be made by other animals or else occur in the ordinary course of natural events, while other kinds of noise can convey but one meaning—man. If you make one of the latter sorts of noise the game will take alarm and move away at once.

A rustle in the grass, a snapped twig, a swaying branch, the fall of a loosened stone; all these sounds may be made by wild creatures as well as by man, and therefore they do not necessarily mean danger. Any one of them will cause an animal to look up on the alert, and if you are conscious of having made such a noise and are even partially in view, you must at once keep absolutely motionless in whatever position you may happen to have at the moment. The animal will stare hard in your direction for a minute or so, and if it sees no suspicious movement it will be satisfied that the noise was made by a snake, a rat, or any small harmless animal.

In all mountainous or hilly country, and more especially the further Himalayas, stones and rocks are continually falling down the mountain sides under the influence of wind, rain, or melting snow. Game animals are so accustomed to these falling stones that they ignore them, particularly as they invariably loosen some themselves when they move. Consequently it is fairly safe to knock stones down a precipice (although of course it should be avoided if possible), because the game will connect the sound with nature and will not be suspicious.

But a cough, a spoken word, the ring of metal (such as a rifle barrel or boot nail) on stone; noises such as these invariably mean man, and game will at once take the alarm.

An incident which was told to me by Mr. W. B. Cotton provides an excellent example of this. He was after yak in the Kuen Lun Mountains and had managed to get within 150 yards of a good bull. He was accompanied by a Ladaki shikari. In working for a position they loosened some stones, but the yak took absolutely no notice. Just then, however, the shikari happened to draw his long leather Tibetan boot across a stone with a rubbing sound. The noise was very slight, hardly noticeable, but the yak at once got up and moved off.

It is well-nigh impossible for a man to do a stalk without making some sorts of noise, but he should always remember to keep motionless wherever he may be, even if out of sight (for an animal may possibly move on hearing something with a view to investigate), immediately after he is conscious of having made a noise ; and above all he should do his utmost to avoid making those noises which must obviously be connected with man alone.

So much for the sense of hearing. We now come to the sense of smell. With the *felidæ* this sense is not particularly highly developed, but with almost all other animals no sense is more delicate, not even that of hearing. Now scent of any kind is carried by the wind ; without wind there is no scent except at very close quarters, far closer than any relative positions which would be occupied during a stalk. If the wind is blowing, no matter how lightly, from you towards the game the latter will get your scent at well-nigh incredible distances. I am quite certain that the *Ovis Ammon* of Tibet, for instance, can easily scent a man at a distance of a mile even when only a gentle wind is blowing from man to beast, and I would not consider myself immune from risk of detection at three miles. If, however, the wind were blowing from the *Ammon* towards myself there would be no fear of alarming them with my scent at 100 yards. Consequently it will be obvious that in planning any stalk the first point of all which must be considered is the direction of the wind. This part may be described as the strategy of the stalk; the precautions which will subsequently be taken against being either seen or heard are the tactics.

Naturally the most favourable wind from the stalker's point of view is one which blows directly from the game to himself, but frequently it is quite impossible to find a feasible line of advance right into the wind's eye, and it will then be necessary to select one which will lead across the direction of the wind. So long as the wind is blowing across the line between stalker and quarry, all will be well, even if the angle made by the direction of the wind with this line is an acute one; but beware of too acute an angle, as all winds have a common habit of changing their direction a few points, when the acute angle may disappear. In that case the wind will be blowing straight from you to the game, and when this occurs the latter will disappear as well as the acute angle on which you had been relying.

The question of the wind would be a comparatively simple one if the "airts" invariably remained constant in direction, but unfortunately this is just what they very seldom do do, and frequently the very best planned stalk will be spoiled by a sudden veering puff, for one puff is quite enough to give the alarm. It is absolutely impossible to guard against sudden changes, but one can be ever on the watch by testing the direction of the wind every few minutes, as one can thus frequently obtain warning of a coming change and quickly alter the general direction of the stalk. The direction of the wind can be tested by throwing up dust into the air, by tobacco smoke, by moistening a finger and holding it up (the windward side will become cold; this sounds simple but it requires much practice before the direction of the wind can be told thus with any degree of nicety), or by carrying a small linen bag of flour or ashes in the pocket, and taking it out and shaking it; the flour will at once show the line of the wind. This is perhaps the best way of all for beginners, but a sportsman must always use his ingenuity; the seeds of grasses or downs are frequently found at hand and seem intended for the very purpose.

There is no law which governs the vagaries of the wind, but in many places there are certain prevailing winds for the different times of the day. Accordingly, when a new bit of country is reached, the first few days will be well spent in studying the local winds and the habits of the game from afar; information will thus be obtained which will be invaluable later on. If you rush off on a stalk the very first morning you may quite likely scare some good heads from the neighbourhood, while a couple of days' observation would have shown you how to avoid the very blunder with which you frightened the game. It may seem irksome and great waste of time merely to watch and wait, but it will pay in the end a thousand-fold.

In most tropical countries the wind settles down for

the day at about 9 a.m. and blows in some fixed direction until about 4 p.m., when it starts veering about for 15 or 30 minutes before settling down into some other direction for the night, and this is particularly true in the Himalayas. It may die away altogether at about 4 a.m. and gradually rise up a couple of hours later, but it will as likely as not be blowing from a different direction from that which it takes in the day. Then it will begin to change and veer about soon after 9.30 a.m., and settle down again at 10 a.m. This programme cannot, of course, be relied upon, but it will indicate the general changes which are likely to occur during the twenty-four hours. As a rule, in mountainous districts the wind blows up a valley during the day and down it at night, but whenever camp is pitched you should start making mental notes, for there is every chance that the wind will behave in the valley just across the ridge where you hope to get some sport in a manner similar to that in which it is behaving above your camp.

The wind is always more changeable and treacherous among mountains than in open plains, and this is one of the factors which tend to make mountain game so difficult to stalk. There is more cover from view, but the wind is far more uncertain. Every gully may cause some peculiar side-eddy which will perhaps betray you. On very gusty days it is really better to stay in camp, as the side-eddies will then be more in evidence, and sometimes they seem to blow from every direction in turn. On occasions such as these the stalker has no chance, and it is far better to keep quiet in camp than to go out and possibly drive some real good heads off the ground.

In all mountains a stalk may often be spoiled by mists which suddenly roll up and blot out everything, rendering visibility impossible beyond a few yards. These mists are a veritable curse, but they sometimes are ready to help if you only realise it. Let me tell you two little stories which will illustrate my statement.

The scene of the first is laid in Scotland. I was far up the glen with the old stalker, and I was due to return to London on the morrow. There was a good stag moving on the bare hill-side about half a mile within the boundary. His position rendered a stalk impossible. The wind was blowing up the glen, that is, from us to the stag. The stalker suggested sending a ghillie round the head of the glen to frighten the stag further down in our direction. I protested against the idea of driving an animal up wind towards the gun, but just then some flakes of mist drifted away from our side of the glen outwards until they were caught in the centre of the valley and carried up. The stalker pointed to them and I understood. The main wind was blowing up the glen, but on our side there was a cross drift outwards towards the centre. The stag would then be driven across the wind and not down wind as I had thought. The mist told us of the existence of the cross wind, and the stag came right past us.

The second story is of the Himalayas. The monsoon was just about to break and the main river valley was filled with rolling mists. I was camped on a side-spur looking down on the sea of cloud. Then one of my men brought news of a black bear not far below the camp. I set off at once and soon saw the bear. In order to get near enough for a shot I would have to cross an open grassy slope for nearly a hundred yards; there was not a particle of cover, and I found myself on one edge of this slope gazing at the bear beyond. It would see us, I knew, if we attempted to cross, so I waited in case the bear should feed toward us. Suddenly a small puff of mist detached itself from the main cloud and was blown towards us. In a moment we were enveloped. I at once darted across the open space hidden in the mist, and when it had passed on I had reached my objective.

In tropical plains it is of little use to attempt stalking during the heat of the day. Quite apart from the unpleasantness of having the sun beating on your back as you crawl, the heated air, or "mirage," near the ground makes all objects blurred and dancing, and accurate shooting under such conditions is out of the question. It is true that these drawbacks do not apply to the Himalayas, but there is another advantage of stalking only in the mornings and evenings, and this applies to hills and mountains as well as to plains. All animals feed in the early morning and evening, lying down during the heat of the day. When they are feeding they are slowly moving and are thus far more easily seen in the first place than they are when sleeping or lying immobile. Also, when the stalk is begun it will be easier to evade their attention because when they are feeding their thoughts are largely occupied with their food, and they are not so much on the *qui vive*. When they lie up for the day at least one sentinel, usually an old female, is always posted. These sentinels

Entering the Zaskar Range. The last of the Juniper Trees, 11,300 feet.

are most marvellously wary, and they never sleep at their posts. Thus it will be realised that not only is it easier to find game in the first instance during the mornings and evenings, but also that it is easier to stalk it when found. Incidentally it should be noted that the mornings are usually clearer than the evenings.

In the hills and mountains game will sometimes take up positions which are absolutely hopeless from the stalker's point of view. On these occasions it is better to wait until another day when conditions may be more favourable, but if time is very short it may be necessary to adopt desperate measures. Such measures should only be used as a very last resource when there is no hope of success without applying them; they may succeed, but they may just as likely fail. They consist in deliberately disturbing the game in the hope that it will move to some more favourable position. The best way of doing this is by sending a spare man, if one is available, round to some spot where he will either show himself to the game or else give them his scent. In either case the game will move, and if discretion is used in selecting the line the spare man should take, it may frequently occur that the game will move in the right direction. It need hardly be explained that the man should only show himself from a very considerable distance in order to disturb the animals rather than frighten them.

Another possible way of achieving the same result is to get above the animals and roll stones down on to them. They will probably think that the stones are falling in the ordinary course of events and will not be alarmed.

A very last resource is to fire a shot at a spot some way below or above the quarry according to the direction in which you want them to move. If you would prefer them to go uphill fire a shot at some point about fifty yards below them, or if you wish them to shift to the right fire to the left, and so on, always aiming at some spot about fifty yards on the opposite side to the direction in which you want the quarry to go. I have never tried this myself, and regard it as only the very last resource of a desperate sportsman : being such it should never be used unless there is no hope of success in any other way.

One more hint. Remember your shadow. In mountains the shadow cast by an object near the crest line of a ridge is frequently projected far below. A moving shadow is not very likely actually to frighten game, but it will probably put them on the alert and arouse their suspicions.

CHAPTER III

STILL HUNTING

STILL Hunting, put in the fewest words, means slowly wandering through the forest in search of game, and taking a shot when a suitable opportunity presents itself. It sounds as if nothing could be more simple, but as a matter of fact there are few arts which need more practice and experience. It is certainly very easy to wander through the jungle. It is not so very difficult, as you do the wandering, to get into touch with game. You can do it by *hearing* animals as they dash away unseen behind some clump of bushes or in thick undergrowth. The trouble begins when you try to catch glimpses, even fleeting glimpses, of the animals you hear. And it grows to its full dimensions when you make it your endeavour to see an animal *when it is standing still* and before it dashes off in alarm. To do this successfully is the art of the still hunter.

An animal on the move is always more difficult to hit than one standing still, and a *sudden* chance at a running animal is more difficult to bring off satisfactorily than one for which you are prepared. A really good rifle shot can make fairly certain of the latter kind of opportunity at moving game, but even the most brilliant shots will be sorely puzzled by the former. Accordingly it will be realised that the successful still hunter is the one who usually gets a standing shot at his game, or at any rate a running shot for which he is prepared, and who seldom has to depend on an entirely sudden and fleeting opportunity.

Now, how can this be done? All a matter of luck, you say? Not a bit of it. The old hand will bring home a head time after time, while the tyro will never get a shot. No, there is no luck about it, but there is method, and, before the method can be grasped properly, there are certain fundamental principles which must be understood thoroughly.

Suppose four men go out still hunting singly in different directions. The first returns having seen or heard nothing. The second says he heard some beast crash off now and then, but he never actually saw anything. The third saw a stag and got a shot, but missed. He declares that anyone would miss an animal when all they see is a sudden vision of vanishing hindquarters as the brute dashed into the thickest bush. The fourth returns to camp last of all, and he brings in a fine head. Yes, he got an easy standing shot at 30 yards.

The first man saw and heard nothing because he gave all the animals such ample warning of his approach that they went off when still beyond his hearing. The second man did not give so much warning of his advent, and the beasts did not take alarm until the would-be hunter was within ear-shot of them. The third man was even more successful: he gave the alarm, it is true, but not until he was so close to the animal that it was actually within view when it darted off, although he did not see it until it had begun to move. The fourth man, however, did not give the alarm at all. He saw the stag before it saw him, and got an easy standing shot. This is the object of still hunting: to see the game before it has realised your presence.

In the previous chapter I explained that animals become aware of the hunter's presence through (1) their sense of sight, (2) their sense of hearing, and (3) their sense of smell, and accordingly it is necessary to avoid being seen, heard or smelt. Everything I wrote concerning these fundamentals applies equally, and in exactly the same way, to still hunting as it does to stalking, but the conduct of the hunting is slightly different.

Let us first take the question of scent. You do not know where an animal may be lying up, and consequently you must be careful not to advertise your approach by walking down wind. If you do your scent will be carried ahead of you, and all the game will move away long before you reach their hiding-places. Study the local conditions of wind just as you would for stalking, and plan your round through the jungle accordingly, so arranging matters that you never move with the wind actually behind your back. If you wish to make a general direction down wind, as you may have to do in order to complete a round and return to camp, it may be advisable to move in a series of zigzags, thus:

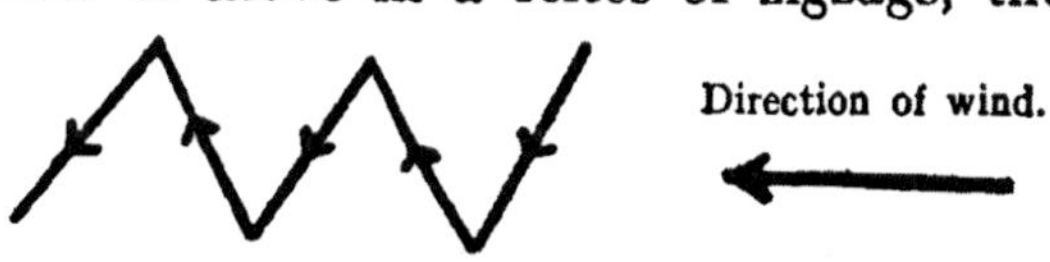

Scent is not carried nearly so far in forests as in open country, the actual danger limit varying with the density of the jungle, but it is ever best to err on the side of caution. A small flour or ash bag, as recommended in the previous chapter, will be found a great help.

Sometimes, when the wind is strong, you may be given warning of some animal's proximity by its smell, but it is not very often that the tables are thus turned, as man's sense of scent is so feeble.

The general direction of the round to be made must be governed by that of the wind, but when this has been determined all else must be subordinated to the other two fundamentals, the arts of being neither seen nor heard.

In order to avoid being heard it is necessary to keep entirely silent and make no noise. I have already shown that there are some noises which alarm animals more than others, but in still hunting *all* noises are nearly equally dangerous. The reason for this is the one which I gave for not attempting a final approach in a stalk nearer than 100 yards. The *felidæ*, the natural enemies of deer and antelope which comprise the usual quarry of the still hunter, attack from close quarters. In the jungle it is impossible to see far on account of the undergrowth, consequently animals are ever on the alert and suspicious of even the faintest rustle in the grass. When still hunting you never know when you may not be within shot of some animal; it is all close-quarters work, both for yourself and the game. You will inevitably pause yourself and listen at the slightest sound: so will the animal you are hunting. And if it takes alarm, as it probably will, it will dash off at once, giving you, at the best, a quick and unexpected snap. Consequently it will be realised that a very slow and careful advance is essential for success, and the utmost care must be taken to avoid making the slightest sound. It is impossible for the ordinary white man to move noiselessly through very thick bush, but he can, at any rate, try. Go slowly and pick out your way; never try to brush your way through dense undergrowth if there is a more open path round; examine the ground carefully before you take a step so as to avoid dry twigs and the like as far as possible; wherever you can, follow jungle tracks or paths, as you will be able to move so much more quietly, and there is every bit as much chance of seeing game. If you have to push your way through dense bush, lift branches past yourself and see that they do not spring back to their original positions after you have done so. Sometimes it is impossible to avoid stepping on some stick or leaf: in such cases a good firm tread with a flat foot is often noiseless when a tip-toe step would be the reverse. If you do happen to make a noise, and at times it is impossible to prevent some dead branch from going off like the crack of a whip, keep still, stock still, dead still. If the noise has attracted an animal it will look in your direction, and if you move you will be seen at once, whereas if you do not move you may perhaps escape detection.

Clothes and footgear make a considerable difference to the noise one makes when moving through the jungle. This is obvious. A hard drill fabric will make a louder scrape against a branch than a soft woollen cloth. But at the same time it should not be forgotten that the soft woollen cloth will tear far more easily among thorns than the drill. A shirt of soft tanned leather is the most soft of all as well as being the most tough. Such shirts can be obtained from various stores in America. They are not so hot in the tropics as one might imagine, but of course the tails should be worn outside the trousers, shorts or breeches, and not tucked in after the fashion of civilisation. But for an Indian hot weather flax shirts are probably the best of any. In India rope soles are usually worn on shooting-boots, and these are very silent and durable, but they slip hopelessly on the slightest patch of wet. Rubber soles are very similar in action but are inclined to draw the feet in great heat, and thick rubber is heavy. Unquestionably the most silent form of footgear of any is a soft mocassin, but this gives no protection against either snakes or thorns.

Mr. Frank Worthington has told me that when hunting in Rhodesia he used to wear soft mocassins with the soles reinforced with sheepskin, the fleece being to the ground on the bottom. These soft soles used to make no noise at all even when treading on dried grass or small leaves, because the fleece yielded to the slightest unevenness on the ground. A dandy brush should be used to brush the soles clean of little twigs, etc. I have found very similar soles most excellent for stalking on the shale slopes of the further Himalayas, but I must admit that I made the discovery by accident. My last pair of native hill shoes were worn completely through, and in desperation I re-soled them with the fresh skin of an *Ovis Ammon* I had just shot. I sewed these soles on with the hair outwards and found them most satisfactory, but they did not wear very well.

After all, however, the best way of all for avoiding noise when in the jungle is to keep still, and this is one of the most important rules of still hunting. Whenever you reach the edge of some open glade or clearing sit down and watch; you will thus be running the smallest risk of detection and will have all your wits available for spotting game. Waiting by some open space is well worth while. You will have an excellent opportunity for a shot should any game appear and you will stand a far better chance of seeing any animals that may be moving in your immediate neighbourhood. It is no use being in a hurry; game is just as likely to be within a few hundred yards of any clearing as ten miles away, and you will be more likely to get a sight of it when you are still and it is on the move than when you are pushing your way through the forest against time in order to reach some supposedly good locality. All beginners make the mistake of going too fast, and the keener the sportsman is the faster he goes. Speed is quite fatal to success. It would not be difficult to make a 10-mile round in three hours in the early morning, but a round of but 2 or 3 miles in the same time would more probably give you a head. It is no use trying to catch the game up on foot; you will never be able to tire it out. Far better to keep quiet and let it come to you. This is the secret of success in still hunting. Let the game come to you.

By sitting down and waiting near open spaces you get every chance of some wandering animal passing within view and shot, and as your hunting instinct is developed you will learn where to wait. The branches stripped of bark where a stag has been rubbing his antlers to get them clean, the droppings, the very tracks themselves—these are all signs which indicate the route usually followed by game. Find out where such routes cross glades, spaces, fire lines, or even jungle paths, and then you will know where to sit and watch during your rounds.

There is another point in favour of sitting and watching: it helps you to elude the third protective sense of your quarry, its sight. I have already emphasised the importance of keeping still in order to avoid being seen: in still hunting this is almost more important than in stalking, if, indeed, there can be comparisons in so vital a matter. So long as an animal is still it may be almost impossible to detect, but let it twitch so much as the tip of one ear, and it is easily distinguished. Its outline merged perfectly into the surrounding scenery and rendered it invisible, until it gave that twitch. Remember —what helps you to distinguish a beast helps the beast to distinguish you. Sit down in front of some bush or tree so as to obtain an uninterrupted view and at the same time avoid making any pronounced silhouette, and having taken your seat, keep still. If there is any game on the move in your immediate neighbourhood you will most likely see it. If nothing stirs in about a quarter of an hour or so, move on to the next clearing and again sit down and wait, always remembering that, so long as you are still, there is every chance of your being neither heard nor seen; but immediately you start moving, no matter how cautiously, the odds are at once turned against you. Of course you must move on, but do not try and break distance or speed records, and spend more of your time waiting than advancing.

Frequently you may see an animal indistinctly: there is just some vague blurr through the bushes, or else the tip of an ear or snout appears through the undergrowth. Avoid risking a shot until you are quite certain of the exact portion of the creature's body at which you are taking aim. Now is the time for patience more than ever: be ready, but do not move a muscle. Sooner or later the animal will change its position, when you may get a shot; or possibly it may gallop off in alarm; always be ready for such an opportunity; the fact that you have seen the animal will have given you warning and you should not be taken by surprise.

Almost all wild animals are afflicted by curiosity, and to a pitch which frequently amounts to their undoing. It is this trait which is the hunter's greatest ally, and which gives him many a chance which he would never otherwise obtain. If an animal is gazing at you through dense undergrowth and is consequently difficult to make out clearly, it is safe to assume that the same undergrowth prevents it from seeing you except as some strange blurr. So long as you keep absolutely still and do not move an eyelid the animal will be unable to make you out. Its natural and insatiable curiosity will make it step out into the open for a clearer inspection, when you will get your shot. But remember, this is a game of patience, and once you have aroused its suspicion as well as its curiosity by some involuntary movement all may be lost. I say "may," because even then there is a chance that curiosity will make the animal halt and look round, just to make quite sure, so to speak, and if that happens you will once more have an opportunity. If any animal has a clear run of several yards before it can disappear into bush it is consequently always preferable to avoid firing immediately it starts off, as the chances are decidedly in favour of its stopping to have a look back before it has taken more than a few strides, and a standing shot is ever preferable to a running shot. If, however, you know that you have given yourself away completely by some blunder it is better to fire when you get a good chance, as in such circumstances the animal's curiosity will probably have been satisfied.

Never forget that curiosity is your quarry's greatest weakness. A sudden whistle will often cause an animal to halt and look round, even after it has been frightened, and this is a tip worth keeping in mind for a moment of despair.

Still hunting, to be successful, must be conducted when the game are on the move, that is during the very early mornings and the evenings. If you go out in the middle of the day all the wild creatures will be lying up resting; it would then be futile to wait at some clearing for one to move into sight. Your only chance would be to find it where it was lying up, and such a chance is too remote even to consider. Long before you had reached its lair you would have given warning by your approach, and even if you did manage by some wonderful good fortune to hit off its favourite resting spot the animal would be certain to see you first, as you would be moving and it would be lying still. Any attempts at still hunting during the heat of the day do more harm than good as they are bound to scare and disturb the game.

In the early mornings and evenings the game are on the feed and are moving about; this means that they will be occupied to a certain extent in grazing, that they will be more easily spotted, and that they will inevitably cross open spaces. At such times, if you exercise care and avoid all noise and unnecessary movement, you will very probably see your quarry before it is aware of your presence, and this is the object of the still hunter. But remember, when you are waiting by some glade do not scratch your nose, or brush away flies, or fan yourself with your hat; you must keep still, really still, and not move. Otherwise you will be seen.

Such are the general principles on which you must go to work, and you must adhere to the principles rather than to any definite rules. For example, if you find that a series of glades lie most suitably on your path during the homeward half of your round, but that in order to take them on your way you will have to walk down wind, do not hesitate, but take the risk. Do not think of zig-zagging through dense scrub, but go by the way of the open glades, only taking care to sit on an edge of the glade so that the rest of the glade is between you and the wind.

I have only attempted to indicate the general lines on which you should set to work; for the rest you must decide for yourself when you leave camp before dawn. Every day will be different, and you must modify your actions according to the immediate surrounding conditions. But of this I am certain: once you have met with success, few forms of hunting will ever appeal to you more strongly, and the excitement will be at boiling point from the moment the camp is lost to view until you come upon it once again. You never know when you may not suddenly get a shot ; the flutter of a startled bird will bring your heart into your mouth with a jump. Everything happens so quickly when once it does happen, and although you are continually straining every nerve on the look out, when you do see an animal, it seems quite unexpected. This is perhaps the greatest charm of all, the excitement which has no break, and the unexpectedness of the expected.

CHAPTER IV

BLACK BEAR (*Ursus Torquatus*)

Native names—*Bhalu, Kala Bhalu, Reech, Kala Reech,* Hindi.

THE Himalayan black bear is one of the most widely distributed game animals of the Himalayas. It is essentially a forest animal by choice, and consequently it is never found above the tree-line, which is generally somewhere about 11,000 feet. The Zaskar and Ladak Ranges are almost barren of vegetation, and consequently black bear will never be found in these systems, though where there was sufficient jungle I have seen them in the trough which lies between the Great Himalayan and Zaskar Ranges. But generally speaking, they are seldom found on the northern slopes of the Great Himalayan Range. They are common in all the lower ranges which lie between the main axis, the Dhauladhar and Pir Panjal Ranges, and are frequently met with in the jungles of the Terai. Westwards their habitat extends to the Hindu Kush Range and eastwards to Assam. In fact they are to be found anywhere in the Himalayas where there is sufficiently thick jungle.

Black bears are not in the least shy of man and choose the neighbourhood of villages as a favourite resort, since they love to feed on the ripening crops and apricot and mulberry trees. They will eat carrion and sometimes kill goats and sheep. A black bear is by no means an antagonist to be despised and should be treated with considerable respect, particularly when wounded.

The Himalayan black bear does not hibernate, and frequently in hard winters large numbers of them come right down into the jungles at the foot of the Himalayas. A few years ago the country round Dehra Dun was infested with black bears in this manner and several were actually shot in cantonments and in the outlying parts of the town itself.

In hunting black bears different tactics must be adopted according to the time of year. To begin with, it must be remembered that like many animals they carry on their main business in life, that is feeding, at night for choice, lying up in shelters during the day. They leave these shelters, which are either caves or patches of dense jungle, when the sun begins to get near the horizon, and return to them soon after 9 a.m. Bears may sometimes be seen during the daytime, but these occasions are the exception rather than the rule, although if the places where they are lying up can be located they can, of course, be driven out at any hour of the day.

In the spring of the year the best plan to adopt is to visit grassy glades in the jungle in the early morning, or to wait at one of these same glades in the evening, taking up a position at about 3.30 p.m. All bears love such clearings, and enjoy rooting for grubs in the luscious grass. It is most interesting to watch them feeding. They will every now and then eat some of the grass, then scratch about apparently in a haphazard fashion,

A Sheltered Camp in the Great Himalayan Range, 9,300 feet.

and then turn over any stones or small boulders there are, and scoop up the grubs which will be exposed. When they have turned over a good-sized stone they usually squat down on their sterns, and sit like a dog, using both their fore-paws for conveying the tit-bits to their mouths. I am less interested in shooting black bears than in any other kind of Himalayan game, but I have never tired of watching them.

When you camp in a nullah after black bear, find out at once from some local goatherd where these glades (or "maidans" (open and level plains) as they will call them, no matter what the inclination to the vertical) are, and get him to show them to you during the daytime. Examine them carefully for tracks and traces of bear, and when you have found one which seems popular, take up your position in cover at about 3.30 p.m. in some spot from which you can command a view of the whole glade. It is always best, if possible, to wait above the glade, so that your scent will be carried over it, as the black bear's sense of smell is highly cultivated. In thick jungle it is most difficult to determine which way the wind will blow; you may think you have avoided it splendidly when just at the critical moment it will change and blow straight from you to the bear; consequently it is always safer to wait well above the spot where you are expecting the bear to appear. Although you are waiting for him he will surprise you when he does come. Bears always seem to come suddenly into view just where you are not looking at the moment. If he does not offer an easy shot or is too far, keep perfectly still and wait.

A movement will probably frighten him as he can both see and hear well. Sooner or later, if you do not betray your presence, you will get a chance, so do not be in too much of a hurry. Remember that the bear has come out on purpose to eat, that grass and grubs cannot really be satisfying to such a big frame, and that he is therefore sure to stay some considerable time unless he is frightened. When you do get a good chance take the neck shot if you are sufficiently close and confident of your shooting; otherwise aim well down just behind the shoulder, or else through the shoulder. Remember that a bear has high withers and long hair, and therefore one is very inclined to aim too high, owing to the false impression of height which is conveyed.

If no bear puts in an appearance when you wait at a glade, visit as many glades as you can as soon after dawn as possible, taking great care to stalk up to each glade, making every allowance for wind, just as if you knew a bear was there. A careless approach will certainly spoil a chance of a shot.

If the glades are thus visited every morning and are sat up over every evening, success is bound to be only a matter of time.

When the crops begin to mature black bears will usually pay attention to them, and in such cases the villagers will be only too anxious to give information. If any bear becomes a regular marauder exactly the same tactics should be employed in visiting his favourite field as have been recommended for the jungle glades.

Still later in the year when the apricots and mulberries begin to ripen, groves of these trees are a sure find for black bears, and here again the same plan should be followed. Bears frequently climb these trees after the fruit. Do not shoot a bear in a tree unless you are absolutely positive at what part you are aiming; it is often very difficult to make out their anatomy when they are in trees. A brother officer of mine was once after black bear in a thick hill mist. He heard one up a mulberry tree, but the mist was so thick that he was unable to make out anything. At last he saw a vague mass against the light when he was right underneath it. The mass moved; he felt sure it was the bear, but when he stepped from under the tree he could see nothing. He accordingly went right under the tree again where he once more dimly made out a moving, dark, indefinite shape. He fired vertically upwards at this lump. The bear—for he was quite right in his conjecture as to the composition of the mass—emitted a fearful yell, and fell to the ground almost on to the head of the bold hunter, and then proceeded to retaliate. G. dodged round the tree to run and then slipped and rolled down the khud with the indignant bear after him. Fortunately G. was brought up by a bush before he had gone far; the bear just missed this bush and not being able to stop, went down fairly headlong to the bottom of the nullah, where it made off. G. recovered his equilibrium and cautiously followed to the bed of the nullah, where he found blood but no bear. He followed the tracks as long as he could, but the blood soon stopped and he lost all traces of the bear and never saw it again. At the beginning of this chapter I said that bears should be treated with respect: I do not consider G.'s treatment of his bear at all respectful, and it might have had serious results. When a bear attacks he usually goes for the head and face, and many Indian woodcutters are disfigured for life, if not killed, by such onslaughts. They frequently disturb bears which are lying up during the day, and the bear, more frightened than angry, at once resents the intrusion.

If you ever are charged by a bear, a shot in the white crescent on its chest will prove instantly fatal.

In 1912 a Sergeant in my battery went for a fortnight's shoot two or three marches out from Mussoorie and captured a young black bear cub alive. He brought it back to Meerut, where it was at once installed as the Subsection pet. It soon became absolutely tame and was a great favourite with the men, some of whom used to spend most of their spare time playing with it. Its appetite was considerable, and loaves of bread used to disappear with amazing swiftness. It was particularly fond of raw eggs, which it used to eat, shell and all, at one mouthful. When it was chained up to a post we sometimes used to place an egg just out of its reach, but it would immediately turn round and scoop in the tit-bit with a hind leg. Lemonade was its favourite drink, and it would swallow half a dozen bottlefuls on end. It always sat up to drink, holding the bottle between its fore-paws. If it was given the bottle without the glass ball being pressed down, it used to get most indignant, and tip the bottle right up vertically in its endeavours to get the sweet liquid. It used to lie in a tank of cold water during the hot weather, but otherwise did not seem to feel the heat very much. It finally died, to everyone's great regret, in the spring of 1914, the cause of its death being unknown, although the farrier declared it was appendicitis brought on by a surfeit of mango stones.

As I have already said, I have personally never derived much amusement from hunting black bear, and have never made any special expedition after them. I have seen a considerable number when after thar and serow. I fancy that most sportsmen will tire of shooting them after having obtained one or two, as they do not tax the hunter's skill to anything like the same extent as do other Himalayan animals. The great thing in their favour is that they are common throughout the lower ranges, and a very few marches will take one to good bear ground. I would, however, never recommend a special trip being made after black bear; they are really not worth it, and are bound to be met with on expeditions after other nobler game, and on the way to and from hunting grounds in the Great Himalayan Range and beyond. However, if you find yourself with ten days' leave in the hot weather and want a breath of cool air, you will have very good fun if you go after black bear. Study the Indian Atlas Sheets (4 miles to the inch) of the country round the hill station from which you intend to start, and follow up to its head any little river which rises at about 6,000 feet within a couple of long marches of the station. Do not take a shikari from the starting-point unless you get a really reliable introduction. Camp at some place such as I have indicated, for choice a spot which people seem to know nothing about, as it is then not so likely to be shot out, and, having arrived, invoke the aid of local talent. You will then have an almost certain chance of success and will have a most enjoyable time.

CHAPTER V

BURRHEL (*Ovis Nahura*)

Native names—*Burrhel, Menda* (rams only), Hindi; *Myalu*, Kulu; *Napu* (ram), *Napu-mo* (ewe), Tibetan.

THE home of the burrhel is Tibet. The species is without doubt distributed all over that great plateau—wherever the altitude is sufficiently high, for the burrhel is never found below the tree-line, and is never known to enter scrub of any sort. The accompanying sketch map shows its distribution as far as the Himalayas are concerned. It will be noticed that its boundary in the direction of India is the Great Himalayan Range, and although it is found on the southern slopes of this range it is never encountered on any of the mountain systems which lie to the south of the main axis, although it occurs almost throughout the huge mountain knot formed by the junction of the Dhauladhar and Great Himalayan Ranges. Burrhel extend along the Great Himalayan Range as far west as the Zaskar River, and they are found in the nullahs surrounding the upper portion of this river, but as the general lie of the country decreases in altitude in the slope towards the valley of the Indus, the limits of the burrhel's wanderings in this direction may be safely assumed to be fixed as marked on the sketch. I am not certain how far their habitat extends along the Karakorum Range to the west. A single head was reported to have been picked up in the valley of the Hunza River near the Mintaka Pass, but I think more evidence is needed before we can assume that burrhel extend right along the Karakorum as far west as this, and that pending the collection of further evidence it will be safer to assume that the boundaries of their distribution are as indicated.

For the purposes of Himalayan sport I would divide burrhel into two classes, Himalayan and Trans-Himalayan. It should be clearly understood that these classes are one and the same species: they have only been so subdivided for the convenience of the sportsman, as they have certain distinctive peculiarities which are of great importance to the hunter of big game, although the scientific differences are nil.

Himalayan burrhel are those which inhabit both slopes of the Great Himalayan Range: Trans-Himalayan burrhel those which make their home in the Zaskar and Ladak Ranges and beyond into Tibet.

Before we consider the peculiarities of these two types let us again turn our attention to the differences in the ranges which form their habitation. I have already mentioned these in the chapter on the geography of the Himalayas, but they are so important that they will bear repetition. First there is the snow-line. On the Great Himalayan Range it occurs on an average at about 15,000 feet, while in the Zaskar and Ladak Ranges it is as high as 19,000 feet. Of course it is not the same everywhere: it will vary on different sides of the same mountain, being higher on the southern slopes than on the northern: the figures given are only a fair average. Next comes the composition of these ranges. The Great Himalayan Range consists of granite, while the Zaskar and Ladak Ranges are made up of different kinds of shales. The third difference has not been emphasised before, and it is that on the Great Himalayan Range the slopes between the tree and snow-lines, which form the home of the Himalayan burrhel, are usually covered with grass which yields excellent grazing. The corresponding slopes in the Zaskar and Ladak Ranges are almost devoid of vegetation, very occasional tufts and patches of coarse grass and moss being all that can be found in addition to the dwarf shrub *boortza*, which is such a common feature in all the barren highlands of Central Asia. This shrub, by the way, is the greatest possible boon to the traveller in these regions which are destitute of wood and other fuel, as it will burn with a cheerful crackling blaze, even when it is quite green: in fact I have often lighted a bush of growing *boortza* when on the march in the early morning and tried to warm myself at the short-lived fire. But however useful *boortza* may be as a fuel I cannot understand it making very satisfying or nutritious food, and it is really about the best food there is in many parts of those inhospitable mountains. That the burrhel live at all is sufficiently wonderful; that they should thrive on this scanty fare is truly marvellous. But thrive they undoubtedly do.

Let us now return to the differences between Himalayan and Trans-Himalayan burrhel. From the foregoing brief descriptions of their respective homes it

DISTRIBUTION OF BURRHEL

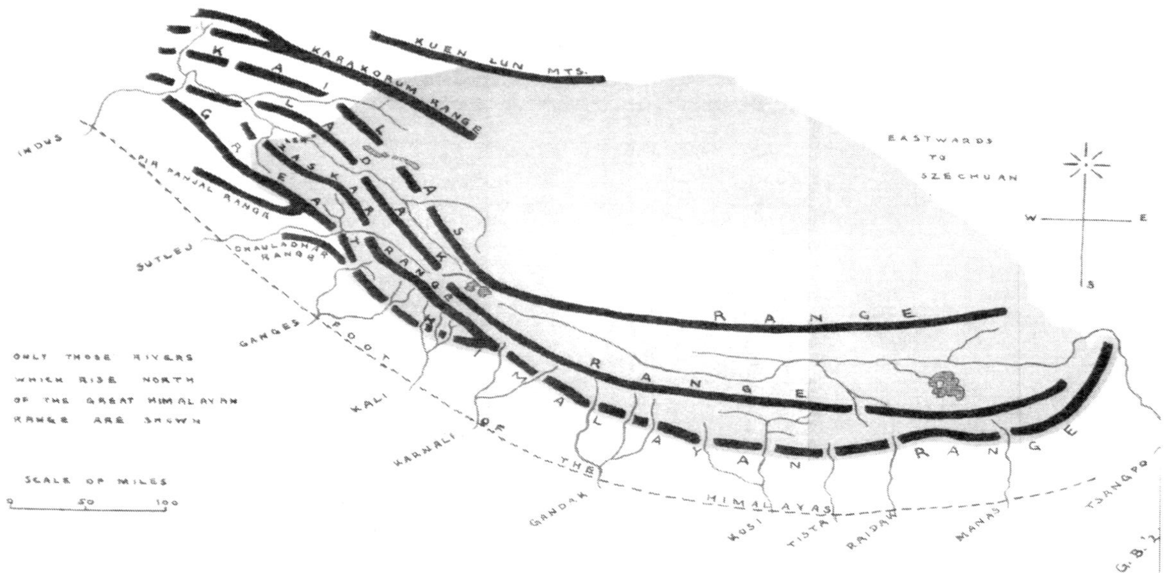

might be imagined that the best heads would undoubtedly come from the Himalayan animals, as the grazing seems so infinitely superior in every way. As a matter of fact just the opposite is the case. Himalayan burrhel never, under any circumstances, carry really decent heads, in fact it is the exception to get even a moderate head, while the heads of the Trans-Himalayan burrhel are very much bigger on the average, and are frequently magnificent. I would consider 23 inches to be almost the limit in size which is likely to be obtained among Himalayan burrhel, while a head of the same size belonging to a Trans-Himalayan burrhel would only just be worth shooting. This difference in the size of heads is extraordinary when it would appear that Himalayan burrhel have everything in their favour. It might be urged that the Great Himalayan Range is nearer to India than the Trans-Himalayan systems, and consequently more easy of access to sportsmen, with the result that these grounds have long ago been shot out as far as good heads are concerned. Also that the Indian population is very much more dense in the main axis of the Himalayas than in the ranges beyond, with the result that there will be more local hunters to kill off the game. But neither of these explanations seems convincing.

When the Indian shikari hunts on his own he kills for the sake of meat rather than for a big head, and ewes and young rams are always found lower down than the old rams. No Indian hunter would ever bother about looking for big heads when tender ewes and lambs were more easily found, and although these men may have decreased the total numbers of burrhel, I do not think that they can fairly be accused of having killed off all the big heads. If the operations of sportsmen were responsible for the absence of good heads among Himalayan burrhel, one might suppose that good heads would have been obtained in the past. But I do not believe this to be the case. I have discussed the matter with several old sportsmen who had shot burrhel in the Great Himalayan Range fifty years ago: I have searched every available old book and record: I have never had direct or indirect evidence of a Himalayan burrhel head of over 25 inches. Surely if big ones had existed there would be some record of them, just as there is of big heads of other species of game and also of burrhel from the Trans-Himalayan districts?

I believe that the real explanation will be found in the fact that the home of the burrhel is Tibet, and that the more nearly their surroundings approximate to the conditions found in Tibet, the more the burrhel thrive in the matter of horns. As has already been pointed out the Great Himalayan Range is composed of granite, which igneous rock probably imparts little horn-building substance to the soil and herbage. The Zaskar and Ladak Ranges are both geographically and geologically mountains of Tibet, the burrhel's natural home, and it is probable that the various shales and stratified rocks which make them up do impart properties to the soil and vegetation which help the animal to its full development. Nature has adapted circumstances to the needs of the creatures which she has condemned to dwell in such desolate regions. Burrhel

Burrhel shot in the Great Himalayan Range at 14,500 feet.

have pushed out their outposts to the main axis of the Himalayas in defiance of Nature, but here the different character of the ground on which they live lacks just that mysterious something which enables them to grow such wonderful horns.

The same phenomenon is found in the mountains in Szechuan, the eastern limits of the burrhel's domain. Here the grassy slopes and general character of the ground seem to be identical with those found on the Great Himalayan Range, and the burrhel also carry small heads. It is true that few sportsmen have shot in this district, but if the burrhel ran large I am sure those few would have found it out. It was only necessary for very few sportsmen to hunt in the Tian Shan to learn that ibex dwelt there with heads far larger than anyone had ever dreamed of finding in the Himalayas. I see no reason why big burrhel heads should not similarly have been obtained in Szechuan if any existed there. Until the Tibet Frontier Mission of 1904 no white man had shot in the hills in Tibet to the north of Sikkim, yet huge burrhel heads were found at once. Why should they not be found as quickly in Szechuan? As it is, all the heads which have been secured there are very small, and exactly similar to those of Himalayan burrhel. I am convinced that the explanation is that they will only attain real grandeur in country which is similar in every respect to the home for which Nature intended them.

Burrhel heads are often described as being particularly difficult to judge. I do not agree with this generally accepted statement. The horns of every kind of animal when met with for the first time are most deceptive, and for some mysterious reason they always seem to be very much larger than they really are. With experience this difficulty is overcome, and the art of judging may be mastered in the case of burrhel horns as easily as with any other species. The important point to remember when judging burrhel heads is that the span must be considered in conjunction with the backward curve of the tips. I have

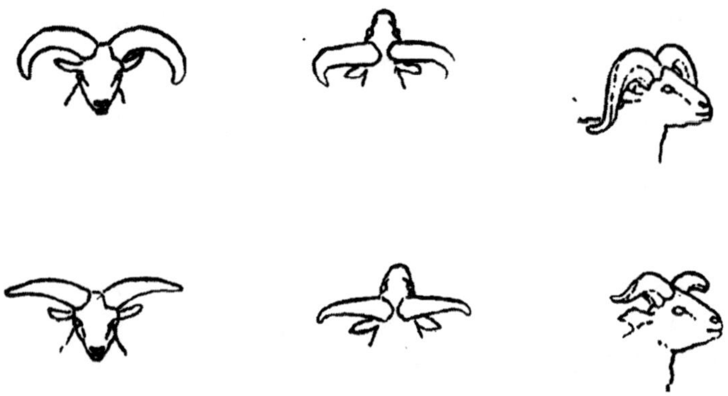

How to judge Burrhel Heads.

The top three sketches show a big ram seen from in front, above and sideways. The bottom three sketches show a small ram seen from identical points of view.

myself been taken in a good many times by a big span, and shot the ram which displayed it to find that the head was only very moderate in size because the tips had no backward curl. A really good ram will always have this curve developed no matter how big the span. If this curve is to be seen the head must be viewed either from the side or from above. When seen from above the spread can be estimated at the same time, but if one is more or less on the same level patience is necessary and one must wait for the ram to turn his head so as to give a chance of viewing the span as well. When rams are sighted they should be carefully studied through a powerful telescope from some considerable distance. Then there is less likelihood of disturbing them than would be the case if the selection of the head were left until just before the shot.

The position of the big ram having been carefully noted, the stalk can either be continued or begun, according to the circumstances; but it should not be forgotten that rams have an exasperating habit of changing places, and so the choice should be verified by a quick look through the glasses before actually firing. I was once very badly deceived by omitting to take this precaution, and shot a small ram in mistake for a much larger one. There is usually time for quick use of the glasses if the stalk has been successfully conducted: if there is not, one must trust to luck. The accompanying rough sketches explain the different positions in which span and backward curve can be respectively seen and judged. With experience I do not think a mistake of more than an inch should ever be made in judging burrhel heads except in very exceptional circumstances. Excellent practice can be obtained by estimating the length of heads on the walls of messes, bungalows and clubs, places where the guesses can be verified.

The burrhel has been frequently described as being the connecting link between the sheep and goats. Its horns are certainly very similar in shape to those of the East Caucasian tur, which is an undoubted goat, but to the unscientific sportsman it would seem an undoubted sheep. It does not possess the strong disagreeable smell which is such a marked characteristic of all wild goats, and its flesh is really excellent, as is that of other wild sheep. It is doubtless somewhat "stockily" built, but so are the shapu and the American big horn.

The horns of the female are small, and they themselves are much smaller than the rams. A full-grown burrhel ram stands about nine hands and weighs about 150 lb. The colour of their summer coats is a definite bluish grey, with white under the belly, on the legs and under the short tail. The rams are marked with a black stripe along the middle of each side and down the front of each leg, and with black marks on the face and chest. All these black markings are wanting in the ewes. Their winter coats are very much lighter in colour and against certain backgrounds they appear almost white. No matter what the season of the year, the burrhel's colour seems to blend most perfectly with the surrounding ground, and there are no animals which are more difficult to pick up, especially when they are lying among some scattered boulders, as is one of their very favourite customs.

The habits of both the Himalayan and Trans-Himalayan burrhel are identical. Like all other wild animals they feed in the early morning and evening, lying up during the day. They are much more easily spotted when feeding than when lying down, and for this reason, if for no other, an early start is always advisable. But one of the greatest charms of burrhel shooting is that they never enter scrub or jungle of any kind, and so are always on view throughout the day. This is a very pleasant trait of the burrhel, as it is most satisfactory to feel that the chances of sport have not been lost for the day if the start has been delayed for some unavoidable reason. One could not have this feeling in all shooting—if the quarry was thar, for instance.

In the spring and summer the old rams generally leave the ewes and collect in bands by themselves, rejoining the ewes in September. These flocks of big rams are usually only met on considerably higher ground than the flocks of ewes and small rams. I have, it is true, on several occasions in June seen mixed flocks of rams and ewes which contained some really fine heads, but in these cases the mature rams always kept somewhat to themselves. If a small flock consisting only of rams is spotted every endeavour should be made to stalk it, as it is pretty certain to consist of the best heads in that particular nullah. This is a golden rule which should never be forgotten.

Burrhel are excellent climbers, and although they are usually found on open slopes they will not hesitate to take to the most precipitous cliffs when alarmed.

Himalayan burrhel, as has already been pointed out, inhabit both sides of the Great Himalayan Range, although they are considerably more numerous on the northern slopes than on the southern. When Dr. T. G. Longstaff was exploring and climbing round Trisul in British Garhwal in 1907 he shot a burrhel on the Sukeram Glacier. In lecturing afterwards to the Alpine Club he mentioned that his Indian shikari did not know what sort of animal it was and called it a thar, while no English sportsmen in Almora had ever heard of burrhel being found in that nullah. The ignorance revealed by this incident testifies to the truth on which I have laid stress: the importance of combining a knowledge of geography with theories of sport. The Sukeram Glacier is a glacier on the southern side of the Great Himalayan Range, and if the geographical distribution of the burrhel had been understood surprise would not have been expressed at finding burrhel just where anyone with properly directed knowledge would expect to find them. They would of course be Himalayan burrhel, and their heads would be small, but they would be burrhel. There is, moreover, another point in this story. The nullah of the Sukeram Glacier is a small tributary nullah of the Pindar Valley, a regular excursion route, yet neither the shikari nor any English sportsman knew what game it contained, which clearly indicates that this nullah had not been shot in for very many years, in spite of the fact that it was only a little more than a week's march out from a popular hill station, while a good road with bungalows along its length led past the very entrance! It only shows how shooting-grounds near at hand may be neglected in the rush to more fashionable districts.

In spite of the smallness of their heads I regard hunting the Himalayan burrhel as one of the pleasantest forms of shooting in the Himalayas, and I think that any beginner in Himalayan shikar could have no better object for a first trip. The shooting-grounds are not very distant—ten good marches should take one into

On the edge of the Tree Line in the Great Himalayan Range, 11,300 feet.

the centre of first-class Himalayan burrhel ground from almost any hill station to the east of the Sutlej—sport is certain, the going is mostly excellent, and not at too high an altitude, for the low snow-line on the main Himalayan axis keeps the burrhel down, and thar may frequently be sought from the same camp. This should be pitched just above the edge of the tree-line in some sheltered hollow, so as to be as near the hunting-grounds as possible. Many of my happiest memories of Himalayan shikar cluster round such camps.

Burrhel always keep above the tree-line, but once in April I saw some on a bare cliff as low as 10,000 feet. This is most exceptional, and as a rule the average height of the shooting-grounds will be about 13,000 feet, which is not too high to be pleasant.

My advice to a beginner who was planning a trip after Himalayan burrhel would be this: Follow any one of the pilgrim roads in Garhwal or Kumaon as far as the Great Himalayan Range, and then try the nullahs in the Great Range. On no account be persuaded by any shikari from one of the hill stations to accept his view as to the best nullahs. Study the map (Indian Atlas sheets, 4 miles to the inch) and select some nullah at the head of which is a glacier. Be sure it is not one to which any hill station shikari has wanted to take you! When you reach the village nearest to this nullah ask for a local man as shikari or guide, and you will be sure of good sport. Of course burrhel may not be always in evidence, and if one small nullah fails, try the next: snow leopards will frequently drive game away from a particular locality for the time being, but you will not have to follow it very far. Such a trip will cost far less than a trip in Kashmir, and will teach you more than would half a dozen shoots conducted by a professional shikari.

The pursuit of the Trans-Himalayan burrhel is a very different pastime. Here, instead of being able to pitch your camp on some pleasant green glade, with an unlimited supply of wood growing in the undergrowth just below, or perhaps round the tents, you will find yourself selecting a site on some barren level surrounded by equally barren hills. The camp fire is no roaring blaze, but just a little crackling flame, *boortza* being the only available fuel, while the very altitude of the camp, even though it is situated at the bottom of the valley so as to be near the stream, is probably considerably higher than the highest level at which you ever stalked burrhel in the Great Himalayan Range. And whereas in the previous year some ten marches sufficed to take you to your camp after Himalayan burrhel, you will now have spent the best part of a fortnight to three weeks on the march before your goal has been reached.

The altitude at which the hunting must be carried on is the greatest difficulty. The snow-line in the Trans-Himalayan regions is so high that there is nothing to keep the burrhel down, and up they go. They seem to delight in getting as high above the sea as possible, and the top of a mountain is their only limit. I have stalked Trans-Himalayan burrhel at well over 18,000 feet, and a friend of mine was once compelled to go over 20,000 feet after them. Climbing at these high altitudes is fatiguing in the extreme, and the going is usually stony and rough. Shooting Trans-Himalayan burrhel entails work which is, as the Russians used to say of hunting in the Caucasus, harder than slavery. But the game is worth the candle, every time; for the heads of Trans-Himalayan burrhel are frequently enormous.

In this country I have only once seen burrhel at a low altitude. It was in May, and my camp was pitched in a ravine in the Zaskar Range at 11,300 feet. I had just had a bath in the evening, and having put on pyjamas was turning into bed, when my men reported some burrhel which had fed their way down on the opposite side of the gorge to the same level as the camp, which was situated several hundred feet above the actual river bed. I at once threw on my poshteen and Gilgit boots and rushed out with the rifle. It was only just light enough to see, but I managed to shoot the ram at about 170 yards, and so provided myself and my following with a very welcome supply of really excellent meat.

I do not think that the Trans-Himalayan burrhel gets nearly as much attention from sportsmen as he deserves. Of course he has not got the horns of the ibex or markhor, and unless the Zaskar Range is actually crossed, his pursuit can rarely be combined with that of any other kind of game. There is, however, to my mind one great point in the sport which is usually overlooked—it offers far more chance of obtaining a record head, or at any rate one approaching the record, than does the pursuit of any other kind of Himalayan game. I firmly believe that 30-inch burrhel heads in

Indian territory are more than a possibility. The actual record burrhel head measures 33¼ inches, and its owner was shot by the late Sir Henry Hayden, F.R.S., in 1904, in Tibet, when he accompanied the Frontier Mission to Lhasa as geologist. Burrhel have been neglected by sportsmen for larger horned animals, with the result that those more popular species have been so thinned that the chance of anything like a record head is now very remote. With burrhel the prospect of that record is decidedly bright. Very few sportsmen have made special trips after burrhel, and what heads have been obtained have mostly been an incidental result of passing through burrhel country on the way to the haunts of *Ovis Ammon*. Consequently I am sure that there is much practically virgin Trans-Himalayan burrhel ground, and the chances of good sport and really good heads in such country are bound to be of the best.

Let us now consider the best way of planning a trip after Trans-Himalayan burrhel, keeping the chances of a record head in view. The Zaskar and Ladak Ranges are our obvious goal, but for political reasons at present the Ladak Range is closed except in Ladak, and here let me say at once that I do not regard Ladak as the place in which to obtain really first-class burrhel heads. It has been so regularly visited by sportsmen for years that the chances of record heads of any animals are small, and also the geological map of the Himalayas shows that there is a large outcrop of granite in Ladak between the Indus and the Pangong Lake, and, as I have said before, I do not believe that granite and big

A broken Snow Bridge in the Zaskar Range. ↑

Altitude 12,300 feet.

The figure of a man can be seen at the junction of the prolongations of the two lines indicated by the arrows. This figure provides a good idea of the scale of the scenery.

burrhel heads go together. In Chang Chen Mo the shales re-occur, but I fancy few sportsmen will devote much time to burrhel there, very rightly preferring to spend the short time at their disposal after Tibetan antelope, an animal which is found nowhere else in Indian territory. South of the Indus shales also break out, but all this country has been very heavily shot over for many, many years.

If we rule out Ladak we see that nowhere can we cross the Zaskar Range without entering Tibet, and so we must be content with shooting in the nullahs of this range. The best Trans-Himalayan burrhel ground, therefore, clearly lies in the Zaskar Range on the line from the basin of the Spiti to Nepal. On the sketch map showing the distribution of burrhel only those rivers which actually rise in the Zaskar Range are marked, and it is obvious that one of these must be selected for following up. At the heads of every one of these rivers there are innumerable smaller nullahs, almost all of which will be found to hold really big burrhel. I have written "almost all," because there is always the possibility that some Indian hunter or else a couple of snow leopards have temporarily driven the burrhel from their usual home.

To give an idea how plentiful burrhel are in these little-known valleys in the Zaskar Range, I need only tell how once, in one short march of 6 miles, I saw five flocks of burrhel from the track which followed the river-bed. On this occasion I believe I was the first white man who had travelled up that particular valley for thirty years: and there are many such valleys in the Zaskar Range. The names of most of them are marked on the Indian Atlas sheets. Make a list of these names and show this list to all your friends. Select the one which no one has ever heard of, and there you will find burrhel, and good heads too.

One word of warning. When you have found your record head do not delay, but stalk it at once. I was once shooting beyond the Zaskar Range, and in the early morning, soon after the start from camp, we spotted a band of six burrhel rams. I examined them carefully through my 40-power telescope. They were huge. Two of them were, I am convinced, over 30 inches. The smallest was 26 inches. They were feeding quietly in a small nullah, and I felt sure they would not leave it. I was after *Ammon* at the time, and was loth to risk disturbing the country with a shot at burrhel. I shot my *Ammon* and returned to look for those big burrhel. I searched for the rest of the available time, but in vain. I have never forgotten that lesson, but I have never again had such a chance so that I might profit by it.

On the whole I do not consider the burrhel a very difficult animal to stalk. This is not because he is a fool in any way, for he is not, and all his senses are as acutely developed as in most other kinds of game animals I know; but because the ground is as a rule in the sportsman's favour. It is easy stalking country, and I have not often missed a stalk. When I have bungled it has been usually on account of a changing wind. But stalking the Trans-Himalayan burrhel is no child's play, and the successful hunter must needs be sound in both wind and limb, for the high altitude will at once find out any flaw in either.

I have treated the burrhel at considerable length, because I have always considered it to be unfairly regarded by sportsmen. It is a fine animal, makes a pretty trophy, and finally that ever present chance of a record head gives it a special place in the sport of the Himalayas. Surely these facts, combined with the pleasure of making a trip into almost virgin country, should make the burrhel one of the most valued game animals of these mighty hills.

CHAPTER VI

GOORAL (*Nemorhædus Goral*)

Native names—*Gooral*, Hindi ; *Pij*, *Pijur*, *Rai*, *Rom*, Kashmir ; *Sah*, Sutlej Valley ; *Gwer*, Kumaon.

THE gooral, a most sporting little beast, is frequently alluded to as the Himalayan chamois. It is certainly about the same size as the chamois, but its horns lack the beautiful and distinctive hook of the real thing, and its habits are not altogether similar. The gooral has little objection to heat, and never moves above the tree-line. It is essentially a species of the Himalayas, and is found in all the ranges which lie to the south of the Great Himalayan Range as well as in the valleys leading off from the southern slopes of that range.

Although gooral occur in the gorges of the rivers which cut through the Great Himalayan Range, they never under any circumstances wander to feeding grounds on the northern slopes of the main axis through these gorges. The main axis forms their hard and fast boundary, and they are not often seen above 8,000 feet, although I once shot one at 9,000 feet. This particular beast had the finest coat I have ever seen on a gooral, much thicker than those usually seen. Southwards they used to extend even to the Siwalik Hills, though

I fancy that few, if any, are now left there: but they still exist on the outermost ranges of the Himalayas. In the west their limit is the basin of the Jhelum, and to the east Assam. Here they merge into different species, the Burmese gooral and the variety discovered by Colonel Bailey when he and Major Morshead ascended the Tsangpo in 1913.

Gooral are not in the least bit shy of man, and frequently live in close proximity to villages: I have on several occasions shot them within a few hundred yards of camps, and have twice missed them from one of the main pilgrim roads.

Although they do not seem to object to heat they certainly dislike the sun, and only come out to feed in the early morning or evening unless the ground is shaded by some higher spur or ridge. In the heat of the day they retire to thick jungle. Like all mountain game they are excellent climbers, and seem to prefer precipitous slopes and khuds which are covered with undergrowth.

In spite of, or perhaps because of, their familiarity with man they are by no means easy to shoot, as they are quick to take heed of the slightest alarm, and a gooral bounding down the khud is an exceedingly difficult mark. Gooral should always be sought on the shady side of a hill or nullah, as they invariably depart to lie up for the day later in the morning and come out to feed earlier in the afternoon when their feeding grounds are in the shade. An afternoon's stroll with the rifle over likely ground is the best method of shooting gooral, and provides the best of fun as well as excellent practice for more serious shikar, when the day's march is done and the camp pitched. I have very seldom had a stalk of any length after gooral, and have generally found them suddenly and had to fire almost at once, frequently when they were just about to move off. If you jump a gooral suddenly, do not fire at once, but wait: it will be almost sure to stop and have a look, thus giving you a better chance.

The great difficulty to be overcome in shooting gooral is distinguishing between the sexes. Both bucks

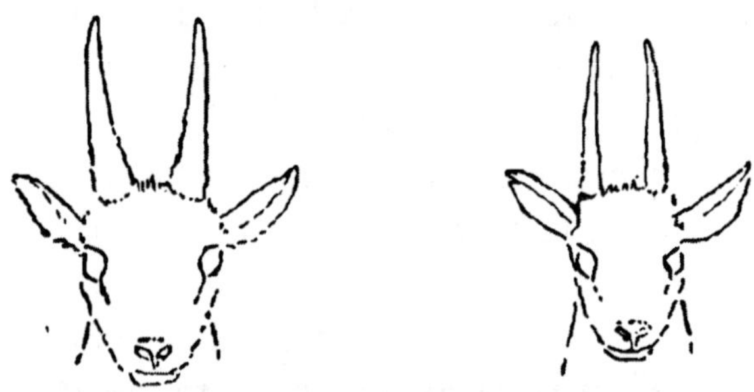

THE DIFFERENCE BETWEEN THE HORNS OF MALE AND FEMALE GOORAL.

The horns of the male (left) are more massive and slightly divergent, while those of the female (right) are slender and parallel or slightly convergent.

and does have horns, and frequently those of the doe are nearly as long as those of a buck, but they are never quite so massive, while apart from being more slender they are parallel or with points slightly convergent; the bucks' horns invariably diverge outwards, and the sketches show the differences. Nevertheless there is often but little time to look, and the horns of the biggest bucks are really very small, and so the difficulty of judging requires years of experience, and even then mistakes are quite likely to occur.

A River Gorge South of the Great Himalayan Range.
Altitude 6,000 feet.

Personally I have always liked gooral meat, although many people do not. It is quite free from any goaty flavour, and is infinitely preferable to village sheep.

Although not worthy of any special expedition being made in its pursuit, the gooral should never be neglected, as it can be usually met with on the march towards the more distant shooting grounds, and so he will not be encroaching on time which might be spent after nobler game.

THE BURMESE GOORAL

By Colonel G. H. Evans, C.B.E., C.I.E.

Burmese—*Taw-Seik* (Jungle-goat)

This fine little animal, so far as my knowledge of it goes, appears to confine itself to suitable localities on some of the higher ranges of hills. It exists in parts of the Arracan, Chin, and Shan Ranges. In time it may be noted in others, for it cannot be said to be definitely " mapped out " yet. I have every reason to believe that it is to be found in certain places in Upper Siam.

My first knowledge of the existence of gooral in Burma was gained in 1889, when I saw quite a number of skulls in the houses of some of the Chin Chiefs in the Northern Chin Hills. Early in the 'nineties I secured a specimen and, suspecting it to be a different animal from the Indian variety, I sent the skull for expert identification. In due course I was informed that the skull was that of a female Himalayan gooral. I was not satisfied, so I asked a friend in India to shoot a gooral and send me the skin and skull. After a long wait I received both; and they satisfied me that there was a considerable difference between the animals.

The next thing was to obtain Burmese specimens, which was no easy matter. Eventually I had the luck to get two, and was able to send the skins and skulls by a friend to the late Prof. Lydekker, of the South Kensington Museum. Later on I received a letter from him and a copy of a note which he had published (*The Zoologist*, March 15, 1905, No. 765: "The Goorals of India and Burma," by R. Lydekker, F.R.S., F.Z.S.). I quote what he reported, as the result of his examination, in this note:

> "In sending these specimens by a friend, he expressed his belief that they indicated an undescribed species, or race. This opinion I am able to endorse, as these skins are certainly very different from those of the typical Himalayan Gooral (*Urotragus Gooral*)."

The late Professor did me the honour of naming this gooral after me, but whether the name remains I know not. "Priority" is to me far less interesting than hunting the animal. Anyway it was many years after my first acquaintance with this splendid little chap that I ever heard of any European suspecting the existence of any other goat-like animal, except the serow.

As a matter of fact very few Europeans have shot one, which is not at all surprising when one considers how seldom anyone has occasion to visit their haunts. I have never found them scattered about the ranges but more or less confined to localities where the hills are rocky and precipitous. The serow, we know, ascends to considerable elevations, but frequently descends and lives at very low elevations. Gooral seem to prefer elevations of 4,000 feet and over. They leave their mountain fastnesses to come and graze during the mornings and evenings. In the day they lie up about the precipices, etc. Occasionally they will lie up out on the hillside even in the open. Serow may be met with on the same grounds, but, generally speaking, gooral show a much more definite preference for precipitous country.

Hunting serow is, for that reason, child's play when compared with the pursuit of gooral. For this game one should be a good cragsman, which I am not. The behaviour of a startled serow on bad ground is alarming, but for real devil-may-care Alpine work commend me to a gooral. The way in which these creatures tear and rush about over perpendiculars where one would not suspect there was foothold for a fly is truly marvellous. I have watched them from the edge of a precipice, while trying to get a shot, and even in such a comparatively safe spot I had no false pride about letting the shikari and gunbearer hang on to me. "Comparatively safe" has different meanings for different people!

A great disadvantage about the shooting is that, owing to the dreadful places to which gooral get, one may shoot two or three before getting a specimen. Human beings simply cannot get at the places, and I hate to see the men trying, when I know that the slightest slip will be fatal, and if it occurs, nothing can save them from being smashed to pieces.

Gooral may be met with singly or in pairs, and occasionally even in small herds.

These animals have a peculiar habit when disturbed. They usually utter a sort of hissing whistle which evidently serves as a warning. The result is that the whistling of one often gives you the chance of seeing others. Like many animals when they have not made out the object of their fear they seem to display impatience. They have an indignant manner of shaking their ears, stamping their feet, and sometimes hissing. The horns are small, faintly ringed, almost smooth, and nearly straight.

Gooral hunting is really very fine sport and one is always certain of a nice cool climate and lovely surroundings. Of course summer is the time to shoot. Any small bore H.V. rifle is good enough. In order to get to gooral haunts it is generally necessary to pass through good game country at lower elevation. Here there may be bison, elephant, sambhur, etc., so it is useful to carry a heavy weapon as well.

CHAPTER VII

IBEX (*Capra Sibirica*)

Native names—*Skin*, Spiti, Ladak, Baltistan; *Keyl*, Kashmir; *Tangrol*, Kulu.

DISTRIBUTION OF HIMALAYAN IBEX

ALTHOUGH the ibex is undoubtedly the best known of all the game animals of the Himalayas, more mistakes have been made in explaining its distribution than in the case of any of its less known friends and relations. In more than one authoritative work it is described as an inhabitant of Tibet, and is mentioned as being found in the neighbourhood of Lhasa. Again it has been repeatedly declared that it is found in " Kumaon as far east as Gangotri " and the sources of the Ganges—quite regardless of the fact that Gangotri is not in the British province of Kumaon at all, but in the protected State of Tehri Garhwal, with the State of British Garhwal in between. It is difficult to understand how these mistakes arose, but I conclude they were made in the course of the collection of hearsay evidence on which some famous scientific naturalists based some of their classification. They provide an excellent example of the errors which can be made through insufficient knowledge of geography and no personal acquaintance of the actual haunts of game. The late General Kinloch, who was always so accurate in all his descriptions of the habitats of animals, never made any such error; nor did the older sportsmen, such as General Markham, and Wilson (Mountaineer), who hunted and shot in the 'forties. The mistakes would accordingly seem to be of a more recent date, and are all the more inexcusable.

The distribution of the ibex, as far as the Himalayas are concerned, is clearly shown on the accompanying sketch. The River Sutlej is its eastern boundary and it is never under any circumstances found on the left bank of this river. Starting from the Sutlej and going westwards, one finds it in the country between the Great Himalayan and Zaskar Ranges, and on both those ranges, but although it is common on the southern side of the main axis it never occurs on the northern slopes of the Zaskar Range. Ibex always live above the tree-line, and extend along both sides of the Pir Panjal Range for some way, but when this system begins to drop towards the gorge of the Chenab they cease, and do not again occur on that range. They inhabit the valley of the Dras and thence to both sides of the western end of the Ladak Range, and northwards to the Kailas and Karakorum systems, and westwards to the Hindu Kush.

The stronghold of the Himalayan ibex is undoubtedly the western end of the Kailas Range in the neighbourhood of Gilgit and Baltistan, and these are the places to go to for the best heads, but the way is long and such an expedition is costly. I am sure that many good heads exist farther east in the Great Himalayan and Zaskar Ranges, in the basins of the Chandra and Bhaga

DISTRIBUTION OF HIMALAYAN IBEX.

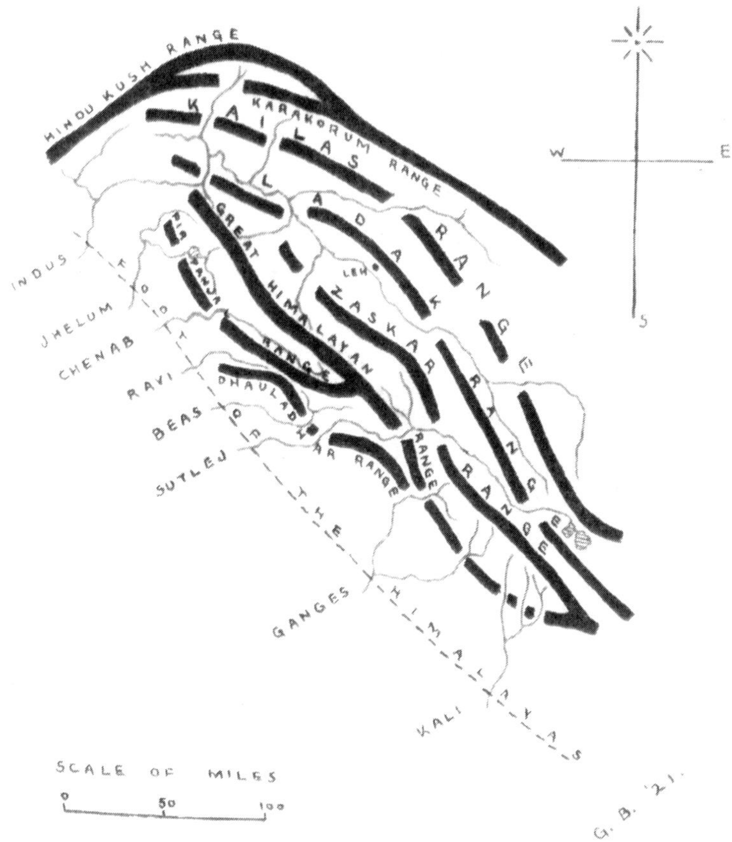

"An outlying boss in an outlying buttress of the main pile."—Kim.

(the two main feeders of the Chenab) and the Spiti Rivers. The grounds on the Great Himalayan Range in Kashmir, such as the Wardwan Valley, have been shot out as far as good heads are concerned. But the nullahs of Lahoul and Spiti are well worth exploring, and there is no reason why heads up to 45 inches, and even more, should not be obtained, particularly in Spiti. Such heads used to be found in these parts, and, as in comparison with Kashmir, all this country has been very lightly shot over, I see no reason why they should not still exist.

The ibex of the Pir Panjal Range as found in Chamba, Bara Bangahal and Kulu have always been small and heads of 37 inches are considered good.

IBEX SHOOTING

By Colonel A. G. Arbuthnot, C.M.G., D.S.O.

(I) *Ibex Country.*

Among the various forms of big game shooting which are open to the soldier, civilian, or traveller in India, the pursuit of the Himalayan ibex and markhor must rank very high, and many true sportsmen will place it before all others. If determination, enterprise, patience, and a quota of skill and nerve, may be accepted as qualities which true sport should demand of the hunter, then the ibex and markhor may challenge any comparison —or if difficulties to be overcome, hardships, risks and excitement, are considered fair measures of sport, the big wild goats of the Himalayas may well claim pride of place. The sportsman who would spend from two to four months on an expedition in the Himalayas and wishes to include ibex and markhor in his bag, will doubtless make Kashmir his first objective. If his purse be limited the sooner he gets to business and leaves the charms and other attributes of Srinagar the better!

Beyond the fair Dal and Wular Lakes, the lovely Sind and Lidar Rivers, beyond that circle of snow peaks that surround the most beautiful Valley of Kashmir, lies a less-known land; a land of rugged beauty where Nature is supreme, life is free, and good sport is the almost certain reward of energy and skill.

South of the above line ibex are getting more scarce, and their horns measure less; but good heads can still be found where the peaks run up to 18,000 or 20,000 feet. In Rupshu and Lahoul, on the borders of Kulu, Chamba and Kishtwar, big ibex can be shot, but they are rare, and must generally be sought for in little-known nullahs that the average shikari passes by.

In Kashmir proper, on the mountains north and east of the valley, in the Wardwan Range, in Suru and Tilel, there are ibex, and good heads too, but they are none too plentiful; the shooting regulations of 1921 were very rightly framed to preserve them.

(II) *Lengths of Horns.*

The horns of the Baltistan, Rondu and Astor ibex run up to 50 inches; any head over 40 inches is a good one, but in these districts nothing under 40 inches should be shot, and the same applies to Ladak.

In Chamba, Pangi and Kulu the horns are perhaps more massive, and 36 inches to 38 inches is a shootable head. Forty-inch heads, however, have been shot in Kulu and Lahoul, and the writer shot a 42-inch on the borders of Chamba in 1908.

To estimate accurately the size of a head before shooting is always difficult, and a novice must at first be dependent on the views of his shikari, who should be held responsible if he advises wrongly. After his first effort, and after much examination of other ibex through glasses and telescope, the novice will soon get a very fair idea of what a shootable ibex looks like. The more complete the curve, the more nearly the points curl round towards three parts of a circle, the longer the horns will prove to be.

Horns that are obviously less than a semicircle are not generally those of a big ibex, except perhaps in the case of the bigger and straighter-horned Central Asian ibex, some of which may occasionally be found in the northern nullahs of Baltistan and Ladak. A head of this description, picked up in 1920 near Arondo, measured 48 inches and was peculiarly straight.

The Kashmir shikaris usually claim that the notches on an ibex horn correspond to his age, a new notch appearing at the base each year. This may very likely be true; the writer has found that in an average ibex fourteen or fifteen notches go to a 40-inch horn, nineteen or twenty to a 45-inch, and so on.

(III) *Routes to Ibex Ground.*

(i) *Baltistan.* Starting from Kashmir, with ibex as chief objective, Baltistan will probably be the best place to make for. From April 1 till about the first week in

July, the longer route will have to be taken, over the Zoji La Pass into Ladak, thence down the left bank of the Indus to Skardo, the chief town of Baltistan, sixteen marches from Srinagar.

The Zoji La is normally an easy pass, open to ponies most of the summer, but a heavy fall of late snow, as happened in 1920, can make it difficult even in May. When clear of snow the road is good throughout and three or four days can be saved by double marches.

The short and direct route to Skardo lies over the Tragbal Pass (above Bandipur on the Wular Lake), up the Gurais Valley, and over the desolate Deosai Plateau, which averages 13,000 feet for over 50 miles. This route is usually open from early July till about September 25, when the first heavy fall of snow closes it for nine months of the year. Skardo can be reached in eight or nine marches from Bandipur, whence pony transport should be obtained.

" Askardo," as the Baltis call their capital, is a large and fertile village set in a broad desert of sand on the left bank of the Indus, nearly opposite its junction with the Shigar River. There is a post and telegraph office, and a few enterprising Indians have some English stores for sale.

From Skardo the sportsman may travel north up the Shigar Valley, famous for the ibex of its nullahs and the apricots of its pretty villages, or west down the Indus, a mighty river even at 8,000 feet, at which level it has carved its hot and sandy bed through the bare mountain masses on either side ; or again, up stream to the east there are ibex in several nullahs on the right bank, and also up the Shyok River, which joins the Indus two marches above Skardo. There are also several good nullahs on the right bank three or four marches above Skardo, some of them belonging to local rajahs who may be willing to exchange permits for 12-bore cartridges.

Shigar Valley. There are ibex in plenty, and good heads are regularly shot in all the nullahs of the Shigar Valley; but it is rather a popular resort, and sometimes disappointing. This was the case in the early part of 1920, when no good heads were shot or seen during April or May.

Four or five marches from Skardo take you to the head of the valley where the river forks; the western branch runs up past Arondo, and the eastern past Braldu Nullah to Askole, "the World's End"; beyond there lie the great glaciers of "K 2," or Mount Godwin Austin, which challenges the claim of Mount Everest to be the highest mountain in the world. Although ibex measuring from 48 inches to 50 inches have been shot quite close to Shigar, it is the Arondo and Braldu Nullahs that are most likely to shelter an exceptional head.

Rondu. Marching west from Skardo down the Indus towards Rondu there are good ibex nullahs on the right bank for four or five marches; some of them are particularly good. Then one reaches markhor ground in Rondu and Haramoosh, and as markhor get more plentiful the ibex seem to get more scarce.

(ii) *Ladak.* The sportsman will not generally visit Ladak especially for ibex, but, when time admits, an expedition to the borders of Tibet after *Ovis Ammon*, and gazelle and antelope, may be combined with a week or so after ibex on the return journey from Leh. There are big ibex in many of the nullahs en route to Leh, and farther north runs the Shyok River where a good head can generally be shot. There are also good ibex and burrhel in Rupshu south of the Leh Road and north-east of Chamba and Lahoul, but this country is difficult and little shot.

(iii) *Astor.* Astor again is chiefly famed for its markhor, but ibex are found in the same nullahs, and run well over 40 inches.

The usual route lies by the Gilgit Road and is described in the chapter on markhor. Astor can also be reached from Rondu over a 16,000-feet pass, open, generally, about July 1.

(iv) *Ibex in other parts.* Excellent sport and good ibex may also be obtained by other routes into the Himalayas, though a big head may not be such a certainty as by the usual but far more expensive Kashmir route.

Chamba. Via Dalhousie, there are ibex on the northern and eastern borders of Chamba State, also in Pangi and Pader, but a 38-inch head in these parts may be considered the equivalent of a 43-inch head in Baltistan.

Kulu. There are several nullahs in Kulu where a decent ibex may be found early in the year, in addition to red bear. Over the Rohtang Pass, or the Kukti Pass from Chamba, one enters Lahoul and Spiti, where there are ibex and burrhel; Kulu can be reached by marching from Simla, or, more directly, via Pathankot and Palumpur to Sultanpur.

Bara Bangahal. North-west of Kulu over the Kali

Hini or "Black Ice" Pass, 17,000 feet, and east of Chamba via the Ravi Gorge, lies the very beautiful little country of Bara Bangahal, whose circle of snow peaks and glaciers provide the sources of the River Ravi. I have no recent information about this most lovely spot, but in 1907 there were several big ibex and plenty of red bear there; I shot a 40-inch ibex and saw some bigger than that. The route via the Ravi Gorge was at that time extremely difficult, and over the Kali Hini was by no means easy. The Thamser Pass, 15,000 feet from Kangra on the south, provides the best approach.

Lahoul, Rupshu, and beyond. The adventurous sportsman with sufficient experience of hill shooting and camping to enable him to dispense with the luxury of a permanent shikari, has a good field for his enterprise in Lahoul, Spiti and Rupshu. With the help of his map and local shikaris he will find good ibex in nullahs little, if ever, shot in, and unknown to the professional shikari. In fact the latter will probably refuse to go, and declare such unknown nullahs are haunted by evil spirits!

(IV) *Habits and Characteristics of Ibex at various times of the year.*

The shooting season for ibex and markhor may be taken as from April to October; few, if any, passes in the Himalayas are open before April, and the majority are closed by the first fall of snow about the end of September. Early in the year ibex are naturally to be found low down below the snow-line, attracted irresistibly by the first few shoots of young grass. The sportsman will be recompensed for his difficulties in crossing passes heavy in snow by finding his game low down; later in the year he will have an easy passage to his hunting-ground, but will have to pitch his camp far up near the head of the nullah, and climb to the crest of the ridge.

In early spring, the time of which varies in different districts, the branch nullahs, beloved of the ibex, are snow-bound and provide but a few twigs for them to eat; the slopes on either side of the main nullah or river, close above the villages, are the first to clear, and as soon as the night frost permits some young grass or herbs to appear, the ibex, if there are any, will be found grazing morning and evening. But it does not necessarily follow that the wary old veteran will condescend to accompany his females and juniors to such low and public resorts!

For example, in Baltistan in 1920, a nullah which has always been one of the best had not a head of 40 inches in it during May. There were plenty of youngsters and females, and several heads of 37 inches or 38 inches, but nothing more.

Searches far up the nullah, beyond the farthest ground free of snow, revealed no living animal bar a wolf that used to come down daily in quest of a young ibex or a village goat. Later in the year, when the favourite ground far up near the head of the nullah was becoming clear of snow, the big ibex appeared from somewhere, and a 43-inch head was shot in August, on the same ground that the writer had shot a 44-inch head in September many years before.

Favourite Ground. By nature the ibex dislikes open grassy downs, and is only found on them when sorely tempted early in the year. He considers them the proper place for the shapu and the village flocks that soon force him to retreat to his fastnesses above.

His favourite abode is high up a side nullah whose precipitous flanks hold small patches of grazing here and there; the herbs and grasses which grow on spurs, and beside a long stony "shute," have a peculiar attraction for him; above are rocky peaks or glaciers, on either side bare and inaccessible rocky ground where safety from the snow leopard or wolf can be quickly gained.

Above his grazing-ground it is a *sine quâ non* that the ibex must have a safe retreat where he can pass his day in peace, with his sentries lying cleverly posted on projecting rocks and ledges, gazing down on all that moves below. After his morning meal he will climb steadily upwards, till his rear is safeguarded by snow and precipice, and his front and flanks secured by those ever watchful sentries, whose eyes are quicker to detect movement than those of almost any other animal.

Here indeed the position of the ibex may well appear to be impregnable. In addition to the protection of those wonderful eyes, the slightest puff of wind from your direction will give him your scent, and you will see your quarry get up, one by one (you had no idea there were so many of them there), and quietly, steadily walk away, springing deliberately from rock to rock, ledge to ledge, out of sight, out of ken, perhaps away to the next nullah for good, or at least for several days!

But the ibex has one weak point in his defence, and

that is, trusting to the natural strength of his selected position, he, or rather she, for the sentries are usually females, seldom looks upwards.

Strength of Herds. Generally speaking, ibex are to be found in herds of from a dozen to forty or fifty, and sometimes even more.

In a small nullah which the map led me to explore in June, 1920, I counted separate herds as follows: (1) seventy-five, chiefly females and young ibex, but with about twelve heads between 30 inches and 40 inches; (2) thirty, comprising all sizes, and including eight heads over 40 inches; I shot the biggest, measuring 45½ inches; (3) twenty, including two heads of about 40 inches; (4) six big ibex, all between 40 inches and 43 inches; these six were generally by themselves, but occasionally joined up with No. 3 party. Similarly the four biggest ibex in No. 2 party nearly always kept together, and occasionally were slightly separated from the remainder.

The reader must not expect that he will always find over 100 ibex in different herds, all within view of his telescope from close beside his tent! the nullah I mention had very seldom been shot in, and was one of the best I have ever been fortunate enough to discover.

In the spring and early summer it will be seen that the old ibex are usually with, or on the outskirts of, herds containing females and young. But later in the year I have usually found the biggest ibex separate, generally from two to six of them together, living a very cautious existence, well away from the herds, and apparently beyond the limits of grass and herbs.

A Shooting Camp at 13,600 feet in the Zaskar Range.

Under these conditions they are deprived of their sentries, and their precautions are increased. They come out later in the evening, and rather earlier in the morning. By day they skilfully place themselves so that all approaches are covered by the eyes of one or other of them. It is a most interesting sight to watch three or four old veterans through a good telescope as they settle themselves for the day.

IN AN IBEX NULLAH

(I) *Preliminary Work.*

Having arrived in your nullah where you hope to find a good ibex, my advice is to be cautious, and, if ibex are spotted, do not be in too great a hurry to shoot. The first few days belong to the field-glasses and telescope; after that you may hope for the rifle to have its turn.

Let us suppose we have reached any typical nullah in Baltistan or Ladak; it is early in the season, say May or early June, and your camp is pitched as far up as snow and a modicum of comfort will permit.

The Local Shikari. At the nearest village to the entrance of the nullah you will have picked up an old man who is introduced to you as the local shikari; be patient with him, for at any rate he knows where the ibex are to be found at different seasons, but his ideas on big and little heads are usually not reliable. Between times he is probably the village poacher, and small blame to him; in his own way he is as good a sportsman as you or I! Above all, take a private opportunity of impressing on him that the somewhat overbearing gentleman who has accompanied you as "burra shikari" will not have any share in the reward which the local man will get when he enables you to shoot the biggest head in the nullah!

Spotting Ibex. Use of Glasses and Telescope. Your first evening you will probably be able to go a mile or so up stream, climb to a suitable vantage point, and spend a couple of hours with glasses and telescope. If you have a second pair for your shikari it will be a great help; the local man too is pleased by an occasional squint through the glasses, but probably sees better without.

Good field-glasses, "sixes" or "eights," and a good stalking-telescope are indispensable. Use your glasses to examine thoroughly all likely ground, dividing it into zones, and going carefully over each zone in turn, time after time; whenever your glass is arrested by a suspicious object that it cannot quite diagnose, take your telescope, rest it on a rock or on your "khud stick," on your hat or your shikari's puggaree, and let it settle the point.

Movement, Colour and Outline. As the evening shadows climb up the mountains it is *movement,* colour and outline that you must train your eye to look for. After you have seen a few ibex, the shape, colour and horns will be impressed on your brain, and any object of the correct colour or outline will at once attract attention. This is so much the case that when looking for and expecting to see ibex, I have several times passed over markhor that were quite visible, but unexpected, and whose portrait was not printed on my brain. Every little patch of grass or herbs must in turn be carefully scanned; if no ibex are visible grazing, then search the rocks and spurs above. Here it will probably be the horns that are most likely to catch the eye, and the telescope must examine every object that may take the peculiar curve of a horn.

The eye that is gifted, or trained by constant practice, to catch movement has, of course, a great advantage; sometimes you will find an ibex lie securely camouflaged on, or under, a grey rock, for nearly an hour, while your glasses pass him over time after time; then a slight turn of his head seems to flash a wireless message to eye and brain; you *felt*, rather than *saw*, something move, and your glasses are swung back at once to examine the area. The curve of the side of that rock is suspicious, and the colouring of the ledge below it is not quite normal.

Fix the spot that your glasses are looking at by naked eye, and then carefully align the telescope on it; now the secret is out! A fine old ibex lies revealed, his massive horns are plainly seen, and you wonder how you failed to see him before!

A further search with the telescope now brings a couple more good heads to light on the rocks near by. Several likely patches of grazing are now in the shade, and half a dozen female ibex suddenly appear some way below; from a stony shute a little farther up the nullah you hear the noise of stones hurtling down to the river-bed; eight or nine ibex, none big, but two fair heads among them, are almost invisibly making their way across, while some babes frolicking on the edge of the shute, cause the disturbance which attracted your attention.

Watching Ibex. Now is the time for you to take stock of the situation; do not be rushed by an over-keen shikari into making a false move that has but a slender chance of success, and if it fails will probably drive your three good ibex right away.

They are a considerable distance away from you, and but an hour and a half of daylight remains. It will take you twenty minutes to reach either of the side nullahs that should provide a hidden line of approach, and then you will have a climb of 1,200 to 1,500 feet to get level or above the ground where the smaller ibex are now grazing, and where you expect the three big fellows to come. That will take you another hour.

Meanwhile you are running many other risks, and the question is whether they are necessary or worth while? If those big ibex remain on their rocks they will see you as you pass along the bottom of the nullah. The wind is still blowing uphill, and will make an approach difficult. You can but make a poor guess at where the ibex mean to travel to during the next hour; it will certainly be better policy to be patient and leave them undisturbed till you know more of their habits, more about the ground, and the vagaries of the wind.

Having drifted into this description of spotting ibex, I propose asking the reader to watch them and follow them for a day, perhaps several days. The first stage of our expedition is accomplished, and we have reached a good nullah, and found at least three good ibex in it.

There is a fascination in watching game through a good telescope that compensates for having to curb our impatience; the information gained will greatly help us to avoid a false move, but at the same time the sportsman must remember that at all times he must be ready to take immediate advantage of a favourable situation, such as when a couple of the biggest ibex separate temporarily from the herd, and lay themselves open to be stalked with wind and cover in our favour and no outlying females to hold up our approach.

Let us now watch our ibex till nightfall. Gradually the youngsters and females work their way downwards, grazing and playing as they go; the three old fellows still remain above, with one faithful young lady standing sentry on a rocky spur close below. The majority have now reached a bit of grazing, and about fifteen can be counted feeding contentedly.

Looking above again, one of the big ibex is seen standing up: he is a grand sight as he gazes fixedly down below, like a statue on a pinnacle of granite. Now he turns his head and reveals the full sweep of his great horns; for many minutes he gazes intently to right, to left, and again below; not a movement, nor a breath of tainted wind will escape him.

Now he is coming down, followed by the other two; now jumping from rock to rock, now walking along what appears to be the face of a cliff, now a short canter down a bit of open ground.

As the light fades the ibex, twenty-two all told, are grazing together about 1,000 feet above the bed of the river. There we will leave them, and unless disturbed by a snow leopard or wolf, you may expect to find them not far away in the morning.

Soon after dawn we make our way up the nullah again, and find a cold frosty wind blowing strong in our faces from the snow peaks above; with this in our favour, we have but the eyes and ears of the ibex to fear, but must try to spot them from as far off as possible.

Taking every chance that offers of a look through the glasses, we succeed in passing some shapu on an open grassy down close above our tents, and farther on eight or nine ibex, females and kids, without disturbing them; but there are still no signs of yesterday's herd.

As we get higher up the nullah the scenery gets bolder; the mountain stream now runs clear as crystal, very different from last night's dull grey torrent, swollen with melted snow. Passing below the slopes where we last saw our ibex grazing, we find their tracks on the sand where they have been to drink.

Cautiously we reach a spur on the left bank whence there is a good view of the upper nullah and several new patches and slopes of likely grazing ground. There are our friends! First a couple catch the eye, then gradually nearly all can be made out, and the three big fellows too!

They have moved a couple of spurs farther up, and are quietly grazing not 600 feet above the river-bed. There is a small nullah this side of them, which should enable us to reach that rock about 200 yards from where they are grazing, unseen and unwinded. It is a fair chance, and with luck should give an easy shot.

In half an hour we have reached our objective, and

with beating hearts peer cautiously round the side of the rock. Not 50 yards away are a couple of small ibex, about 30-inch horns, lying down; then a few females grazing; on the crest of the opposite ridge, about 300 yards off, stands a young female gazing fixedly in our faces! fortunately we blend well with the rocks, and little but the tops of our heads are visible—for a long ten minutes we lie motionless, and the ibex neither moves nor takes her eyes off us.

Meanwhile, scarcely daring to turn even our eyes, we see the three big ibex grazing steadily up the spur, but out of reasonable range. At last the small female decides she has made a mistake, and moves on; but all the other ibex are now between us and the three big fellows. They are crossing over towards our side of the nullah, and we can but watch them gradually make their way towards the rocks above us.

It is now past eight o'clock, and we become aware of an occasional puff of wind coming from below us, instead of the steady cold breeze from above. If we can extricate ourselves without doing harm we shall be lucky; it would be courting disaster to try to follow up our quarry with a changing wind; had we been more sure of their line of retreat we might have done better, but now our best plan will be to get back across the main stream and try to pick up their movements from the opposite side.

From some rocks above the left bank we watch our friends working their way bit by bit up the mountain; now pausing to graze, now climbing; mark well their route, for it will be useful to know it exactly. Here and there a few think they have gone far enough, and lie down, but the three big fellows are still moving on till they have left the last bit of grazing behind them, and have reached the bleak jumble of rocks and snow patches below the peaks that crown the ridge.

At length, at about ten o'clock, they have all settled down. Two of the three big ones are visible; a little below them are three or four females, and a bit farther down to the right about half of the remainder have been marked down, blending almost invisibly with the grey-brown rocks. Now we may leave them and return to breakfast feeling we have done a good first morning's work, gained some very useful information, and left our ibex still unconscious of our intrusion.

We must not, however, take it for granted that they will not move till evening, and it will be best to leave a good man to watch them. It is quite possible that as the sun reaches their present position they will shift to a shadier place.

(II) *Plan of Action—Methods of Approach and Stalking—The Shot.*

Having described a typical day or two of watching ibex, we will now consider the next move. It may take several days to locate any shootable ibex, and several more to watch them, before we feel we know enough to venture on a difficult approach. Three days, however, should generally suffice to tell us whether there is anything fit to shoot in our nullah, and if we cannot find any after three days' hard work, it will be best to clear out and try other ground; but we must not fail to search the difficult higher branches before we quit.

Presuming we have found our ibex, and made up our minds with the help of the telescope as to which of them we mean to shoot, we must sit down and carefully think the matter out. What is now required, to use a military term, peculiarly suitable to the case, is a clear "appreciation of the situation." We must remember that Himalayan stalking is not like East African shooting, where any number of "misses" and careless attempts at stalking in no way prejudice the chances of a lucky shot next day, or next hour. We have come many hundred miles, and surmounted many physical difficulties, prepared, as true sportsmen, to be recompensed if we succeed in securing one fine ibex head, and leave none of God's creatures maimed or dying behind us.

Appreciation of Situation. Now to our "appreciation of the situation." First we have our "information regarding the enemy"; our day or two of careful watching tell us: (1) The rocks and recesses where our ibex usually pass the day, and whether they generally shift position after noon; (2) The feeding-grounds they come down to in the evening, and those they retire from in the morning; (3) The routes generally taken to come down and go up; (4) The habits of the big ibex, whether inclined to separate from the herd at any time, when approach may be easier.

Next we must consider "the courses open to the enemy," and "the course open to us."

Our ibex are very mobile; to make a flank march and stalk them in position will entail a maximum of climbing difficulties, and very possibly lead to our finding they have shifted out of sight; or perhaps the big "heads" are invisible, being securely masked by their outlying sentries.

The courses remaining are either to stalk them in the early morning or the evening, when feeding, or to "manœuvre for position"—by the latter I mean to stalk their feeding-grounds; in fact, to lie in ambush for them.

Wind. But there are other "factors affecting the situation" to be taken into consideration before arriving at a decision. First comes the wind, a factor, as in modern war, of great importance. In the afternoon and evening the wind will nearly always be found to blow up the main nullah, and also from the bottom of the main nullah up the side nullahs; in the late evening, the time varying in different seasons, the wind changes and begins to blow down hill; this continues all night, and usually till the sun is well up next day. In the cold early morning the wind is most favourable, as a steady breeze blows directly down the main and all side nullahs.

On misty or stormy days the vagaries of the wind make stalking very risky; the advice of a very old Kashmir shikari, the best of many I have met, was to stop in camp and do no harm on these occasions! Throughout a stalk, of course, the wind should be frequently tested by throwing up a handful of dust, or wetting a finger and holding it up; this is especially necessary when emerging from a ravine on to more open ground at its side or head.

Time. Time is another important factor. Your ibex

are likely to quit their morning ground when the sun reaches it, except very early in the year. You must carefully calculate the time it will take to make your approaching climb ; an aneroid reading heights to 20,000 feet will be found most useful in all mountain-shooting, and a stiff but straightforward climb of 1,500 feet should be normally accomplished in under the hour.

Detached Herds. A third " factor " which has upset many a well-attempted stalk, is the presence of some small detached herd of ibex. If such a herd has been detected they must be considered when choosing your route, and throughout your approach, as they will soon communicate the alarm to your quarry if they see or wind you.

The Morning Stalk. After carefully considering the above courses and factors we must make our decision. There are many who swear by the morning effort, but it depends on circumstances ; personally I have shot most of my ibex in the evening, and am inclined to consider the early morning as a time to find and to watch our game. The morning stalk, if we are lucky in locating our ibex very early, has the advantage of the most favourable wind and light. Its disadvantages are that you have to stalk upwind from below, while the ibex are all moving upwards, with their sentries looking downwards covering their retreat. Probably time does not admit of your getting above them on their leeward flank. The result, in my experience, has often been that I have followed them till the wind changed, with all the small ones between me and the big heads, unable to get a fair shot.

Sleeping Out. Another method that circumstances may require is to take a small bivouac tent, bedding and food, and sleep up above and to a flank of your ibex feeding-ground ; you may then find a position that will give you an easy shot as they come up hill in the morning.

I remember a nullah in the Shigar Valley in Baltistan one September many years ago, where, after spotting four big solitary ibex, and watching them for several days, I found it completely impossible to approach them at any time of day without a certainty of being seen or winded !

They were extremely wary ; never began to descend in the evening till nearly dark, and their day position commanded every possible line of advance. At dawn they were usually grazing about one-third of the way down the mountain, but within an hour were back in their impregnable position near the crest of the ridge.

There was only one solution : I must get over the impassable ground by moonlight, and, climbing up the nullah short of their usual feeding-ground before dawn, wait for them in a position that would command, but be to leeward of, their return route.

There was a favourable moon, and starting at 3 a.m. a couple of hours' climb brought us before dawn to the spot on the ridge which we had selected. Luck was with us. Soon after the great snow peaks around us were lit up by the coming dawn, we made out all four ibex grazing near their usual place. The ground made an immediate approach very risky, so we decided to wait. The ibex fed steadily upwards ; after nearly an hour two of them appeared not 100 yards from us, and the bigger fell to a single bullet between neck and shoulder. He had a very massive pair of horns measuring 44½ inches.

We all lay motionless after the first shot, and presently the other two ibex, not knowing whence came the danger, suddenly appeared 50 yards below us! Here of course they winded us and were off at once full speed, but as they breasted the steep part of the opposite ridge I was able to shoot one of them, a very nice 43-inch head.

The Evening Stalk. Personally, the course I have most often found successful has been the afternoon "approach," and evening stalk.

The plan I would recommend to the consideration of the novice is to locate and watch your ibex in the early morning and mark them carefully back to their day retreat. Utilise the afternoon to "manœuvre for position"; that is to say, move quietly up the nullah in the middle of the day, and climb up a side nullah till you reach a selected spot that commands, and is well to leeward of, their downward route and probable feeding-ground. Here you should be able to continue watching your game, or at any rate the ground they must pass over as they descend; they may come within shot without your moving, but if they do not, at any rate you are in a favourable position for a final stalk.

The Final Stalk and Shot—Hints to Novices. A few hints on this final stalk and shot may be of some assistance to the novice until, by practice and experience, he has awakened his latent power of doing instinctively the right thing; and he would not have the enterprise to be wandering in the wilds of the Himalayas had he not the dormant instincts in him!

So far let us assume you have "manœuvred for position" and obtained it. Your ibex have left their rocks and are coming downhill, grazing and playing. Do not be in a hurry, but let them come to you, or at least as near as they intend to. When they seem inclined to come no nearer the stalk must begin.

Pick your line of advance carefully before you start, and be sure there is no "sentry" left behind who will see you leave your hiding-place. Search thoroughly with your glasses as each new bit of ground comes into view, and constantly test the wind, especially as evening draws on.

Use the butt end of your "khud stick" when crossing stones and rocks, as the metal end makes an unnatural noise; feel with your foot for loose stones before you put your weight on them.

As you reach the crest of the next spur nothing but your glasses and the top of your head must be visible; search up and down both slopes beyond you; if a single outlying ibex sees you your stalk is doomed! Should one suddenly come into view while you are on the move, your only chance is to drop to the ground and remain motionless. These hints may read as very elementary, but until they become second nature many a hard week's work will be thrown away.

Down below you as you peer between the rocks, the ibex are again visible grazing on the opposite slope; one or two are passing over the next crest; the two biggest, one of whom you mean to shoot, are not to be seen for

A Cantilever Bridge in the Zaskar Range, 11,300 feet.

the moment; probably they are still on the near slope where you cannot get a shot without being seen by the others; probably also, in due course, they will take the same line as those females that are now crossing the next ridge, and would give you about a 250-yard shot.

You have two hours of good light left and every advantage in your favour; the ibex is a very tough animal, and if you hit him in the wrong place the chances are you will lose him and leave him wounded. Wait for a deadly shot. Watch them all over the next ridge, and then drop down the nullah below you and be after them, but make quite sure before you start that none have remained where they can see or hear you.

Now the two big ibex are crossing over the next crest; for several minutes the leader stands and scans the ground below and beyond; then he moves on out of sight, followed by his companion. A female and two kids only remain.

At last these have also crossed over, and you are hurrying after them; go steady as you breast the opposite side; it is a stiff climb. Make for those few rocks about 50 yards above the spot where the last ibex crossed. Load your rifle at "safety," and put some cartridges in a pocket where your right hand can easily get at them.

The Shot. A very cautious peep round the side of the rocks reveals the two best ibex placidly grazing not 80 yards below you! Get your shikari's puggaree and place it on a suitable rock as a rest if you can; slide your rifle slowly into position; be sure it is not still at "safety" and glance at your sights to make certain that the 200- or 300-yard leaf has not been accidentally raised. Believe me, all these things happen to the most experienced sportsman!

That climb and the excitement have winded you, and your heart is beating violently; in East Africa animals are missed, or wounded, from carelessness, in India from over-anxiety and excitement. So take plenty of time, and do not shoot till hand, and heart, and eye are steady. Pick the bigger ibex of the two, even if the other is slightly nearer, and wait till he gives you a shoulder, or neck and shoulder shot. Aim a trifle high and *through* the shoulder rather than behind it. Never allow your shikari to say "Maro, sahib (Shoot, sahib)"; take your time, but as soon as your foresight steadies on the right spot, a gentle, steady, continuous squeeze of the trigger —"That's got him!" He's down! Now up again, and away he goes, hit perhaps a trifle too far back. Another shot, and a miss, clean over his back; you would have done better to have waited; probably you forgot you were shooting downhill and wanted a finer sight than on the level; now he is close to the next crest about 150 yards off, and before crossing suddenly stops and looks back; I hoped he would! He does not yet realise whence your shot came! Another shot and he disappears over the ridge with a stagger.

Away after him, and make for the next spur, just above where he crossed it; by the way he went off, with his head rather low and back slightly humped, he will not go far or fast.

Having reached the next crest, for the moment there is no sign of him. Follow down to where he got your last shot—there he lies! he must have fallen almost at once and slid 300 feet to the bottom of the nullah below. Let your shikari go off at once in the hopes of being able to cut his throat in the orthodox manner before the last glimmer of life is extinct, and so provide an honourable meal for your Mohammedan servants. But warn him not to spoil the head skin by cutting too high up.

The stalk is over, and a fine trophy secured; a 43-inch ibex is no mean prize, and an ample reward for a month or more of marching and climbing, hardships and disappointments; but independently of the trophy secured, you have shot the ibex you had marked down, the biggest head in the nullah; you have scorned to pull trigger on any other; you have pitted your brains and skill on level terms against those of one of the wariest of wild animals, and may justly feel proud of your success. The trophy you have secured will in years to come bring back to you many happy moments, and irrevocably some day, call you back to Nature's wilds.

Incidentally you have improved your mind, strengthened your manhood, widened your views by contact with Nature's grandest scenery, and, if a soldier, have unquestionably quickened those instincts and attributes which are invaluable in peace, but above all in war, to a leader of men.

I have endeavoured to lead the reader through some of the incidents and pitfalls which will be met by the hunter of ibex, and much that I have said is equally applicable to markhor and other mountain game. Probably there are many points I have missed, but the description I have given of locating, watching, and shooting an ibex, may, I trust, help the novice to work out his own scheme and not be entirely dependent on his shikari. It is this that gives to Himalayan shooting a character, fascination and value of its own.

CHAPTER VIII

KASHMIR STAG OR BARASINGH (*Cervus Kashmiriensis*)

By Colonel A. G. Arbuthnot, C.M.G., D.S.O.

Native names—*Hungal, Barasingha,* Kashmir.

HABITAT. As autumn settles on the Valley of Kashmir the dense fir forests that clothe the mountains on the north and north-west ring to the war cry of the barasingh ; it is a wonderful and awe-inspiring cry, more like a long-drawn-out shriek than the genuine " roar " of the Scottish red deer. Soon after mid-September, within a few days of the first heavy fall of snow, you may hear him signal his arrival, with antlers clear of " velvet," and ready for battle, among the sea of pine-trees beyond the Wular Lake ; he is returning eastwards to his winter haunts from his secluded summer retreat.

From late September the barasingh may be found in most of the nullahs from west of the Wular Lake to Kishtwar, and as far east as the borders of Chamba State. Here he spends his winter, till in March or April he begins to yearn for higher altitudes, and the more lonely forests farther west. There, in peace and solitude, he sheds his great antlers and grows a finer pair in " velvet."

It is generally believed that the same stag returns,

like the nightingale, to the same place each season. There are, however, certainly some, perhaps many, that remain all the summer in the same nullah, but they are seldom seen. I have found their tracks in May in Sonamarg, and beyond Baltal.

Antlers. The antlers of the Kashmir stag are peculiarly beautiful; very similar to the Scottish red deer, but considerably longer, heavier, and usually more symmetrical. The bez-tine is usually longer than the brow, while in the true red deer the brow-tine is generally longer than the bez. The normal number of points is ten, but a twelve- or even fourteen-pointer is not too uncommon. The pair of antlers, unlike the red deer, form more or less of an ellipse, with the terminal points curving inwards. A good head measures from 40 to 45 inches along the curve, the record being 53½ inches.

Where to Look for the Stag. To get the best chance of securing a good barasingh, the sportsman should pitch his tent by September 20, fairly high up the mountain where the fir forest begins to give way to the more open ground. With the first heavy snowfall the stag are supposed to appear north-west of the Wular Lake, and very shortly afterwards in all their favourite haunts in the Erin Nullah, Sind Valley, Lidar Valley, and Wardwan Range.

They travel high, and their tracks will soon be found in the snow high up above the forest. Here is the place to look for them in the evenings, and you may be rewarded by a stalk in the open.

In the early morning search the open glades in the forest, or the grazing-ground on the edge of it; if you have followed down fresh tracks in the snow the previous evening you will have a guide where to look.

The miles and miles of dense firs and grand deodars might conceal a thousand barasingh, but if you work on sound lines and mark down where they entered the forest you have a fair chance of a shot. Some will stop in your nullah, though many whose tracks you see may be on the move further east.

As a sport there is perhaps too much forest work and too much chance, to allow barasingh-shooting to be compared with ibex or markhor. Perhaps this is as well, for the shot, when you get it, is usually an easy one.

I once spent three weeks in vain efforts to get a shot at a fine fourteen-pointer not far from the Tragbal Pass. I was camped in a lovely spot, just above the forest-line, with a fresh fall of snow all round me; at first nearly all the stags that came into my nullah were passengers; they went down into the forest and on again next night. Then one day I tracked a very big fellow with several big others. Next morning he was "roaring" quite close to my camp. I went after him and heard him in the forest polishing his horns on a tree. In the course of an exciting morning stalk I came upon him suddenly, but he was off like lightning, without giving a chance of even a snapshot! Nearly every morning I heard his roar in the forest below. I took my bivouac tent and followed him for days; one clear moonlight night I was woken up by a piercing "roar"! I jumped up, seized my rifle, and through the open end of my tent saw my friend for one second, with his magnificent antlers clearly defined, not ten yards away! Just a fleeting glimpse, and he was gone, and I never got another sight of him.

In the course of my three weeks, however, luck did not altogether desert me, although I failed in my main effort. I came unexpectedly up on a fine ten-pointer stag, and a red bear in excellent coat, both of which I shot. I also was fortunate in getting a 40-inch ibex near the head of my nullah, rather unusual in that locality. I heard of my friend the fourteen-pointer being shot in the same nullah two years later.

KAKUR (*Cervulus Muntjac*)

Native names (Himalayas only)—*Kakur*, Hindi.

The kakur or barking deer is by no means a purely Himalayan animal, for it is found all over India and Burma, wherever conditions are suitable, that is wherever there is a combination of hills and dense jungle. In the Himalayas kakur are only found in the outer ranges which lie to the south of the main axis, and they never ascend to high altitudes. The greatest height at which I have ever seen them is 7,600 feet, and I should say this was rather exceptional, somewhere about 6,000 feet being their normal limit, while the majority will be found between 2,000 and 5,000 feet. They live in dense jungle, and are usually only seen in the early mornings and evenings. They can seldom be legitimately stalked, and a quiet stroll is the most likely way of getting a shot: owing to the thickness of the jungles they usually inhabit they are not often seen out of shot unless they are on one side of a valley and the sportsman is on the other. A path running along one side of a narrow nullah is the best form of hunting ground, as the kakur can be more easily seen on the opposite slopes.

Their colour is a bright red, and in certain lights they show up wonderfully against the surrounding green, but in the shade they are by no means easy to pick up.

The loud, dog-like bark, from which they derive their name, is usually a cry of alarm, and is frequently an indication that a leopard is in the neighbourhood. On one occasion when I was after gooral and was following a path which led along the face of an almost precipitous cliff in company with my shikari (a very good local man) we heard a kakur bark, and saw him (for it is only the bucks which bark) in some thick bushes on the edge of a flat grassy glade almost directly below us. The little animal stood out wonderfully in the evening sun, and although the range was nearly 300 yards I was tempted to have a shot. I accordingly sat down on the path, put the rifle sling round my left arm to steady myself, and handing the glasses to the shikari took careful aim. I allowed nothing for the bullet drop owing to the fact that the horizontal range was certainly not more than 50 yards, if as much, and pressed the trigger. The kakur never moved a muscle. "Just over his back, Sahib." I sighted again and now I saw the whole of the little red body above the fine platinum bead. Again the kakur never moved to the shot, and this time my companion told me my bullet had gone just under him. Having got my bracket, I could not resist another shot, and was just settling down to aim when something caught my eye jutting out from the precipice about 300 feet below us. Still holding the rifle with my left hand, I took the glasses with my right to examine the little protuberance which had caught my eye. I thought it might be a gooral, and I would far sooner have a shot at a gooral at 100 yards than go on firing at three times that range at a kakur which refused to be frightened away. One glance was sufficient. What I had seen was the round bullet head of a big male leopard, and it was obviously stalking the kakur. This explained the original bark of alarm which we had heard. Before I could bring my rifle to bear the head had been withdrawn and all signs of the leopard had disappeared. We waited five minutes, ten minutes, and then I noticed something on the green glade below us which I have already mentioned. One glance through the glasses showed it to be the leopard, looking almost as red as the kakur in the glancing sunlight. He was crouching down gazing up at us, and his great tail, which seemed as thick as one of his legs, was slowly moving to and fro. I had got my range on the kakur (which was still in the same spot, although not more than thirty yards from the leopard: it seemed too hypnotised to move) and took a quick but careful aim. I have already said that the leopard was crouching. As I pressed the trigger I saw it stand up. The bullet struck the ground immediately under its belly, and it gave a great vertical leap like a cat, all four paws off the ground at once and back arched, and then bounded away before I had moved my rifle from my shoulder. The spell was broken for the kakur also, and it, too, vanished.

I think I have registered more misses with kakur than with all other kinds of animals put together, and can put forward no excuse for it. They certainly offer a small mark, measuring as they do but a bare 2 feet at the withers, but they are no smaller than several other species of game.

The kakur being a member of the deer family sheds its horns every year, usually some time in May. The new horns grow quickly and are generally clean of velvet about the middle of August. The horns are usually about four inches along, and the hairy pedicle from which they grow is about 3 inches in length. The buck has long canine teeth which protrude from the jaw nearly three-quarters of an inch. Another peculiarity is the very long tongue. The young are spotted.

The flesh of the kakur is excellent, and will provide a most welcome change on the march through the Himalayas. The sportsman should make a very early start and take a round through likely ground, the coolies following by the ordinary route. Kakur will frequently be met when one is after black bear in the outer ranges. When one is seen there should be no delay in taking the shot.

KYANG (*Equus Hemionus*)

Native name—*Kyang*, Tibetan.

The kyang cannot in any way be considered a game animal, and I am unable to understand any sportsman ever wishing to shoot one except in a spirit of revenge. The mildest man may, I confess, be roused to extreme fury at having a stalk spoiled by one of these animals. Their habitat may be taken as being identical with that of *Ammon.* They blend curiosity and timidity into an extraordinary mixture, and it is almost as difficult to escape their detection as the detection of a monal pheasant or a peacock. Once they have seen an unfortunate sportsman, their curiosity overcomes all other feelings and they trot up for a closer inspection. As soon as they have satisfied themselves as to the identity of the intruder their timidity asserts itself and they dash away at full gallop, thus attracting the attention of every wild animal in the neighbourhood to the cause of their antics.

Kyang are particularly annoying on *Ammon* ground, and when any are sighted they should be stalked just as carefully as the great sheep if the sportsman would escape their notice.

I have heard the kyang described as a wild horse, but this appellation is an insult to that noble friend of man, and "wild ass" is more suitable in every way as well as being more accurate. Their heads and ears are large and heavy, and their shoulders are particularly straight, but behind the fore-hand they are undoubtedly well made.

MUSK DEER (*Moschus Moschiferus*)

Native names—*Kastura, Muskhanafa,* Hindi; *Rao, Roos,* Kashmir.

This tiny little member of the deer tribe is distributed throughout the Himalayas and Tibet wherever the country suits its requirements, which are steep slopes covered with scrub and jungle, and an elevation of at least 8,000 feet. That grand sportsman

Amidst Silver Birch and Pines in the Great Himalayan Range at 10,000 feet.

and great naturalist, the late Mr. Philip Mackinnon, told me that he once shot a musk deer on his estate in Mussoorie, but they are seldom met with as far away from the main axis of the Himalayas as this.

Musk deer have no horns, but the males are armed with abnormally developed eye-teeth, sometimes as much as 2 to 4 inches long. These eye-teeth are very difficult to distinguish except with the help of a powerful glass and bright sunlight, and consequently it is more difficult in stalking to tell the sex of a musk deer than of any other animal. The hind legs are longer than the fore, which raises the croup about two inches above the withers. The height at the latter is about 20 inches and the weight is but the same number of pounds. The males have an abdominal pod in which there is usually about an ounce of musk. All natives know this pod perfectly well, and it is to be feared that your shikari will try to palm off the scrotum on you, keeping the pod for himself, if you are not very careful.

When marching through and beyond the Great Himalayan Range you are certain to come on heaps of their droppings, which are quite unmistakable owing to their minute size. The droppings of the male, even when dry, smell slightly of musk. The Indians declare that musk deer always return to deposit their droppings in the same place, but I have never been able to verify this statement. If it were true, such an easy road to the shooting of musk deer would be provided that I fancy they would have been exterminated long ago, in the Himalayas at any rate, for Indians poach them everywhere. The wait which would be so tedious to a white man would be nothing to an oriental, and musk pods will sometimes fetch as much as Rs. 30, a huge sum to a hillman.

The flesh of musk deer is excellent and is entirely free from any flavour of musk.

CHAPTER IX

LEOPARD (*Felis Pardus*)

By W. B. Cotton, I.C.S., F.R.G.S., F.Z.S.

Native names—*Cheetah, Baghera, Tandour, Lugger Bagha,* Hindi; *Mirg, Brag,* Kulu.

THE leopard, or panther, is the most widely distributed of the great cats, and is likely to be the first species of dangerous game encountered by the sportsman in India. It occurs throughout the Himalayas wherever there is a sufficiency of jungle. Members of the species are probably most common in the outer Himalayas, and frequently abound round many hill stations. (I have seen tracks of a leopard beyond the main Himalayan axis, and I believe their boundary depends entirely on comfortable quarters; they do not like hill-slopes devoid of vegetation.—G.B.). No serious work on natural history, and very few practical sportsmen, admit that there is more than one species of this animal, of which adult specimens may vary from the size and weight of a heavy spaniel to that of a mastiff; the well-known black variety is an undoubted melanism confined almost entirely to heavy jungle in the tropics; specimens shot on the North-West Frontier and in Persia suggest an approach to the ounce; and the African leopard usually carries more spots and fewer rosettes, particularly over the back and shoulders, than the Indian animal. Any leopard, however small, may be distinguished at a glance from any of the lesser cats by the length of its tail; the smallest leopard cub will show an amazing development of the claws and the canine teeth; and the leopard, in common with all of the great cats, has a circular pupil, whereas the serval, the tiger cat, and every species of lesser cat, has a vertical pupil resembling the domestic animal. Concerning this same length of tail, I heard a story which illustrates the character of the leopard among those best acquainted with him. I once asked a village shikari in Bundelkhand whether a particular leopard was cunning. The reply which I received was: "Sahib! where that leopard walks he brushes out his tracks with the tip of his tail!"

No more beautiful and graceful creature walks the earth, but none save the tiger excites a more universal detestation, and this not only among his natural victims, but even small birds become uneasy in his presence. This also may be said for the tiger, that one must invade his domain before he becomes a menace, and that domain is for choice very far from the haunts of men. The leopard, however, takes the measure of his human adversaries, and will hold his own alike in the jungle, where every animal either hates or fears him; in a pile of rocks, of which the lower slopes are covered with the houses of Indian villagers, through the roofs of which the marauder will often break a way at midnight, and carry off a calf; and in the fringes of a hill cantonment full of sportsmen thirsting for his blood, whose dogs will be carried off from the public road or the verandah under their owners' eyes.

The attributes of the leopard have hitherto saved him from the fate that has overtaken almost every wild animal in these days of arms of precision, and whereas the lion has disappeared from every corner of Asia save a single forest within the memory of men still alive, and the number of tigers is as well known to many district officers as the number of their revenue assistants, there are probably as many leopards in India now as there were in the days of muzzle-loaders. His survival is due to the fact that with strength and ferocity marvellous in an animal whose weight rarely exceeds 9 stone, are allied caution, patience, wariness, stealth, and an unmatched faculty for noiseless movement and concealment. The sportsman without experience of these animals should understand that he is dealing with a most formidable antagonist, and when shooting in the Sudan, where the Arab hunters fear nothing, they were careful to warn me to take no chances when dealing with the leopard and the buffalo. I have known a full-grown Indian cow weighing about 400 lb. killed by a single female leopard, which I subsequently shot, and I have been told a circumstantial story, which I fully believe, that a large male killed one of the camels of a former collector of Banda, and was shot by sitting up over the head and neck of the camel. A few leopards make a practice of dragging their prey into the forks of trees, having probably suffered by the depredations of hyænas, and I have seen the bodies of dogs fully 20 feet from the ground, and on one occasion the better part of a buffalo calf at a greater height than my head, and these feats of strength are explained by the remarkable development of the muscles of the neck in the leopard. The largest leopard ever shot by me taped 24 inches round the neck, being the same as a tigress whose measurements approached a record, and whose weight was more than double that of the leopard. One hears occasional stories of sportsmen who come to close quarters with leopards and strangle them with their hands. I have never met with any of these fortunate individuals, and I recommend that the experiment should be conducted upon the throat of a dead specimen, upon which my own fingers have never been able to produce the least impression. Incidentally one may note that the carnivora are the usual hosts of an extremely poisonous variety of tick, and that measurements, etc., should be conducted with the greatest of caution when these parasites have decided upon migration, and before they have dispersed themselves.

The curious detached collar-bones exist alike in the leopard, the tiger, and the lion, and lie embedded in muscle, an inch below the surface, at the points of the shoulders.

The call of the leopard to his mate is a well-known sound in the Indian jungle, and precisely resembles the sawing of wood. The grunt of an angry leopard so closely resembles the "ough ough" of a boar, that I have known experienced sportsmen deceived, and he charges to the accompaniment of a series of short growls, the first of which should warn the sportsman of the approaching crisis. He can snarl with considerable vigour, but although I once kept a leopard cub from the size of a kitten until it was nine months old, and as heavy as a greyhound, I never heard it purr. They make delightful pets when young, being totally fearless, and in this instance remarkably good tempered and playful. This cub ran practically wild, and when it spent a night in the garden was to be found in the morning asleep in a tree. However, the feral instinct was there, and it never saw a goat or a fowl without beginning a stalk, and when it got hold of anything which it fancied, whether a fowl, a helmet, or a pillow, trouble began at once, and a blanket had to be thrown over it before attempting a rescue. As they approach maturity they become more and more untrustworthy with the realisation of their own powers, and my cub was sent to the Calcutta menagerie later than is safe with these animals.

Fully 75 per cent of leopards are shot over baits, some 20 per cent by beating, and 5 per cent turn up in the most mysterious manner from nowhere. And here I will recount a couple of my own experiences in the Etah district of the United Provinces, of incidents falling under the last category, which illustrate the character of the animal. The one which was brought to a satisfactory conclusion occurred when I was marching from camp to camp along the Kali Nadi, accompanied by a few attendants who were bringing along my greyhounds, one or two hogspears, my rifle, and my shotgun. We beat out a fringe of tamarisk along the Kali Nadi about a hundred yards long and ten yards wide, and turned out a hare, which gave me a circular course and finally returned to the same patch of jungle, which my attendants beat out for the second time without success, but disturbed a number of quail and partridges, so that I dismounted and took my shot-gun, and we beat it out for the third time. I fired a shot at a quail, and immediately some large animal jumped up and broke back between the beaters, who shouted "Sher!" and my sweeper, who was standing with the greyhounds at the end of the cover, told me that a leopard had galloped past him within arm's length. The surrounding country was entirely open, and I mounted my horse, took a hogspear, and rode out into the open ground, but the villagers who were working there told me that nothing had broken across. I then dismounted, took my rifle, and turned my attention to the fringes of tamarisk along the river, which I proceeded to beat out one by one with the help of my attendants and a few villagers. The first beat proved blank, but the leopard was in the next beat, and passed me at a gallop at 60 yards, the bullet telling loudly as he disappeared into a field of arhar. Examination showed blood, and that the leopard was obviously lying in the arhar, part of which had been killed by frost. I took up a commanding position where the dead stalks gave a fair field of fire, and ordered my sweeper to let loose the greyhounds. This was done, and the dogs rushed at the leopard, who took not the least notice of them, but charged me from a distance of 20 paces, and a bullet from a ·500 Express by Rigby dropped him practically dead when he had covered half of it. The first bullet had broken a hind leg, and the second struck fair between the neck and shoulder, but he still struck out at the dogs, and a third shot finished him, a fine male, and I remember the villagers saying that at last a visit by a Government official had been productive of some good. No regular jungle which could hold leopards exists within a hundred miles of the Etah district, but the point of the story seems to me to lie in the fact that beaters must have walked within a few feet of this leopard three times in succession, and even then a shot-gun had to be fired over his back before he would move.

The second incident occurred on the Lower Ganges Canal, where a leopard was drinking, and two Indians happened to pass. The leopard attacked them without the least provocation, and seized one of them, whilst the other climbed a tree. However, the leopard dropped his first victim, and proceeded to climb the tree after the other, and mauled him in his turn.

I received the news through the police, and was on the spot within forty-eight hours. The tree was smeared with blood up to a height of 20 feet, and it was obvious that the unfortunate man had been dragged down inch by inch, resisting the whole time. This man died, and the first victim recovered, but the leopard vanished completely, and neither I nor some sportsmen to whom I wired in Aligarh were ever able to trace it.

Although beating, either through grass with a line of elephants, or up to guns with a line of beaters, is not recommended as a means of securing leopards, a good many are turned out and shot by these methods among other animals. When a beat is suspected to contain a leopard, the sportsmen should undoubtedly be seated on machans, not on account of the danger, though this is a consideration where the party includes ladies, but because the field of fire from a machan is so much less restricted. A portable machan measuring 5 feet by 4 feet, the frame to be of setium wood with a section of 2½ inches by 2 inches, and the webbing of newar dyed green or khaki, with the corners crossing and projecting about 4 inches, and with two stout iron rings 3 feet apart in the middle of one of the 5-foot 8-inch lengths, should form part of the outfit of every hunter of big game in the plains of India, and a sporting landowner in India will often own a dozen of these machans. The two iron rings can be attached with a rope to any forked tree in a few seconds, after which the machan is pulled up to the horizontal by passing ropes over the corners, and can be made perfectly secure in a few minutes, and all that remains to be done is to provide a screen of leaves in the direction from which the beat will approach. Upon such a machan the sportsman, seated upon a "mora" (stool) 9 inches high, will be screened from the view of everything except the peafowl, which overlook nothing, and can swing his rifle round a complete semicircle, and he will, I am convinced, eschew for the future makeshifts such as charpoys or cut branches, which invariably creak, or sag, or are uncomfortably cramped. If a beat contains a leopard, the sportsman will nearly always become aware of its presence, not by the noise made by the leopard himself, for the sound of its approaching footsteps will very rarely be heard, but by certain cries uttered by the birds and beasts which have detected its presence; and a repetition of these cries may be taken as a certain sign that a leopard or a tiger is on the move. Violent excitement is produced among the monkeys, which utter hoarse barks and shake the branches, and this is so well known in the jungle, that when possible a herd of spotted deer is certain to place itself under the protection of these strange guardians. The spotted deer themselves will bell most persistently, and I have watched a herd of these animals following a tiger in daylight for a considerable distance, and another time shot a leopard which had been signalled for some minutes by a fawn standing five yards from my machan. A peafowl surprised by a leopard will rise with a screech like a startled pheasant, but the regular warning call is a grating cry repeated at intervals of half a minute, quite distinct from the well-known catcall of these birds when they go to roost.

The leopard rarely moves far ahead of a line of beaters, and may be expected towards the end of a beat, but he does not come out literally among the beaters, which is by no means unusual with an old male tiger, and unless a shot has been fired in his immediate vicinity, he never seems to be in the least hurry; but he has an annoying trick of leaping over sunk roads and the like, and in fixing the site of the machan and deciding where the shot will be fired, this peculiarity should be remembered. And with this animal more than any other it is necessary to lop away superfluous bushes which obstruct the view, and to obtain two clear lines of fire, one on the right, and one on the left of the machan, neither of which should conduct straight to the next machan, and from both of which the cut bushes should be sedulously removed and piled under or behind the machan itself. Should a beat for a leopard prove unsuccessful, and the jungle contains a kill, that kill should invariably be sat over towards sunset; and within my experience a leopard has eaten a considerable portion of his kill whilst the beat which failed to drive him up to the guns was actually in progress.

My own view is that unless it is desired to provide sport for a party, the leopard should be shot over a bait by a single sportsman; and here it is as well to warn the novice that the business is not so simple a matter as may appear, and when I was young, and full of ignorance and enthusiasm, I tied up baits for an entire year among the rocks of Bundelkhand, and must have sat up over them nearly a hundred times, and shot several hyænas, before I secured my first leopard. However, this apprenticeship was of the utmost value, for I learned by repeated mistakes, and during the next fifteen months I shot ten leopards over the same ground, some of which were cunning in the extreme, and one of which was a man-eater. The story of this man-eater illustrates the incalculable element in the character of the leopard, which is well known to all tamers of wild animals. The first hint which we received of the presence of a man-eater was the disappearance of a villager, whose body was found half devoured in the jungle, and who was reported by the Superintendent of Police to have been killed by some wild animal; and I well recollect the annoyance of this officer, himself an experienced sportsman, when he was told by superior authority that the case was one of murder. At that time a severe famine was raging in Bundelkhand, and relief works had been started by the excavation of tanks, and some 3,000 men, women, and children were working by day and sleeping at night in and around a tank in this neighbourhood. The hot weather was far advanced, the tank was bone dry, and water exceedingly scarce, and it was stored for the workers in small shelters each of which was in charge of a Brahmin, and I afterwards learned that some animals had been making free use of the water stored in these shelters, entering them by night and drinking the water, whilst offering no sort of molestation to the occupants, who had come to disregard its visits. However, one night towards ten o'clock a loud shriek was heard in a small grove of mango trees close to the tank, and the occupants of the grove fled in the darkness and gave the alarm, and it is certain that within a few minutes hundreds of men were collected on the embankment within 50 yards of the mango grove. Taking courage from numbers they attempted a rescue, but were met with a series of growls from the darkness under the trees, which effectively hindered them from prosecuting their search, and during the entire night the whole party of workers occupied the embankment, whilst their visitor maintained his position in the grove. My own camp was a couple of miles distant, and at early dawn I was aware of considerable excitement, and learned that some "janwar" (animal) had been the author of a tragedy upon the famine work, and hastening to the spot I was told that in the early dawn an animal the size of a dog with a long tail had been seen to walk away from the grove into the jungle, and that the body of a woman was lying in the grove. I examined the body, which was that of a young woman, and came to the conclusion that she had been sleeping on her side, when she had been stalked by a leopard, which had approached along a shallow trench which led into the grove, that the leopard had sprung upon her, placing a paw upon her shoulder, and that she had attempted to push it off with her other hand. That hand had been taken by the leopard into its mouth, and most of the fingers had been bitten clean off, and with its disengaged paw the leopard had seized the woman by the head, and had inflicted such a wrench as not only broke the neck, but tore the whole of the flesh off one side of the woman's face. Apart from the missing fingers I was unable to discover any marks of teeth above the waist, but the whole of the flesh of the legs and of the lower portion of the body had been completely devoured, and the contents of the stomach removed through a hole in the side large enough to admit the paw. The bones were stripped bare, and had not been broken, and I was confident that a leopard was the culprit, and forthwith erected a machan in a tree in the grove, and spent the night watching over the body by the light of a lantern. However, nothing approached but the village dogs, which made a grisly meal, and finally severed the rope with which I had secured the remains, and carried them away. Next day duty called me to another part of the district, and it was some weeks before I could return, but meanwhile I had been pursuing a train of thought which led to the final destruction of the leopard. One thing was obvious to me, that on the fatal night the leopard had not drunk out of the Brahmin's huts, and yet he had eaten a full meal and walked away into the jungle at the hottest period of the year, and this indicated the presence of water in the jungle in the vicinity. When I was able to return to the neighbourhood, nothing more had been heard of the leopard, but I followed the direction which he was said to have taken, and I found a villager who was able to show me a small spring at the foot of a valley a mile away from the tank. The sides of the valley were thickly overgrown with thorn, and as soon as I saw the spring I knew that I had found the lair of the leopard. I had business which took me into Allahabad, but I told an attendant to tie up a pariah dog by the side of the spring towards evening, to visit the place next morning and to let me know the result. I returned from Allahabad next day, and found my attendant in a state of the greatest excitement, and he told me that he had tied up the dog in the evening as ordered, and had visited it in the morning and found it alive and well. He had then begun to search for tracks, and after some minutes had returned to the dog, and found it with the head bitten clean off, after which he fled. Three p.m. saw me in the valley, which was totally destitute of trees which would support a machan, and there I found the headless body of the dog, and made the screen of leaves known in those parts as a "putwa," behind which I sat down when the sun was within an hour of setting, when my attendants tied up a kid over the body of the dog, and hurriedly left, and I made a mental resolve that nothing would retain me at my post after the sun had reached the horizon. However, my courage was not to be severely tried, for within twenty minutes a leopard sprang out of the bushes upon the goat, and dropped to my first shot, although I gave it a second barrel to make sure. Having secured the leopard, I called up my attendants, and we searched the neighbourhood of the spring, and found the remains of three human beings, all of whom had presumably come for water, and met with the fate which my attendant so narrowly escaped, their disappearance being overlooked owing to the famine. This leopard was quite a small female, and was in milk, though I was never able to find the cubs.

However, the man-eater is fortunately rare, and in twenty-six years' experience of two continents I have not come across another specimen; and the temperament of the leopard is such that an unwounded specimen is usually glad to make off when he detects the sportsman, and is far less likely to attack than a bear or a crusty old boar; and in the scrub jungle and piles of rocks which leopards largely affect, the device which I have described as a "putwa" may be used with confidence. The apparatus then required will be simple in the extreme, consisting of no more than a church hassock, a square of felt, a hatchet, and a trowel. The object of the hassock and the felt is to ensure complete silence, and the first point to recollect is that the hearing of wild beasts stands on an entirely different plane from that of human beings, and can only be compared with the microphone. The faintest sound that proceeds from the sportsman is detected instantly, and recognised as unnatural, and since the most common stratagem of all the cats is to flatten themselves out within 20 yards of their prey, and listen and watch intently, from a place of concealment, and this vigil may be extended for hours, I am convinced that nine times out of ten when the sportsman is unsuccessful he has been heard by his quarry, and that the reputation enjoyed by many leopards and tigers of never revisiting a kill is undeserved. My own belief is that almost every kill is revisited, and that almost every bait tied up in a hill which contains a leopard is reconnoitred and that this reconnaissance is often made in broad daylight whilst the preparations of the sportsman are in progress. However, the stealthy visitor is unnoticed and a fruitless watch is all that finds an entry in the journal. The clothes worn by the sportsman in the " putwa " should be of neutral tinted flannel, the helmet should be replaced by a cap, boots and gaiters by soft slippers, and one need hardly say that white shirts and collars should be abjured. Seated upon his hassock, with his feet upon the felt, he can then hope with practice to attain that deathly silence which is essential for success, and which explains why in a beat the animals seem invariably to run up against the experienced guns and to avoid the novices. The choice of a " putwa " or of a site for a machan has always seemed to me to be a crucial test of the skill of the sportsman, and a satisfactory selection seemed to me more than half the battle. For a "putwa" I always looked for a thick and thorny bush, which must be particularly thick on the side from which the leopard is expected, and in these localities is usually found a bush known as the "karaunda," which has the additional advantage of being an evergreen and possessing small leaves, a large dead leaf upon a hot weather evening being as noisy as an empty tin. Within this bush the sportsman must scoop and hack a space within which he will be able to sit upon his hassock upright, with his left shoulder in the direction from which he expects the leopard. He should then take branches, which ought to be of the same character as the bush under which he sits, and wedge them into the interior of the bush from the inside, until he is completely surrounded by an impervious leafy screen, with a single egress on the side from which the leopard is least likely to arrive, namely his right. This screen should be so high that his head will be quite invisible even from the top of the hill which is often the home of the leopard, and no projecting sprays must interfere with slight movements on the part of the sportsman or of his rifle. The next step will be to make the aperture through which to shoot, and for this an 8-inch diameter will be a good average size, and it should be carefully lined with twigs of the same character as the rest of the bush. The object of sitting with the left shoulder to the hill will now be apparent, for when the sportsman sits upright the bait should be completely concealed from view, and should come into sight as he assumes the firing position. The "putwa" should then be examined from the outside, and any branch that appears to be twisted or unnatural should be removed, the leopard having a limited range, and a correspondingly close acquaintance with the details of his usual haunts. In fact, complete concealment must be combined with as little interference as possible with the natural features of the landscape, and I once outwitted a leopard by making a "putwa" out of a pile of sleepers at the edge of the Rohilkhand & Kumaon Railway, the aforesaid leopard having acquired the extraordinary habit of living on the right bank of the Sarda River by day, and hunting on the left bank by night, crossing the river towards 9 p.m. by means of the trestle bridge which then supported the permanent way, to the accompaniment of a chorus of barking by the dogs of an adjoining village. When the villagers told me this story, I declined to believe it, but I thought it worth while to leave the carcase of a swamp deer which I had shot, close to the bridge head, and this carcase was speedily visited by the leopard, which was shot by me next night. This incident impressed itself the more upon my mind because I spent the whole of the night in the "putwa," and an hour after I had fired the shot I heard a series of furious grunts proceeding from the quarter where I knew that the leopard was lying, and these sounds were repeated at intervals until dawn. I supposed that the leopard had come to life, and spent the night in the expectation of an attack. However, when it was light enough to see, and silence was restored, I approached the grass into which the leopard had retreated, and there I found him lying dead, and realised that my second visitor had been a boar, which had cut and slashed the carcase of the leopard in every direction with his tusks, and wound up by making a meal of his stomach.

The "putwa" having been completed so far as the outside is concerned, the interior should be levelled and scraped and brushed clean of all fallen leaves, and in order to secure comfort in sitting possibly for hours upon a hassock, I finally made a practice of digging a hole to a depth of about six inches, sufficiently large to contain my two feet. Should one prefer a 9-inch mora to a 4-inch hassock, this last refinement will be unnecessary, but on the other hand one's head will be 5 inches higher, and the "putwa" correspondingly more conspicuous. In case it is proposed to remain in the "putwa" after nightfall, a small tree well provided with thorns may be cut down, and placed in readiness to be dragged into the entrance behind the sportsman, but this precaution is not essential, and I have shot my leopards behind screens which merely provided shelter in the direction from which the leopard was expected.

The bait should be tied up six yards from a "putwa" or ten yards from a machan, and it is an advantage if there is a thick bush behind the bait, which will prevent the leopard from looking into the hole through which the shot will be fired, until he has seized the bait, and his attention is fully occupied. I always preferred to attach the bait to some natural object, such as the stump of a tree, but occasionally a peg must be hammered into the ground, and the whole of the operations up to this point must be conducted whilst the leopard is still asleep, and never after 4 p.m. Delay in the construction of " putwas " or in the tying up of machans is one of the commonest causes of failure in this branch of sport, and I have known the best Indian shikaris drive away tigers by the use of an axe near the kill towards sunset. A stout knife and a small saw have for some years formed part of my own equipment, in order that any belated operations may be performed in silence, but this much may be said for the leopard, that when he means business, nothing seems to drive him away.

In forest country nobody attempts to shoot leopards from " putwas," because machans are easier to construct, afford better concealment, and are very much safer to use by night. One usually sits over an actual kill, and the leopard may approach from any quarter. The kill of a leopard may be distinguished at a glance from that of a tiger, because the leopard invariably makes his first meal of the soft parts about the stomach, whereas the tiger first eats the buttocks. The track of a large leopard is so like that of a young tigress that I have known the best shikaris mistaken, but there is no possibility of a mistake between the tracks of adult animals, and the only real resemblance between the track of a leopard and that of a hyæna is in size, the former being round with the sole and the toes wide apart, and the latter diamond shaped with the sole and the toes close together and faint marks of claws. Claw-marks on the ground by a leopard or a tiger will only be seen where he has grappled with his prey, or when he has made a convulsive spring after being wounded. The same amount of camouflage is not required for a machan as for a "putwa," but over a bait it is very much better to construct it in the heart of a tree with dense foliage such as a jhamon, and it should always be screened with leaves all round to a height of 3 feet at the back and sides, and 2 feet in front. One device may be used from a machan which I would never recommend in a "putwa," namely, an orilux electric torch may be tied with a handkerchief below the left knee, and a ray of light directed at will upon the kill. It is a remarkable fact that if one waits until the bait has been actually seized, this ray of light has not the least disturbing effect upon either lions, tigers, or leopards, and on the very few occasions when they have trotted away, they have invariably returned. All that need be attached to the rifle is an ordinary night-sight, which consists of a circular white head the size of a small pea, which slips over the foresight, and this will show up plainly against the illumination below. I have always found moonlight a most deceptive aid to shooting by night, but this electric torch defines the outlines of the object, and up to ten yards I have found it most effective, though a portion of the screen must be removed before it can be used. If the sportsman prefers to lie down in the machan the torch must be fixed to some rigid object above his head, such as a branch, but the alignment will present difficulty, whereas in a sitting position the left knee can be moved at will either vertically or horizontally, and still support the left elbow and the rifle. Should the sportsman desire to shoot by the light of the moon he should try to site the machan so that the moon will be behind him, when it will show up the white disc of the night-sight, and will not illuminate the face of the sportsman. Should he attract the notice of the leopard, which may be done by a mere movement of the eyebrows, the only policy to pursue is to sit like an image of stone, until its suspicions have been allayed, which may be a quarter of an hour; and no greater mistake can be made than the gradual withdrawal of the head whilst one is the object of intense scrutiny.

As regards baits, large numbers of leopards are shot in India over the carcases of young buffaloes which have been tied up as baits for tigers, but the regulation bait for a leopard is a live male kid, which can still be purchased for one or two rupees, whereas a buffalo calf now costs from five to ten. I always preferred kids on the small side, which can be relied upon to bleat when separated from their mothers, and the colour white for choice, in case of a shot after dusk. More rope should never be allowed than will suffice for it to stand with its head well raised, or it is quite likely to strangle itself, and the rope must be stout enough to resist the rush with which the leopard attacks a live prey, and although there is no objection to picketing a kid by the neck, a new white rope should be avoided. On no account must the kid be allowed to see the sportsman, or it will refuse to bleat, and if it can be arranged for other goats to be grazed in the vicinity, and to be gradually withdrawn, the leopard may be induced to seize the supposed straggler at once. However, many cunning leopards know all about picketed goats, and I acquired much useful knowledge during my first year in Bundelkhand from an ancient female leopard of this description which had its home in a pile of rocks upon a metalled road 12 miles from my headquarters, and which had come no doubt to expect the arrival of my dogcart on Sunday afternoons. However, this leopard made a mistake, and chased a dog into the village street, when I was actually encamped in the village, and like Cromwell at Dunbar, I felt when I heard the news that the Lord had delivered it into my hand, and towards dawn of that night it met with its fate. The tying up of a pariah dog should be avoided unless no other animal is available and it is essential that the neighbourhood should be rid of a dangerous pest. Apart from all reasons of sentiment a dog understands the motive, and goes into paroxysms of terror, whereas I am convinced that a kid feels no more than the absence of its mother until the leopard actually arrives, when it ceases to bleat and stares intently. Should it be necessary to tie up a dog, this is best accomplished by boring two holes in the ends of a stout stick, and attaching two cords, one for the peg, and one for the dog's neck, but even then the wood is likely to be gnawed through in the course of a night. I used a chain with success to tie up baits for the unsophisticated lions and leopards in the Sudan, but a chain would undoubtedly arouse the suspicion of a cunning animal that needs to be taken off its guard. The habits of an exceptional animal must be watched; and if it proves to be partial to pork, one might pen up a pig in a tempting situation, but the sportsman should be himself a strategist, and a cut-and-dried formula cannot be prescribed.

Leopards in general have not the same detestation of the scent of human beings that characterises the tiger, which I have heard approach my machan at midnight from the rear, sniff loudly and repeatedly when it struck the trail by which my attendants had retreated, and then move away never to return. For this reason it is not necessary to allow the sun to burn the scent, and the machan or the "putwa" need not be occupied more than an hour before sunset in the case of a live bait, or two hours when sitting up over a kill. However, they are much more diurnal in their habits than the majority of tigers, and leopards are shot over baits in broad daylight very much more often than not. Indeed when the sun has reached the horizon, if none of the jungle warnings have been heard, one may generally go off home, and find the bait untouched next day; whereas a tiger rarely appears before 8 p.m., and obviously retreats into far more remote solitudes than the leopard. It is characteristic of both, that a clean miss on the part of the sportsman frequently fails to produce permanent alarm. A most remarkable instance of this kind occurred in the Philibhit district, when a brother sportsman fired four shots at a single tiger within my hearing in the course of the night, the last shot only, fired at sunrise, striking the tiger and proving fatal; but I have myself twice secured leopards in this way, of which the first returned to a goat within five minutes and the second returned to a kill within an hour. It is a very different matter should the sportsman be himself detected, when the animal which makes the discovery becomes cunning for life, and never approaches another bait without infinite precautions. It should also be recollected that when a leopard is approaching the bait, his senses are intensely upon the alert, and that the faintest movement by the sportsman is liable to be detected; but when he has actually seized the goat, or begun to devour the kill, he has then made up his mind that the coast is clear, and the sportsman has his opportunity. A shot from a ·500 Express or a ·350 H.V. cordite rifle will often stretch the leopard stone dead upon the ground, but a shot through the ribs generally sends him away with a series of low growls, and one finds him dead forty yards away. The greatest caution should be exercised until it is certain that the leopard is dead or has got clean away, and on one occasion I recollect that I broke a leopard's back, but this leopard retreated down a nullah for nearly a hundred yards, and concealed himself in a side nullah, and wound up by a charge which landed him four feet from the muzzle of my rifle before I fired into his head and killed him, and examination showed that the whole of the fur had been rubbed off the stifles by friction with the ground. A first shot from a "putwa" may be fired nine times out of ten with impunity, but a second shot is almost certain to provoke a charge, and the sportsman is likely to remember the tenth time, when the leopard recovers his feet after the shot and begins to search for his opponent. This happened to me once when using a solid bullet fired from a 16-bore rifle, and a shot fired into almost complete darkness was followed by the most blood-curdling series of growls. I decided to reserve the second barrel until the leopard actually got into the "putwa," and this appalling concert continued for fully ten minutes, when the leopard lay down on my right, sighed, and became silent. I sat in that "putwa" for two hours until the moon rose, and then emerged to find the leopard dead. Upon another occasion I fired a charge of slugs into a leopard from a "putwa," with a somewhat similar result, except that the leopard made less noise, and finally made off, and was never recovered, and I strongly advise the sportsman to use a powerful rifle upon these animals.

Upon two occasions I recollect that the death of a leopard was followed by the most laughable consequences. The first occurred after I had shot the enormous leopard, to which I have already referred, in Nepal. The leopard disappeared into the forest after receiving the shot, and I judged that it was lying dead some 30 yards to the right of the machan, but far beyond the range of my little electric lamp. I therefore whistled up my elephant, which presently appeared carrying my two Pathan orderlies, and from my machan I directed the mahout to the spot. The elephant shuffled along and all of a sudden detected the leopard, when it uttered a loud scream, turned right about and fled through the forest in the darkness, whilst the orderlies clung to the pad, dropping shoes, pugarees, etc., as the elephant crashed through the branches. Nothing would then bring that elephant up to within 50 yards, and I had to climb down from the machan after pacifying the two irate

Pathans and retrieve the leopard with the aid of the electric torch. The second occurred when I was sitting over a waterhole in the Bahraich district, and would have been worth hundreds of pounds to a cinema company. A party of bears were in the habit of visiting this hole in the sand which was the size of a basin, and as the moon was near the full I tied up a machan in a commanding situation and seated myself therein an hour before sunset. My shikari directed my attention to the cries of the spotted deer, and said that a leopard was undoubtedly on the prowl, and within half an hour a female leopard followed by two cubs the size of terriers approached the pool. I killed her stone dead at the edge of the pool without causing the least alarm to the cubs and then decided to try to effect their capture. They retreated into the jungle when I descended from the tree, and I returned to my camp which was only half a mile off and brought along a large meat-safe, which I buried in the sand on its back and set like a sparrow-trap, with the body of the leopard inside, the door being supported by a stick to which I attached a cord which reached up to my machan. However, the cubs showed no disposition to return, and I regret to say that I never secured them. What actually happened was that towards 9 p.m. a party of three bears climbed down the high bank opposite and were approaching the water, when they smelt the leopard. They immediately turned and fled up the bank, with growls of alarm, but the path was both steep and narrow, and each of the bears was determined not to be last, with the result that the entire party rolled down the bank with loud cries of fear, and fled in three directions, and I was too much amused to fire a shot. Towards midnight the father of this family arrived alone, and approached the trap, when I fired in something of a hurry, and wounded the bear, but he too fled, springing my trap, and I was never able to find him.

One final story will serve to illustrate both the method of approach of a cunning leopard, and a device which I have since employed with success. I had constructed a "putwa" among some low hills in Bundelkhand, and had sat over a goat for an hour before sunset, when a peafowl uttered the grating call to which I have already referred, and repeated it at intervals when the light had disappeared, and the jungle was only lit up by the moon. This was a certain warning and I decided to continue the sitting indefinitely, and actually sat for fully two hours, when over a rock which was behind the goat I became aware of a black silhouette, which presently took the form of the square head and round ears of a leopard staring intently into the aperture through which I was to shoot. By this time I knew too much to move, although my face must have been strongly lit up by the moon, and after a mutual scrutiny of some ten minutes, the head of the leopard was slowly withdrawn. My "putwa" was open in the rear, and whether I was subjected to a similar scrutiny from that quarter I never knew, but after a space of time which seemed to me half an hour, the leopard suddenly rushed at the goat, and I realised that owing to the rock and the shadow of a tree I could distinguish nothing. Presently the cord snapped and the leopard vanished with the goat, and it seemed to me that no more was to be done, but I was determined at least to induce the leopard to believe that he had robbed a sleeping goatherd, so I sat for ten more minutes, and then began to imitate to the best of my power the call of a goatherd to his flock, and then crept out of my "putwa" and rejoined my attendants without allowing them to approach. We returned to camp, which was distant about a mile, but I found myself utterly unable to sleep, and towards 3 a.m. I arose and told my shikari that I was fully determined to return to the "putwa" and tie up a second goat. At that time I had a thoroughly good man in my police orderly Madho, and he fully approved of my resolve, so we left the sleeping camp with a fresh goat and sat out in the open country until there was sufficient light to distinguish one's sights, and then I sat down once more in the "putwa," and Madho very silently tied up the goat and disappeared. I sat until the sun had fully risen, and then became aware of a white blur some 30 yards away in a path which led straight towards the rock under which I had tied the goat, and when a square head and round ears defined itself above the white, I knew that I was again looking into the eyes of the leopard. That leopard approached up the path with a movement so slow as to be imperceptible to the eye, and he must have taken fully half an hour to reach the rock below which I had tied the goat. At one time I blinked an eye, and the far-away look which is so characteristic of the great cats changed at once into an intent frown, and a couple of minutes must have passed before I saw the scrutiny relax, and the head swing round to where the peafowl were scratching on the hill. Then it was slowly withdrawn from above the rock and presently the goat sprang erect and tugged at the rope, but the leopard had fed and walked slowly up to the terrified beast, flung itself over on its back and proceeded to caress the goat between its uplifted forepaws. At this moment I fired and the leopard recovered its feet and disappeared in a flash, but I waited for five minutes, and then whistled up my men, and we found him dead 30 yards off. The goat had only received a slight scratch on the top of the back, but he too was dead before night.

CHAPTER X

MARKHOR (*Capra falconeri*)

Native names—*Markhor*, Kashmir, Afghanistan, Punjab ; *Sara* (male), *Buzkuhi* (female), Baluchistan.

DISTRIBUTION OF MARKHOR

THE home of this grandest of all the goats is not confined to the Himalayas proper, as it extends to the Hindu Kush Range and to the Suleiman system which runs along the north-west frontier of India north of Quetta. Geographically, the habitat of the markhor can be accurately described as the valleys of the Indus and its tributaries from the peak of Haramosh in Baltistan downwards to the plains of India, but it must not be assumed that markhor exist everywhere in this region.

Early sportsmen classed markhor into four types and gave each of these types a geographical name. Unfortunately the names were not strictly accurate, but they have continued in general use and it would be a pity to attempt a change. It should, however, be clearly understood that the names do not necessarily signify the districts in which the different types are generally found. The four different types are known as Astor, Pir Panjal, Kabul and Suleiman.

Let us now consider the geographical distributions of these four types.

Astor. The valley of the Astor River is its stronghold, but heads of this type are also found farther north in Baltistan, as well as nearer its home in two or three valleys to the south of Astor, all of which join the Indus on its left bank. It has been stated that the variety is never, or at any rate rarely, found on the right bank of the Indus, but this is not correct, as it occurs in almost all the nullahs running into the Indus on its right bank

The horns on the left are those of an Astor Markhor and those on the right of a Pir Panjal Markhor. It will be noticed that both types of horns possess both a twist and a spiral. In the Astor variety the spiral is very wide and sweeping in comparison with the Pir Panjal head. In the Kabul and Suleiman types the spiral is almost entirely wanting and the horns are only twisted and nearly straight.

from Rondu in Baltistan down to Chilas. It is true, however, that heads of this type are in the minority in these nullahs. It is also sometimes found in the Gilgit Agency.

Pir Panjal. This variety is found, as its name indicates, in the Pir Panjal Range, but only where that system lies in Kashmir proper; it also occurs in the Kaj Nag and Shamsberi systems, both of which lie entirely within the vale of Kashmir and are off-shoots of the Pir Panjal Range, and even in some of the nullahs which run down into the lower part of the Kishengunga Valley on the left bank of the river. In addition to being a feature of the grounds in Kashmir, the Pir Panjal type is the common variety which occurs throughout Baltistan, Gilgit and Chitral, and it is also found in the nullahs of the Astor Valley, but here it is not so common as the Astor variety. Its northern limits appear to be: in the Lutkho Valley at a point halfway between Drusp and Shogot; in the Chitral main valley and valleys joining it on the left bank at Mori (about 10 miles above Chitral). In Chitral proper its southern limits are said to be on the right bank of the Kunar River at Chigar Serai, and on the left bank at Nari (Narsat). In Chitral, horns of over 50 inches are very rare, but they run considerably bigger in Gilgit and Baltistan, while Kashmir itself used to provide magnificent heads, and only last year (1924) the record markhor of 65 inches was shot by Colonel A. B. Souter in the Kaj Nag. But big heads are by no means common.

Kabul. In this variety there is no imposing spiral, the line of the twisted horns being almost straight. Such animals are first found in the hills on the northern edge of the Peshawar district, and they are the variety which occurs in the Kabul Valley and all the hill ranges of the North-West Frontier of India down to the Gomal River, which may be said to be its southern limit.

Suleiman. South of the Gomal River we have a few markhor of the pure Suleiman type, the horns of which are even straighter than those of the Kabul variety. But generally speaking the markhor found to the southward throughout the mountain ranges of Baluchistan, as far as Quetta, are curiously enough of two mixed types—one resembling the Astor with its pronounced span, and the other the Pir Panjal with its more modified curve. In one case two heads were found locked together, the markhor having died fighting. One head was akin to the Astor variety, the other to the Pir Panjal. But about 1910 a head was obtained in the Zarghan Range near Quetta, which was even more of a curiosity, for each horn was a representative of the two different types. These facts will indicate the hopelessness of attempting to distinguish the various varieties by geographical names and attributions.

There is yet another type of markhor which is not so well known. It is quite distinct as the section of the horns is extremely flat. It is called the Chialtan variety, and specimens were originally obtained in the Takatu and Zarghan Ranges. Subsequent research, however, has shown that it is the characteristic type for the area comprising the Chialtan, Takatu and Zarghan Ranges, and almost all the hill systems situated between Quetta and Chilas. It also seems to exist in some of the Chilas nullahs of the Gilgit Agency which lie towards the Babusar Pass, but it is not numerous here, and is entirely restricted to this one small district. It has been stated that the Chialtan variety is a hybrid between markhor and domesticated goats, but this is not the case. A strong argument against the theory is to be found in the fact that the twist of the horns is the same as that of all wild goats, and in the opposite direction to that of all domesticated varieties.

MARKHOR SHOOTING

By Colonel A. G. Arbuthnot, C.M.G., D.S.O.

The markhor is generally considered by sportsmen to be the stalker's greatest prize. As a trophy, when well set up, with his long flowing beard and magnificent spiral horns, and as a stalker's achievement, he deserves to rank first.

Markhor are still fairly plentiful in Chitral and Chilas, and round the slopes of Mount Nanga Parbat; in the Gilgit Mountains are found some of the biggest and most rugged heads, the best being 60¾ inches. Nearly all the nullahs in Astor hold good markhor as well as ibex; following up the Indus Valley from its junction with the Astor River, Haramoosh is famous for big markhor, and they inhabit most of the nullahs on either bank as far east as Rondu.

As one travels upstream, however, markhor become scarcer and ibex more predominant, till the last remaining markhor is found on the right bank, a day's march below Shardo. Rondu, however, may be taken as the limit, as none are allowed to be shot east of the village of Mendi.

The horns of the markhor are measured along the spiral, and are deceptive. The broader the spread and bolder the spiral the finer the head appears to be, and is; but the sharper spiral will measure more. For example, in 1920 I spent five or six days watching and stalking two big markhor in a nullah between Rondu and Haramoosh. Both were good heads, but the one which attracted me most had an unusually wide spread and massive horns, almost like an Indian buffalo! The other was a head of the "intermediate" species, rather nearer the Pir Panjal variety. To watch the two together through the telescope there appeared to be no doubt which was the bigger, and I set my heart on securing the one with the broad spread; but I was wrong!

After several failures, as the ground was extremely difficult, I succeeded in outwitting the pair, and took the shot at my favourite, though he was further off than the other. He fell to the first bullet, got up, and a second sent him sliding and crashing down 600 feet. He was a fine old specimen and satisfied all my expectations, but only measured 46 inches, though the spread and weight of his horns were exceptional. A friend of mine, Major Weatherbe, followed me to the same nullah a month later, and shot the remaining one, which I recognised as my discarded friend; he was a beautiful head, with two complete spirals, measuring 50 inches.

Routes to Markhor Ground

Probably the best place to secure a good Pir Panjal markhor is in the Kaj Nag or Shamsberi Mountains; Baramulla, 30 miles short of Srinagar on the Rawal Pindi—Kashmir road, would be the best starting-point, and several good local shikaris are to be had near there.

Another route to the Kaj Nag, and also farther afield towards Chilas, runs from Abbotabad, but the novice may find difficulties.

Permits for the Kaj Nag and Shamsberi Ranges have to be applied for specially, and only a very limited number are issued for the first and second half-seasons. In

1920 the application had to be made in Kashmir territory, so it was advisable to wire from Kohala, where the Rawal Pindi—Srinigar Road crosses the Jhelum into Kashmir.

In addition to markhor there are plenty of black bear near Baramulla, and there are red bear in the Shamsberi Mountains. Fifty inches is an exceptional head and nothing less than 43 inches should be shot in the Kaj Nag.

Astor and Gilgit. To reach Astor the sportsman travels by boat to Bandipur, north of the Wular Lake, where pony transport should be arranged for. Thence by the main Gilgit road over the Burzil Pass.

The Burzil can be crossed most years before the end of April, though a late fall of snow may necessitate some bribery to obtain porters.

Astor is in the Gilgit Agency, and passes to sportsmen from Kashmir are limited. In addition to this, visitors are warned that the village headmen are not bound to give them any assistance in transport or supplies for their men, so it is advisable to bring all requirements with them. This naturally adds considerably to the difficulties and expenses of the expedition, and points to a certain amount of unnecessary jealousy between Gilgit and Kashmir.

Nearly all the nullahs between Astor village and the Indus hold big markhor and ibex too. Forty-five inches should be taken as the smallest shootable head in this district.

Four or five marches below Astor the Indus is reached, and beyond lies the Gilgit district; the shooting is mainly reserved for the small garrison of this distant outport, but special permit may be obtained.

Haramoosh and Rondu. Haramoosh and Rondu can be reached either via the Astor and Indus Rivers, or by marching down the river from Skardo. There is a short cut over a 16,000 feet pass from Astor to Rondu, which is open " when the apricots are ripe," generally by the end of June.

The road on the right bank of the Indus from Haramoosh to Rondu is extremely rough and not normally passable for ponies; but it was being improved in 1920. There are rope bridges above and below Tahr, the chief village of Rondu.

Habits and Special Characteristics of Markhor

Most that I have said about the habits of ibex is equally applicable to markhor, so it will suffice to note any peculiarities or differences. Markhor are not so plentiful as ibex, and are peculiar in their liking for special nullahs, and even particular bits of ground in those nullahs.

In several places where ibex predominate about half a dozen apparently isolated markhor may be found year after year, and they seem to reserve certain spots for themselves. In some nullahs in Astor and Haramoosh they may be seen in large herds, but the old veterans generally live apart, sometimes alone, sometimes a couple of good heads along with four or five others.

Early in the year markhor are to be found low down near the entrances of side nullahs, and if there are ibex in the same nullah, the former will be the lower of the two. They are, however, even more averse to open ground and " maidans " than are ibex, and usually select the most broken precipitous country with small strips of grazing here and there. To such places they show great attachment, and will often return a few days after having been scared away. There is a nullah in the Shigar Valley where an isolated family of markhor lived for many years, and maintained their claim, among all the ibex, to certain bits of ground, far from the rest of their kin.

Later in the year the markhor in many places seem to change positions with the ibex, pass above them, and inhabit the highest precipices near the head of the nullah.

As far as alertness, eyesight, and scent go, I have never found the markhor in any way inferior to the ibex, and I think the solitary old markhor deserves the palm for difficulty of approach. If he suffers any disadvantage it is probably due to his devotion to certain definite bits of ground.

He selects his day retreat with the same care and cunning, and it has struck me is even a greater adept than the ibex at " camouflaging " himself as he lies among the rocks. When grazing, his lighter colouring, longer hair, and the black and white of his flowing beard, make him more conspicuous. As a rule he grazes later in the morning, and comes down earlier in the evening than his confrère.

Locating and Stalking

All that has been written regarding locating and watching ibex applies with equal force to markhor ; the value of watching your game from morn till night, and very carefully choosing the best line of approach, is even greater with the latter, owing to his more regular habits, and to his usually being found on more difficult ground.

In many places the ground is the chief obstacle to your most obvious plan of approach. To the thar of Chamba and Kishtwar is usually accorded the palm for selecting the most dangerous abodes, and in this I agree, but the markhor in his higher and remoter altitudes is no mean second!

We must look for him not so much on the big spurs and sides of small nullahs beloved of the ibex, but on the more precipitous slopes falling abruptly from the rocky peaks above. In crossing such slopes his route will naturally vary day by day, but he will have more or less the same objective, the same few patches of grass or herbs to reach soon before dusk, and there will be certain points in his route that he will *always* pass; possibly because there is no other way he can go!

As regards the approach and stalking of markhor, I have nothing to add to what I have written in the chapter on ibex. The same rules and the same ideas apply to both; both require all the skill and cunning we can produce, and a carefully thought out plan of action.

I have laid great stress on locating and watching game, but the necessity for caution must be remembered. Many a time have I remarked how low down ibex or markhor have been grazing the first day I spotted them on reaching my nullah, and how they have never come so low again! Carelessness on the part of one's shikari or coolies, or indifferent use of glasses and telescope by oneself, may easily waste many days, or lead to quitting a nullah empty handed and disappointed.

General notes. A few general notes may be of use to sportsmen who are thinking of making their first expedition to the haunts of the markhor and ibex, but space does not admit of more than a reference to one or two points.

Expenses. I would fain say that the cost of a two or three months' trip to the Himalayas is well within the limits of a subaltern's pay in India! It is a fact, but I feel bound to warn the novice that his first expedition is likely to be expensive. Experience has to be bought, and it sells for an unduly high price in Kashmir.

The journey to Srinagar is costly; rail fare to Rawal Pindi and the cost of a seat in the mail motor, and "ekka" or "tonga" for your kit and servant, can be found in the railway time-table.

Arrived in Srinagar, there is no limit to what you may spend; I can only advise a limit of three days while awaiting your luggage and servant; your shikari will expect a coat, and probably ask for a complete trousseau, but the latter is not necessary. Your tiffin coolie and, say, two or three permanent coolies, want a blanket and "*chaplies*" and "puttoo" socks for snow passes. If early in the year, a pair of snow-spectacles apiece is also necessary.

All prices in the Valley of Kashmir have, of course, gone up since the war; stores, flour, rice and wages have all risen about 50 per cent, but once you are clear of the valley the monthly cost of an expedition is little more than in pre-war days.

Rs. 250 a month may be taken as a fair estimate of monthly expenditure including stores, food, wages, and flour for coolies, after leaving Srinagar. In my shooting diary of 1901 I have the total cost of a three-months' expedition to Kashmir from Jhansi in Central India, Rs. 900, including rail journey. Many subsequent shoots in other parts of the Himalayas averaged Rs. 200 a month after leaving the starting-point. In 1920 a three-months' trip to Baltistan and Haramoosh with my wife averaged Rs. 350 a month after leaving Srinagar. This covered an average of sixteen to twenty-two coolies, and all stores, wages, etc.

As every old campaigner knows, it is possible to travel light and yet be comfortable. The essentials are few, but we cannot dispense with *one* of them; the non-essentials must be ruthlessly left behind.

Camp Kit. Tents and all camp equipment can be hired at Cockburn's agency, or from other agents in Srinagar. If possible it is wise to take one's own camp bed, chair, table and bath, as those provided are heavy, rickety, and uncomfortable. If hiring a tent, be sure you insist on one of not over 80 lb. to 100 lb.; that, with its pegs, will make two easy coolie loads; see it pitched, and have all doubtful ropes and rope attachments renewed.

In 1920 I found awaiting me in Srinagar a spacious 250-lb. tent, and had some difficulty in exchanging it for one of 100 lb. On my return from Baltistan I met an unfortunate subaltern stranded in Ladak with that 250-lb. tent; pony transport failed, and he could get no further!

Footwear. A couple of pairs of stout, well-oiled and nailed shooting boots are the backbone of one's requirements. In dry weather "*chaplies*" and leather socks made in Srinagar are the lightest and best for marching, but boots are best over grass or snow. For actual stalking on ibex or markhor ground there is nothing to compare with the native grass shoes, bound on over puttoo socks and quilted boots. A pair or two of each of the latter per month should be bought in Srinagar. The grass shoes are made up as required by one's own shikari; a pair last about three days, and a spare pair should be carried on every occasion.

Rifles. The vexed question of small versus heavy bore rifles is one on which writers and sportsmen still fail to agree. The introduction of rifles with accelerated velocities, producing the so-called paralysing effect, has perhaps added to the agreements in favour of the smaller bore. The best advice I can offer is to buy a good medium-bore high-velocity rifle, and try it well; try it on the range, and if possible on blackluck and gazelle. If it fails to inspire you with confidence, get rid of it and try another. The one point on which all sportsmen will agree is that it matters little what calibre of rifle you use if you fail to hit your ibex or markhor in a fatal or disabling spot, and to do that you must have a good weapon that suits you.

Where to Aim. The secret of clean shooting is to concentrate all your efforts on your stalk, and a careful, well placed first shot. Forget that you have a magazine behind you; there are several vulnerable places open to you, and it is very seldom worth while to risk a doubtful first shot. Ibex and markhor are tough customers and can carry a lot of misplaced lead, especially the former.

My advice to the novice is to endeavour to obtain the following conditions:

(1) A shot at not more than 150 yards.

(2) Either, a broadside target—aim below the withers with a view to a fatal shot through the spine, or at any rate smashing the shoulder blade.

(3) Or, the animal facing you at an angle of 45°—aim between the neck and shoulder blade.

(4) Or, the animal facing away from you at an angle of 45°—aim rather high, and close behind the shoulder blade.

The neck-shot is also very fatal, but like the heart-shot gives but a small target, and a miss will not necessarily disable.

CHAPTER XI

OORIAL OR SHAPU (*Ovis vignei* or *Ovis cycloceros*)

Native names—*Shapo* (male), *Shamo* (female), Ladak, Baltistan; *Urin*, Astor; *Roch, Gadh*, Baluch; *Oorial*, Punjab.

THIS handsome sheep is essentially an inhabitant of the valley of the Indus. It is found in hills and mountains on both banks of that great river, and also in the basins of most of its tributaries from Ladak to the Plains of India, but it never occurs in the basin of the Jhelum in Kashmir. Otherwise the basin of the Indus in the immediate neighbourhood of the river is a most accurate description of its habitat. In Ladak it is found on both sides of the Zaskar Range, and Kinloch mentions seeing shapu and *Ammon* feeding in the same nullah near Gya, which is about 35 miles due south of Leh. Hence it follows the valley of the Indus down stream, although it is much more common to the south of the river than to the north, as far as Chilas. Between Chilas and Attock the Indus is unexplored, but as oorial occur in the hills in the neighbourhood of both these places I see no reason to doubt their being found on both banks of the river in between.

To the north-east they extend up to the Hindu Kush Range beyond Chitral and Gilgit, and I believe they are found in Afghanistan. At one time they were common in the hills round Quetta, but they have been rather shot out in this neighbourhood. South of the Indus in the Punjab Salt Range they are still fairly plentiful, and the best heads probably come from this range and from Ladak.

SHAPU SHOOTING

By Colonel A. G. Arbuthnot, C.M.G., D.S.O.

Shapu and Oorial Horns. A good head measures from 30 to 35 inches. The set up head is a fine trophy, and the shapu is no easy game to circumvent, whether it be on the steep slopes of the Indus or on the bare, rugged Punjab Salt Hills.

Favourite Ground. In Ladak, Baltistan, and on the Indus banks, you will find shapu on their favourite ground, quite unlike that chosen by the ibex; in fact "sheep ground" rather than "goat ground." Where the rocks, ravines, and precipitous cliffs are less predominant, and steep grassy slopes appear, the shapu will probably be found.

Following down the Indus from Ladak or Dras towards Skardo and beyond, there are shapu on either bank, wherever their favourite conditions exist. Generally they are found on the more open headlands at the entrance of nullahs, while the ibex live higher up.

Near Skardo on the borders of the Deosai Plateau, and in the nullahs running down from the Deosai to the Indus, there are good shapu, but a big head always takes some finding. Certain nullahs of the Shigar Valley hold a few shapu, but I have never seen a good head there, though a march or so east of Shigar, on the right bank of the Indus, heads of 35 inches have been shot. Shapu are not likely to be the main object of a shooting expedition, but on the road through Ladak to Leh in search of *Ovis Ammon* the reader should be able to get a good head, and with four or five days to spare from Skardo, should be able to get a fair one.

Stalking Shapu. Though shapu ground may be comparatively easy climbing, these wild sheep are lively animals to stalk and admit of no liberties. If they get your wind or view they will clear off at a great pace and go a long way. Though constant to a certain locality they are far more variable than the wild goats in their feeding-grounds, and seldom graze the same place two days in succession.

Living as they do on more or less open, downy spurs, they are very ready to take alarm; a suspicion of a leopard in the vicinity will often drive a herd right away, and leave you wondering if they have winded you.

Should your herd be scared away like this, instead of searching for them higher up, as you would for ibex under similar circumstances, you are more likely to find them lower down.

One year, having a few days to spare on the way back from Baltistan, I went up a small nullah on the left bank of the Indus, about twenty marches above Skardo, in hopes of getting a good shapu. I found a herd of about twenty and another of about six or seven, but not a head over 26 inches among them. While watching the big herd, well to windward of me, I suddenly saw them cease grazing and begin to shift uphill; in another minute they were all tracking off as fast as they could. They passed not far above where I was lying, and I watched them for 2 miles till they had crossed over into the next nullah, and could only guess they had seen a leopard or wolf.

Next day I took a bivouac tent and searched all the ground at the head of the nullah, but failed to see any shapu. On my return the day after I found the frightened herd peacefully grazing on the headland close above my camp beside the Indus.

CHAPTER XII

OVIS AMMON OR NYAN (*Ovis Ammon Hodgsoni*)

Native names—*Nyan* (rams), *Nyanmo* (ewes), Tibetan.

THIS magnificent creature essentially belongs to open, undulating country, rather than to precipitous mountains; and the flat plains, tilted levels and round-topped hills of Tibet form its home. Like all wild sheep it can climb well, but it is seldom found in precipitous places, although it is frequently met with in broken ground. The chief point which impressed me when I first saw *Ammon* was their wonderful length of leg, compared with such animals as burrhel, thar, ibex, or shapu. They seem built for galloping over open country, and without doubt the best places in which to find them are vast open spaces interspersed with hills in which there are valleys to provide shelter from both sun and wind when they lie up during the heat of the day. From this it will be obvious that the Zaskar Range must certainly be crossed before *Ammon* ground is reached, and the sketch map shows their distribution as far as it is at present known. In the description of the geography of the Himalayas it was pointed out that from the basin of the Karnali to that of the Bhotia Kosi the country between the Ladak and Great Himalayan Ranges was mountainous and similar in general character to that lying between the Zaskar and Great Himalayan Ranges farther west. Consequently here *Ammon* will not be found to the south of the Ladak Range, but for the rest of its length in Tibet *Ammon* are found on both sides, except, perhaps, where it forms the boundary between Tibet and Bhutan. Here our knowledge of the geographical features is decidedly limited.

As soon as the mean elevation of the country falls much below 14,000 feet *Ammon* are no longer found, which accounts for the boundaries of their habitat being fixed as they are in the valleys of the Tsangpo and Indus. Their eastern limits are unknown, but they probably extend northwards up to the Kuen Lun Range.

Curiously enough there are two spots in which *Ammon* rams will sometimes cross the crest of the Zaskar Range, although they will never wander far down the southern slopes of that range. These two places are: first, just to the south of the Tso Morari (lake), where they may be occasionally found at the head of the Kibber Valley in Spiti; and secondly, in the neighbourhood of the Kangri Bingri Pass on the borders of Kumaon and British Garhwal. Why they should choose these two places and no others is most extraordinary. There are several other parts of the Zaskar Range which seem equally suitable for their requirements, but I have never been able to find any evidence or traces of rams anywhere else. Ewes and kyang will now and then cross into the head of the valley of the Jadhganga branch of the Bhagirathi, and Wilson mentions this in *A Summer Ramble in the Himalayas*, but rams never seem to follow this lead. It should be noted that *Ammon* rams only now and then cross into British territory at the two places mentioned, and a sportsman who made a special trip to either of them for the special purpose of getting an *Ammon* would probably be disappointed. Still, that these grand beasts do occasionally select these crossing points is an undoubted fact.

Ammon are big animals standing quite twelve hands at the shoulder, but they do not weigh so much in proportion to their size as ibex or thar. The average weight of a full-grown ram would probably be some-

HOW TO JUDGE AMMON HEADS.

The sketch on the left shows a big ram with massive points to its horns, and that on the right a small ram with slender points.

where in the neighbourhood of 210 to 220 lb., and occasionally one might weigh as much as 250 lb.

The colour is a very light brown with darker withers. Ewes and young rams have dark heads and necks, but full-grown rams develop a white ruff or mane, and in the distance they can be easily distinguished by the light colour of their heads and necks, for the horns, in spite of their great size, are light in colour and very difficult to see. If *Ammon* are spotted and the glass reveals dark heads they can be left alone, while if the heads are light they should be stalked forthwith in order to obtain a closer inspection, for although a white ruff means a mature ram it does not necessarily indicate a good head,

DISTRIBUTION OF "OVIS AMMON"

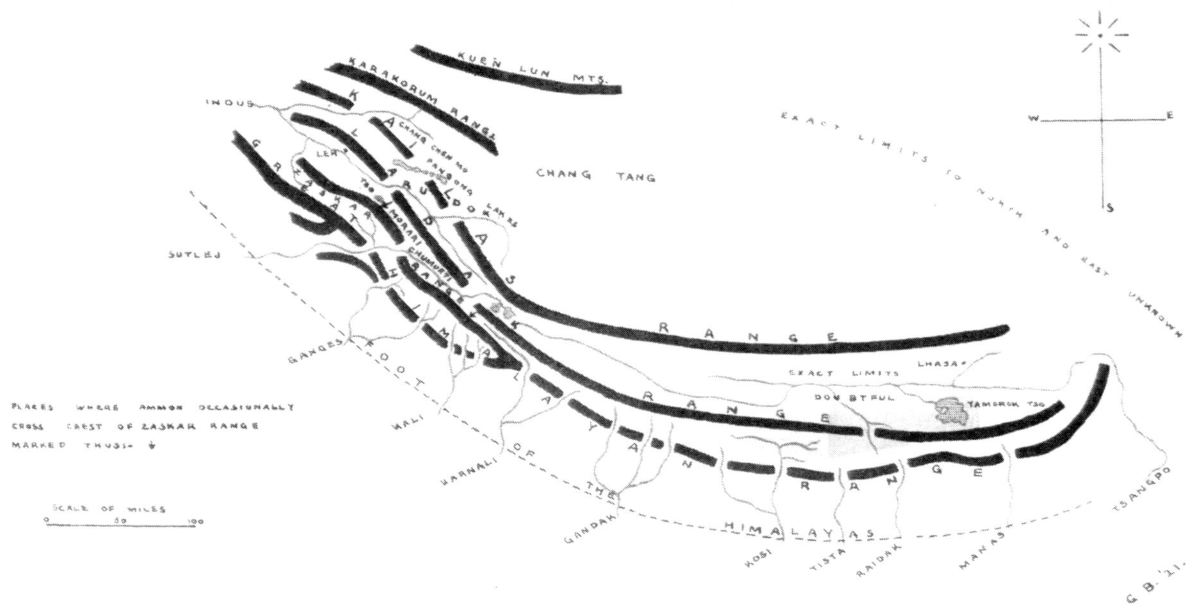

and there are many rams with white ruffs which do not carry worthy trophies. At first comparatively small *Ammon* horns will look enormous, but once a really fine head has been seen and studied mistakes should not be made. If the horns taper rapidly from a point near the base they can be assumed to be small, while if the massiveness is maintained throughout the greater part of their length (in which case they certainly do convey the impression of the fossil after which they are named), a shot can be taken with confidence. The two little sketches show this more clearly than mere words could. Unfortunately it is very seldom that an old ram is shot with perfect horns, the tips having usually been broken off for several inches. I realised the great difference that this damage could make to the measurements of a horn when I picked up the head of an old ram which had been recently killed by wolves. The left horn was quite perfect, and measured with a steel tape was 49½ inches; the right horn showed the usual broken tip and only measured 45 inches. In each case the girth was 18 inches. I believe that the tips get broken partly through fighting, for the rams are very pugnacious among themselves, and partly when scrabbling in snow or earth to get at some such tit-bits as moss or short wiry grass.

The heads one picks up are often very fine and much larger than those which are usually seen on live animals. Tibetans have explained this to me by saying that when the horns are fully grown they are so large that the ram is prevented from reaching the grass with his mouth because the horns hit the ground first, and consequently he dies of starvation! This ingenious theory is palpably absurd because many of the horns I picked up did not protrude nearly as far down as the broken nose bone of the skull. I believe that the real explanation is that in hard winters when food is scarce the rams with the biggest and heaviest heads find the burden of them too much to carry easily and are unable to gallop as fast as the others, and so fall a prey to the wolves. I have almost invariably found tooth marks on heads and bones thus picked up, but of course it is impossible to say whether the wolves which made the marks actually killed the ram or found it dead.

The old rams keep studiously apart from the ewes and youngsters during the summer months, and the rut does not begin until September. Ewes may be seen constantly when one is hunting for *Ammon*, but the bands of rams are exceedingly difficult to find. They seem to be most particular in their selection of ground, and after the country has been traversed again and again without result the rams may suddenly be found lying up in some small hidden nullah. They usually lie up at about 10 a.m. and begin grazing again soon after 4 p.m., but I have once seen rams moving to the nullah in which they intended to lie up for the day as late as 1 p.m.

I regard the *Ammon* as the most difficult of all animals to stalk and shoot. Not only has it every sense abnormally developed, but it has the open nature of the ground entirely in its favour, in addition to its natural wariness. Further, the winds in Tibet are at the best an uncertain quantity, and have a most exasperating way of changing just at the wrong moment. The old proverb about more

Typical *Ovis Ammon* ground beyond the Zaskar Range.
Altitude 15,100 feet.

haste and less speed is truer in *Ammon*-shooting than in any other form of sport I know. On very windy and gusty days it is better to stay in camp or go after burrhel than to risk spoiling a stalk after *Ammon*, in which case they are sure to clear out of the country. And when actually looking for game do not be in too much of a hurry and try to cover a vast tract of country, but search minutely every nook and cranny in a small area, taking bits at a time until the whole ground is covered. Thus shall you meet with success. Remember that your ideas of ideal resting places and those of the rams may not necessarily coincide, and what you have got to do is to find out what they think about it, not to determine what they ought to think about it. Frequently the band of rams in any particular locality will select some insignificant little side nullah in which to lurk by day : no fold in the ground is worth neglecting.

If *Ammon* see you first you will be indeed lucky if it is not a case of good-bye for ever. I was once crossing a broad nullah which I thought I had examined most thoroughly before my party entered it. We were almost across when we spotted four rams standing up and gazing at us about 1,000 yards away. Where they came from I do not know, but there they were. I insisted on my little band continuing its way until hidden behind a low spur when I cried a halt and crept up alone until I could just see the *Ammon*. I watched them for ten minutes and then one lay down ; a second soon followed its example, and at last all four seemed nicely settled for the day. It was only 11 a.m. and I felt sure that they had recovered from their alarm and would stay where they were. I accordingly reconnoitred for a stalk, and found a small nullah running parallel to the big one which we had just crossed, the head of which should bring me to a spot just over where the rams were lying. The wind was right and steady and I never felt more certain of a stalk, but just as I was about to look over the crest from the spot where I hoped to get a shot an exclamation from my Tibetan guide drew my attention to four rams retreating over the sky-line nearly a mile away. Now until that moment we had been entirely hidden from view ever since we began the stalk—there could be no question of that—and as I have already said the wind was in our favour. The *Ammon* were not galloping as if wildly alarmed but just steadily covering ground, and at the pace they were going when we saw them they must have left the spot where they lay down soon after we had started our fruitless stalk, for it was but a short one. No, it was simply their intuition or instinct, call it what you will, which had warned them that the humans they had seen promised them no good. So, even after they had lain down once more, their caution got the better of their desire for comfort and they felt that they could not rest in peace where they were. This reasoning may seem far-fetched, but I believe it to be correct, and can think of no other explanation.

On another occasion I was most anxious to reach a certain grassy basin which my Tibetan guide assured me was a sure find for rams and rather hurried my examination of a smaller nullah which had to be crossed. My feelings can be better imagined than described when suddenly just as we were about half-way across, four rams appeared from nowhere, wheeled round, and galloped for the next province.

I have purposely dwelt on failures, as the lessons to be learnt therefrom are more instructive than any which will be acquired by success, which frequently tends to make one underestimate the difficulties. Let me now describe a success, for it too will provide its lesson.

There were four of us altogether, at least four humans and a pony, and we were a somewhat mixed party. First and foremost there was Roop Ram. Of course this was not the name with which he was christened, or whatever the corresponding function is called in Spiti, for the province of his birth is decidedly Buddhist ; but he was a rolling stone and had fulfilled all sorts and conditions of posts throughout the Himalayas, Ladak and Tibet during a decidedly chequered career. I had hit on him quite by chance and discovered that his real *métier* was undoubtedly that of shikari—he had all the instincts, and the most wonderful eyesight I have ever known in a human being. He lacked the experience which is necessary before the excitement of a really keen hunter can be properly controlled, but he was indefatigable, brimful of zeal and ambition to become a shikari proper (this was his first experience with a sahib), and made an intensely amusing companion. His ideas on religion were decidedly convenient. In Tibet he was a Buddhist and would eat yak's flesh with the best of them ; but once the frontier had been recrossed he was a devout Hindu, and regarded all cows (including yaks and jibboos, or half-bred yaks) as entirely sacred and holy, and altogether as animals against which it would be utter desecration to lift a hand. He was quite a good cook in a rough way, and on one trip for over a month he acted as my bearer and cook combined. In spite of his love of wandering his domestic instincts were very strong, and I have never met a hillman who was fonder of his wife and three children than Roop Ram. He was ever talking about his family and extolling the virtues of Mrs. R. R., whom he invariably treated with a courteous kindness which is rare in the further Himalayas.

Next in importance was Chiang, my Tibetan guide. His chief characteristics were sparkling good humour, gleaming white teeth, a filthily greasy pig-tail, and a most appalling odour. His business was to lead and look after the shaggy little Rudok pony and generally act as guide.

Yonghdu was a Bhotia who had travelled much. He was really the head man of my little expedition and had accompanied me out shooting at his own earnest request.

I myself was the fourth.

We had covered a good many miles since the start at dawn, for it was now nearly 1 p.m. On arrival at a little plateau which was hidden by a higher ridge from the ground which we intended to cover in the afternoon we stopped for our mid-day halt, and I was just about to have my tiffin of chappatie and burrhel sandwiches washed down with cold tea when Roop Ram said "Nyan," and my first feeling was one of thankfulness that I had insisted on Chiang keeping the pony in a hollow just below us. Over the crest of the ridge I have mentioned and quite two miles away there appeared the summit

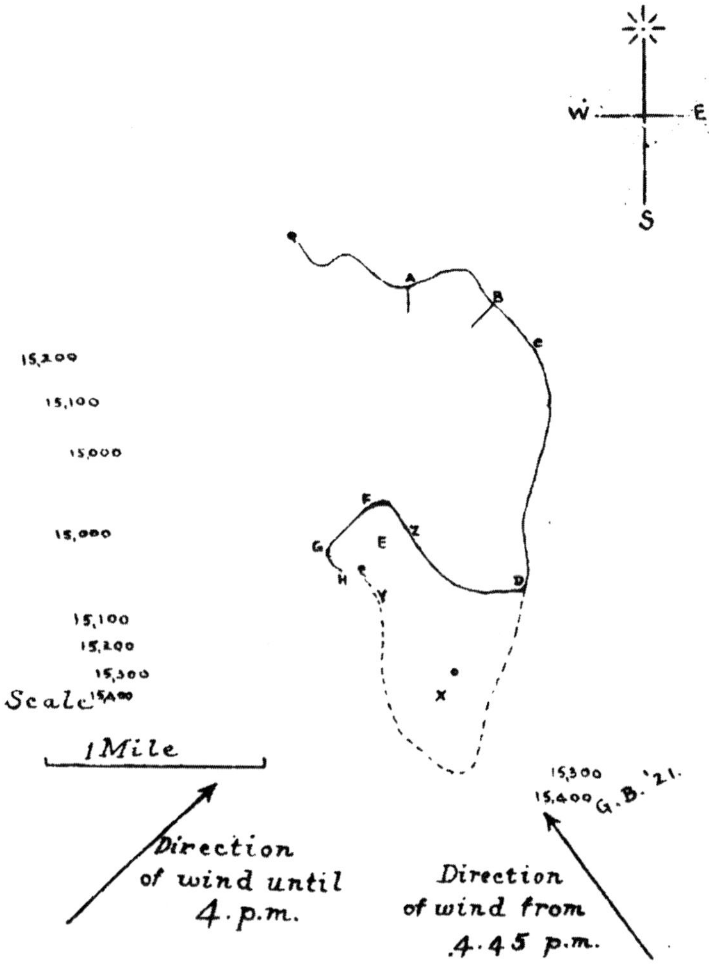

Stalk after
Ovis ammon hodgsoni

References.

Ammon first seen at O

Ammon lay up at P

Ammon first seen from Q

Route followed on stalk ——

Alternative route -------

of a round-topped hill. On this hill Roop Ram declared he could see two animals which must be nyan, but he honestly added that he could not tell if they were rams or ewes! With my eight-power glasses I could just distinguish two little dots, which might be anything until I saw them move, when I knew they must be *Ammon*. I did not expect them to be rams, as they were on the move in the middle of the day, but my forty-power telescope showed them to be undoubted rams, as they had light coloured heads and necks, but of course I could not distinguish any horns. I saw they were slowly descending the hill, and we did not dare risk a move until they were hidden by the ridge. I felt sure they were on their way to some nook in which to lie up during the heat of the afternoon, and doubted their being alarmed considering the great distance which separated them from us.

The accompanying sketch map gives a plan of the country and the route taken for the actual stalk.

All thoughts of food vanished and I instructed Chiang to remain where he was with the pony, which was laden with the remains of our food and my cast clothes, for the thermometer had indicated 35 degrees of frost when we left camp, and now the sun was so hot that I had been sitting in my shirt sleeves. Yonghdu was to accompany Roop Ram and myself on the stalk for as long as I considered safe, and when this point was reached was to wait until he heard a shot or we returned to him. If he heard a shot he was to locate our position and then return and bring along Chiang and the pony. In fact he was to be the "connecting file."

Roop Ram took my rifle, a single-barrel falling-block action ·280, the telescope and the camera, while I carried my glasses. We first advanced straight towards the aforementioned ridge, but soon saw that it would be too risky to attempt to cross it at once, and so turned to the left and followed the line of the crest but keeping well down below the summit. At A I decided to reconnoitre, because it must be remembered that so far we did not know where the *Ammon* had gone, how many there were in all, or even whether there was a good head amongst them. Leaving Roop Ram and Yonghdu with strict injunctions not to attempt to follow me, I crawled to the crest of the ridge, selecting a place where was a slight hillock, until I could just see over the top, taking good care to keep well down on the side of the hillock. It was some time before I found the rams, but at last I spotted them lying down in a tiny side nullah, which was an offshoot of one of many parallel and larger ones, all of which gave into a huge open basin. There were now four rams, but they were all lying down facing me and I could not see their horns properly at that distance, for I did not dare use the telescope here for fear of it flashing in the sun, since the blacking had become rather worn. I accordingly rejoined my companions and we continued our way along the side of the ridge as far as B, where I decided to reconnoitre once again. Taking the same precautions as before, but this time pulling out the draws of the telescope before starting and tying a couple of khaki handkerchiefs round it, I again crawled to the top. From this position I could see the *Ammon* from a slightly more favourable angle, and could now see that there were six rams, and the telescope showed two to carry massive tipped horns. They were still all lying down and seemed perfectly unconscious of danger. At C I left Yonghdu to fulfil his part and went on as shown in the sketch with Roop Ram. We arrived at D at about 3.15 p.m., and here I think I made a mistake through not being acquainted with the country. I think we should have continued our way round the hill X, as indicated by the dotted line, when the convex slope of the ground would have hidden us from the *Ammon*, but neither of us knew what lay beyond, and I had obtained a good general knowledge of the ground to our right when I made my two reconnaissances. Accordingly we crossed the ridge by a little coll which was hidden from the *Ammon* by the side of the little branch nullah in which they were lying, and dropped down into the larger nullah Z which was one of the parallel valleys already mentioned. We were now in the next main nullah to the rams. I thought of trying to get a shot from E but decided that the distance was too great and so determined on crossing the mouth of the larger nullah Y in the sides of which the *Ammon* were lying up and working for a shot from just above them. With this end in view we got to F at about 4 p.m., and here the wind which had been wonderfully steady so far, started veering about and blowing from every corner at once. I at once drew Roop Ram back into the nullah Z, because as long as we were in there the chances against our scent being taken to the rams were decidedly good. I felt sure that the wind would settle down soon and blow down the nullah Z and all those parallel valleys, in which case we could cross from F to G in safety, but I also feared that the rams might soon begin to move and prayed for a quick ceasing of this veering air. Roop Ram became fearfully impatient, and was all for risking it, but I refused to budge, and at last at 4.45 p.m. my patience was rewarded, for the wind suddenly stopped its antics and began to blow steadily in the direction I had anticipated. We quickly darted across from F to G, where I rested to regain breath, for the altitude was over 15,000 feet, and our dash had made me blow like the proverbial grampus.

We were now on the last lap, and began the short ascent towards H. This was but half completed when we suddenly saw four more *Ammon*—two ewes and two small rams—walking down the centre of the valley Y towards us, and we had to waste several precious minutes until they had entered dead ground. At the time I did not think they had seen us, but looking back I think that their suspicions must have been aroused by something. At last we were within a few yards of H, the spot from which I hoped to get a shot at about forty yards. Again I waited to get breath, and then took the rifle from Roop Ram and drew off the muzzle cover and put up the Lyman sight. With the rifle in one hand and the glasses in the other I was just about to crawl up the final half dozen yards when an exclamation from Roop Ram made me look up. There in the centre of the big nullah, and quite 250 yards away, were all the *Ammon* together, the six full-grown rams we had been stalking, and the two youngsters and two ewes which had recently arrived. They were standing gazing at us, and I knew that in a moment they would be off. A quick look through the glasses showed me that the left hand one of all carried horns with massive tips, and as it presented as good a target as any, being nearly broadside on, I took a quick aim and fired.

Then ensued one of the finest sights I have ever seen. Off went all those ten *Ammon* at full gallop: it was like a start for the Derby. I felt my bullet had gone over the ram's back, and mechanically I worked the lever of the falling block and jerked out the fired case. Another cartridge was slipped in and the lever rammed home. It was the work of a second. I swung just clear of my ram's shoulder as he was stretched at full speed up the nullah. This time there was no doubt, for he staggered and started moving downhill away from the rest. Again the falling block was worked mechanically, and at the third shot the noble beast collapsed in a heap. My second shot had caught him too far back, while the first was a clean miss. I looked at my watch: it was now 5 p.m., just four hours since we began the stalk.

After taking a photograph I sent Roop Ram back for Yonghdu while I set about skinning and cutting up the *Ammon*. At the end of half an hour Chiang arrived by himself; he was smiling as usual and started to talk hard. I could not understand a word of what he said, as he naturally knew no Hindustani at all, and my knowledge of Tibetan was of the most elementary nature imaginable; but at last I gathered that the pony had escaped and departed back for camp and the others had gone after it. This was indeed cheerful news, for now the sun was dropping, I was beginning to get bitterly cold, and I knew that this was nothing to what it would be in a couple of hours' time. I had had nothing to eat since a few mouthfuls snatched during a brief halt at about 10 a.m., and I now realised that I was very hungry. My warm wraps as well as my food were on the pony, so I looked forward to a joyful tramp back to camp, which was anything from 10 to 15 miles away. However, the great horns beside me made up for everything, and I decided to give Chiang the head to carry, while I shouldered the rifle, which Roop Ram had left with me.

Soon after 6.30 p.m. I heard a bell, and looking up saw Yonghdu, Roop Ram and the delinquent pony, which they had succeeded in catching after a long hunt. I have seldom been more thankful for anything in my life, and at once threw on my sweater and poshteen and greedily fell to on my interrupted tiffin. By the time I had finished the others were ready, having disposed of the *Ammon* meat in a sack which was pulled from off the pony's back in some mysterious manner. This was left cached for the next day, and the protesting Chiang was given the head to carry as a reward for letting the pony escape, while I mounted the culprit in question, and we all set back for camp. There was a full moon, and I felt very happy. We reached our little home at 10 p.m., just sixteen hours after we had left it in the morning. It was one of the longest and most tiring, but also one of the most exciting days of my life.

The only regular habitat of *Ammon* which exists in Indian territory is a part of Ladak, and unfortunately, this has been so heavily hunted for very many years

A 40-INCH *Ovis Ammon* SHOT AT 15,300 FEET.

past, that rams with shootable heads are not common. In 1911 a friend of mine traversed Ladak from Chang Chen Mo in the north to Hanle in the south, and saw but one ram worth shooting, and even this one did not carry a good head, only measuring 37 inches as far as I can remember. It has already been pointed out that *Ammon* will occasionally cross into Spiti and Kumaon, and they are also sometimes to be found in the neighbourhood of the Tso Lhama (lake) at the head of the Tista River in the extreme north of Sikkim, but here again they are only occasional visitors.

If the political restrictions on entering Tibet are ever removed some grand sport will be assured. I do not believe *Ammon* to be at all plentiful in the Chang Tang, or great desert of northern Tibet, but they occur in greater numbers farther south. Rudok will probably always be a district somewhat jealously guarded by the Tibetans on account of the goldfields which exist there, and I fancy the best *Ammon* grounds adjoining Indian territory will be found from Chumurti to Yamdrok Tso (lake).

The flesh of the *Ammon* is excellent, quite as good as, if not superior to, that of burrhel, which is always supposed to be the best meat of any Himalayan or Tibetan game.

No efforts should be considered too great in attempting to get an *Ammon* head, and exploration in the Zaskar Range up to the extreme limits of Indian territory are worth while. Although I know of no other places where the rams cross this range other than those mentioned, I have always felt that they may sometimes cross it elsewhere, and I am sure explorations on the lines I have suggested in the section about Trans-Himalayan burrhel would be well worth while ; but localities where there is one well-defined and easy pass should be avoided, as these places are known too well. The game is decidedly worth the candle and an *Ammon* head obtained in such a manner would ever be trophy cherished beyond any obtained in Ladak or other well-known locality.

CHAPTER XIII

RED BEAR (*Ursus Arctus Isabellinus*)

Native names—*Lal bhalu, Safed bhalu, Sialareecche*, Hindi; *Harput*, Kashmir.

THE red bear or snow bear of the Himalayas is the same animal as the brown bear of Europe. Red bears are generally found from slightly below the tree-line to some way above it on both sides of the Great Himalayan Range and also on both sides of the Dhauladhar and Pir Panjal Ranges wherever these two systems attain a sufficient altitude, but they do not extend farther to the west on the Pir Panjal Range than the Chenab River, while Bara Bangahal, the peculiar basin at the head of the Ravi, forms the western limit on the Dhauladhar Range. On this last system they do not occur between the Beas and Sutlej Rivers, nor on that part which lies immediately east of the River Sutlej. They exist in small numbers in the mountains beyond the Indus and south of the Gilgit River, but their western boundary is the valley of Chitral, where they are sometimes, though rarely, encountered. Their eastern limit seems to be the basin of the Bhagirathi. It can be safely assumed that they are never found on the slopes of any mountain or range the summit of which is not crowned with perpetual snow.

Unlike the Himalayan black bear, red bears hibernate during the winter, and rarely descend below 10,000 feet, but in many other ways their habits are very similar to those of their black relations. For example, early in the spring they invariably visit grassy glades in the jungle, feeding on them in exactly the same way as has already been described in the chapter on black bear, the only difference being that in the case of the red bear the favoured glades are always comparatively near the edge of the tree-line, and those should be selected which are just clearing from snow. A glade half clear is generally a more likely place than one entirely free of snow.

But red bears are seen above the tree-line, even early in the season, just as often as below it, and in this case the favourite spots are the sites of old sheep pens. These can always be spotted by the very bright green of the grass which grows over them ; it is much brighter than that on the surrounding ground. The grass on old pens is always much richer than anywhere else on account of the constant manuring it receives from the droppings of the sheep when they are in residence. Red bears cannot resist such spots, especially when they are just clearing of snow, and all these green patches should be carefully watched from some vantage point.

A nullah which faces south will obviously clear from snow earlier than one which faces north, and consequently the programme for hunting should be arranged accordingly.

When feeding above the tree-line red bears are frequently followed by a flock of crows which greedily

DISTRIBUTION OF THAR

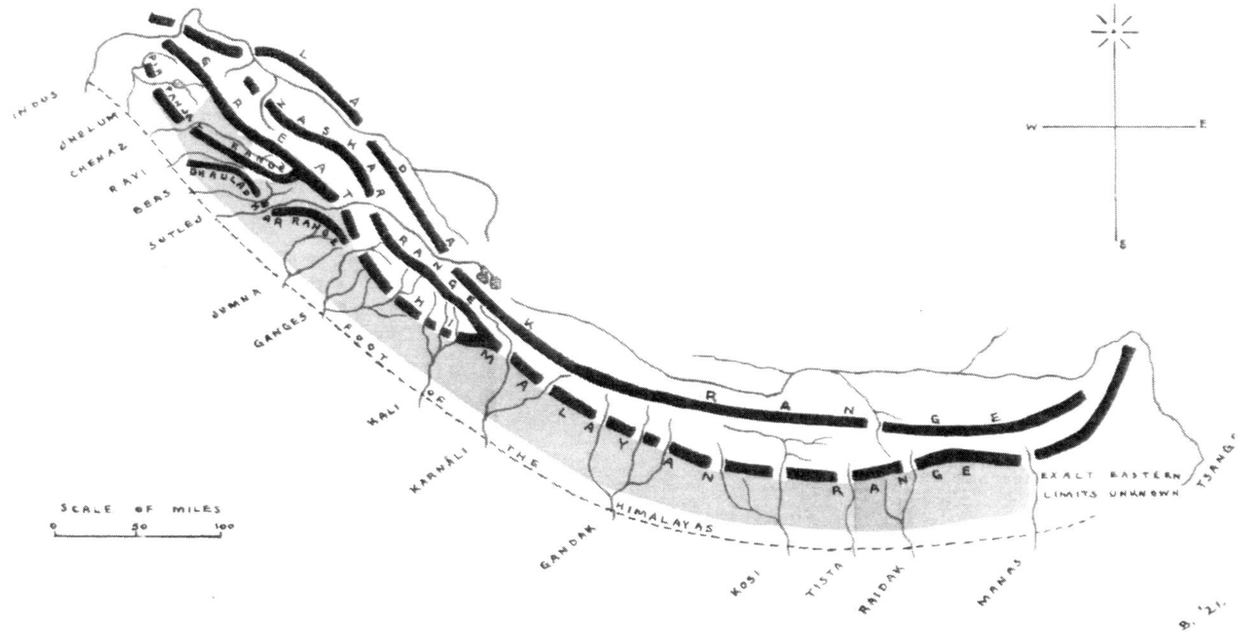

settle on the spots where the bear has overturned a stone or rooted about as soon as he moves on. It is most interesting to watch the crows waiting until the bear has taken all he wants. Directly he leaves the spot they all dart at it. This habit of the crows can be rather embarrassing for the bear, because it will often give his position away to a sportsman who would otherwise never have seen him, owing to his being hidden in some fold of the hill side. I once thought I had missed a stalk because when I reached the position from which I expected to get a shot I could see no bear at all on the bright green patch of grass. Then I saw a crow momentarily appear out of a hollow and disappear into it again. This was quite sufficient. Sure enough I found the bear in the hollow in question.

Although red bear generally feed chiefly in the early mornings and evenings they are not nearly so particular in this respect as most other Himalayan animals, especially early in the season when they have just come out from their winter quarters, and I have seen them at all hours of the day.

The eyesight of red bear is undoubtedly poor, but their sense of scent is very acute, and I believe their hearing to be far quicker than is generally supposed.

When they are in their winter coats their colour varies from pale, almost light yellow-brown, to a brown so dark that at a distance it appears black. I once saw a bear in April which looked like a black bear, but I could not understand any black bear feeding above the tree-line, and an inspection through a powerful telescope proved it to be a so-called red bear. They lose their winter coats towards the end of May or early in June, according to the direction in which the nullah they inhabit faces: the later the nullah clears of snow the later the bears wake up from their hibernation and lose their winter coats. In the summer they frequently are far redder in appearance, but "brown" or "snow" bear would be a much more suitable name. They put on their full winter coats towards the end of September and retire for their long sleep in November. From the point of view of a trophy the best time of year to shoot them would undoubtedly be the end of September or October. In the summer they are not worth shooting unless living at some very considerable altitude, when they keep good coats all the year round as they do on the Deosai Plains. But hard and fast rules are impossible, and I once shot a red bear in absolutely perfect coat on a 31st of May at an altitude of 10,700 feet.

Red bears are mostly inoffensive creatures living chiefly on grass, roots, grubs, and such simple food, but occasionally they depart from their blameless lives and develop a taste for meat, when they become quite a scourge to the flocks of sheep and goats. There are many instances of their eating carrion, and one famous example of red bears eating human flesh. Some men were crossing the Burzil Pass, I think it was, during the winter, and were destroyed in an avalanche. Their bodies could not be recovered from underneath the deep snow until the spring had set in, and it was then found that a couple of red bears had found the bodies first and had partly devoured them.

There have been undoubted instances of red bears

BEYOND THE GREAT HIMALAYAN RANGE.
Photographed from an altitude of 10,300 feet.

becoming dangerous customers and charging courageously, but such bold beasts are very rare, and the majority are timid animals, intending evil to no one and loth to assume hostilities even in extremities.

Red bear shooting has never appealed to me very much. I do not think it can compare as a sport with the stalking of ibex, thar, or burrhel, and I think most lovers of Himalayan shikar will agree with me. No animal has been more persecuted, and in places where it used to abound it is now very scarce. It is probably still most plentiful in Kashmir and Chamba, and in both these States the number allowed to be shot is very rightly strictly limited. But I do not think the red bear is nearly so rare as many sportsmen think, and I am sure that there are plenty of hunting-grounds where it exists in numbers never suspected by those who annually dash off to fashionable Kashmir. In searching for red bear grounds the same plan should be adopted as I recommended for burrhel. Study the geographical distribution, and follow up to its source some river which rises in one of the ranges which form part of that distribution. At the heads of all these rivers there are many branch nullahs, and the number of these which hold red bear would surprise many men.

One final word of warning. Monal pheasant frequently abound on red bear ground. No finer bird flies, but they are perfect fiends for getting up with a great whirr and sailing down the khud, uttering shrill cries the while. It is as difficult to elude the vigilance of a monal as of a peacock, and all other animals know and understand its warning.

CHAPTER XIV

SAMBHUR (*Cervus Unicolor*)

Native name—*Jarao,* Hindi.

SAMBHUR occur on the densely wooded ranges which lie entirely to the south of the Great Himalayan Range and the foot of the Himalayas. They never ascend higher than 8,000 feet, or thereabouts, and are usually found considerably lower. In the Himalayas they do not exist west of the basin of the Jumna, and they undoubtedly extend into Nepal, but there their eastern limits are unknown. They are essentially animals of the lesser Himalayan ranges, and as has already been said, are only found in dense jungle.

Their habits and the methods of shooting are identical with those of the plains, but a sufficient number of beaters will never be obtained from the small villages of the hills to organise a drive on a large scale, and the hillmen do not possess sufficient woodcraft for the conducting of a small silent beat. The only chance of bagging a hill sambhur is by "still hunting." If one is ever actually located in a small nullah a beat may be tried, but even then I doubt whether such a plan will be successful.

I have never shot a Himalayan sambhur, although I have seen them on several occasions when on a round over the hills during the march up to the higher hunting grounds. Those that I have seen had in every case shed their horns.

Himalayan sambhur never carry such big heads as those of the plains, but a common characteristic seems to be great massiveness combined with very long brow tines.

SEROW (*Capricornis Bubalinus*)

Native names—*Serow*, Hindi; *Yamu*, Kulu; *Ramu Halj*, Kashmir; *Gaya*, Sikkim.

This ungainly animal is distributed throughout the Himalayas to the south of the main axis, and is found in thick jungle on all the Ranges which lie to the south of the Great Himalayan Range, and on the southern slopes of the Great range itself, but never on the northern slopes, and seldom, if ever, much below 5,000 feet. It is a solitary animal and is nowhere common, being probably most plentiful in Kumaon. It is not met with to the west of the basin of the Jhelum, but it extends eastwards through Assam to Burma, Sumatra and China with but slight alterations of type. The minimum altitude limit I have placed refers only to the Himalayan serow. Serow are usually met with by chance and are shot more often by accident rather than by design. Both males and females have horns, those of the male being somewhat longer and stouter. Sometimes a drive may prove successful if a serow can be fairly accurately located, but more often than not drives will draw blank. At least this has been my experience, and I am sorry to say I have never shot a serow, and I have only once seen one at a distance of over four hundred yards, when I studied it carefully with my glasses, but of course all thoughts of a shot were out of the question.

If a chance at a serow is ever obtained it should be taken at once, as although they cannot possibly be described as having grand heads they make rare and interesting trophies which are not often obtained.

Many sportsmen who have shot serow maintain that they will charge viciously when wounded, and there have been one or two cases of Indians being killed by a wound from their short, yet stout and sharp horns. Accordingly a wounded serow should be approached with caution.

The average height at the shoulder is slightly over 3 feet, and their colour is dark. Their horns are not unlike those of a very large gooral, and they possess a distinct mane and large ears. They are indeed curious animals, and I will always regret that I never succeeded in obtaining a specimen in spite of many days of fruitless searching and frequent drives.

THE BURMESE SEROW (*Capricornis Sumatrensis*)

By Sir Otway-Wheeler Cuffe, Bart.

It was in February, 1899, while stationed at Thayetmyo on the Irrawaddy, that I first became acquainted with this remarkable animal and his haunts.

From Thayetmyo I had gone out by cart road three stages to Mindon, a small town on the right bank of the river of the same name. From there I collected coolies to climb the slopes of the Arakan Yomas, that fine range of mountains which divides the valley of the River

Irrawaddy from the western coast-line of Burma on the Bay of Bengal, and rises to an altitude of 5,000 feet and upwards. My shikari and I had done two days' tracking without any very great success on the eastern slopes, which are fairly rounded and wooded. On the 28th we started early from our camp and made our way up for 4,000 feet to the crest of the range. The western slopes of these hills are very precipitous and rocky, and offer the most magnificent and picturesque scenery one could wish for.

Our first look round showed no game, but on mounting to the highest pinnacle of rock, I spied what at first sight I took to be a large goat some 200 yards below me; there was no possibility of getting nearer, so from the lying down position, with my rifle (a ·400 Winchester Express) resting over the edge of the precipice I took my shot. The beast jumped high in the air, ran a few paces, stopped, looked round, and uttered that peculiar cry which is characteristic of the serow, a cry not unlike the mewings of a cat, very loud and penetrating. My second shot was then delivered, which rolled the animal over the precipice. No sooner had I fired my second shot than another serow made his appearance from behind a rock, and my third shot simply caused him to drop where he stood; a fourth shot I do not think touched him, but struck the ground beside him. However, to make quite sure of him I fired my fifth shot, which caused him to roll over the ledge on which he lay, and disappear from view. After a desperate scramble we found him wedged in between two projecting rocks, about fifty feet below the ledge on which he was shot;

the other beast, which we adjudged to be the female, we never saw again, as she had fallen many hundreds of feet below us.

The male, which we secured, thanks to those projecting rocks, proved to be a most magnificent specimen, the record for Burma, as far as I know, of the rufous variety. He measured 3 feet 1½ inches at the withers, and his horns 10½ inches, with a girth at base of 5 inches. His head is not unlike that of a goat, but the nose and nostrils resemble those of a calf; body and legs like a pony, but with cloven hoofs; the hair is coarse and of a deep bay colour all over, with a mane some 6 to 8 inches long, hence his name in Burmese of "Taw myin" (jungle-pony).

This trophy was well mounted for me by Rowland Ward, and now adorns the walls of my Irish home. Two years later I secured a live black specimen from a Burman villager, who had caught him, when a small kid, on the slopes of the Pegn Yomas, the range of hills to the east of the Irrawaddy, and had reared and tamed him. He was more than three years old when he came into my possession, and was perfectly tame, and absolutely fearless of dogs or anything else, including my pet panther. He died of heart disease, brought on, probably, by living an unnatural life in the heat of the plains, although he was perfectly free and wandered about at his own sweet will. This beast was in build and structure exactly similar to the rufous variety already described, but with black hair tipped with white, and red legs. He stood 2 feet 9 inches at the withers, and had horns 8½ inches long; he was omnivorous so far as vegetable food was concerned, and he repaired to one particular place to deposit his droppings, a peculiarity I have never yet seen stated.

The Natural History Museum, Dublin, accepted his mortal remains, and he may now be seen mounted in a glass case there.

The serow, which, as at present specified by zoologists, belongs to a group intermediate between the goats and antelopes, is known in the Himalayas as *Capricornis Bubalinus* and in Burma and the Malay Peninsula as *Capricornis Sumatrensis*, no distinction being recognised between the rufous and black varieties. The former I am inclined to think are confined to the hills west of the Irrawaddy; I have never known or heard of a red serow having been killed or even seen east of the Irrawaddy. Serows have also been shot in Burma by the following: In the Arakan Yomas by W. Thom and H. A. Kelso, Burma Police; on Popa, a large extinct volcano, in Central Burma, by the late Sir Bertram Carey, C.I.E.; and in the Ruby Mines district by Lieut. Sant Fournier, Col. Evans, Veterinary Department, and Mr. Bacon, of the Burma Ruby Mines Co.

In the *Journal* of the Bombay Natural History Society, Vol. xxviii, No. 1, published December 30, 1921, page 267, Mr. C. E. Milner, Forest Department, gives an interesting account of the distribution of serow in Burma. He describes that he shot a red serow in the Maigthorn Hills of Mu Forest Division, north of Shevebo, and his remarks bear out my theory that the red variety are only found west of the Irrawaddy.

SHOU (*Cervus Wallichi*)

Native name—*Shou*, Chumbi Valley.

The alternative name for the shou is the Sikkim stag, and I suppose it was given this name because it is never found in Sikkim! After all, this is a very good reason, for with the exception of this one fact very little is known for certain concerning its habitat. It undoubtedly inhabits the Chumbi Valley, which is the basin of the Ammu River, a tributary of the Raidak, which flows through Bhutan. The shou is also found in Bhutan in the valley of this last river, and it is believed to occur again in Tibet, but between its haunts in the basins of the Ammu and Raidak there are many miles of barren mountains and uplands devoid of vegetation. All deer like forests, and no shou are found in these desolate regions. Exactly where it occurs in Tibet again, if indeed it does, is really not known. The Indian explorer, Kinthup, reported finding deer of sorts on some wooded mountains to the east and north of Lhasa when he made his famous journeys in 1880 to 1884. In 1914 I interrogated him about these deer, but he could tell me nothing beyond the fact that they were deer and had big antlers. He said that some he saw were spotted, but these were probably young ones. Whether Kinthup's deer were shou or Thorold's deer I would not like to say; they might quite possibly be either, or even both.

The shou has also been repeatedly described as inhabiting the "neighbourhood of the Manasarowar Lakes, Tibet." I am convinced that this statement is absolutely incorrect. The neighbourhood of the Manasarowar Lakes is an open country, absolutely barren and traversed by high and equally barren mountains. The mean elevation is 15,000 feet, and no one who knows anything of the habits of deer would expect to find them in such a locality. I believe the idea originated in the narrative of some traveller who reported finding the antlers of a shou in one of the numerous monasteries which abound round Manasarowar and Kailas. But this head might easily have been brought from Chumbi, or elsewhere, and such an explanation seems to me far more reasonable than the assumption that it belonged to a stag which lived in an absolutely barren and treeless waste. Many sportsmen and travellers have journeyed all over Tibet around the Manasarowar Lakes, and not one has ever succeeded in killing a shou, or even in seeing a live one in those parts, although other game animals such as *Ovis Ammon*, Tibetan antelope, and Tibetan gazelle have all been shot. How anyone professing to a knowledge of natural history can imagine that deer, essentially forest animals by nature, will be found on the same ground as these animals is hard to understand.

Shou may possibly be found in Nepal in the basin of the Karnali, but there is no evidence in favour of this, and, even if they were, such a country could not possibly be described as being in "the neighbourhood of the Manasarowar Lakes, Tibet," with the slightest degree of geographical accuracy.

The shou is allied to the Kashmir stag, but is considerably larger, and the beam of the antlers suddenly bends forward immediately above the trez line, thus overhanging the face.

SNOW LEOPARD (*Felis Uncia*)

Native names—*Safed Baghera, Safed Cheetah, Burreyl,* Hindi.

The snow leopard, or ounce, is probably the most beautiful of all the big cats. It is found from the Hindu Kush on the west to the extreme eastern end of the Great Himalayan Range, and extends right into, and probably throughout Tibet; but its southern boundary is generally the Great Himalayan Range, and it is not nearly so common on the southern slopes of the main axis as on the northern side. It extends in limited numbers a few miles along the Dhauladhar and Pir Panjal Ranges from their junctions with the Great Himalayan Range.

Snow leopards always live above the tree-line and never enter scrub or jungle. They are almost entirely nocturnal in their habits, and it is on this account that they are so seldom shot by sportsmen. During the day-time they seem to vanish, probably lying up in little caves or crevices among boulders.

In the Zaskar Range snow leopards abound, and levy a heavy toll on the burrhel and ibex, frequently clearing a nullah of game for the time being. When marching and shooting in the Zaskar Range I have day after day come on fresh tracks of these creatures, but I have never seen one, and I am sure that it is only on account of their nocturnal habits that they are so seldom encountered, not because they are in any way rare.

I once found fresh tracks of a snow leopard which

had come to drink from the pool at the snout of a glacier, at an elevation of 13,000 feet. The pugs were very plain in the semi-frozen sand surrounding the pool. I tried sitting up that night as there was a good moon, but never saw a thing, and was very nearly frozen as solid as the glacier.

Occasionally snow leopards are seen by day, and when this occurs they are frequently in pairs. If the sportsman is quick to appreciate the situation, and the rifle is at hand, he will have a chance of bagging a right and left.

If a fresh kill is ever found it would certainly be worth while sitting up, but this is not an amusement which will appeal to any but extreme enthusiasts on account of the intense cold.

TAKIN SHOOTING IN BURMA

By F. C. Lowis

The takin is only found in the high hills on the extreme northern borders of Burma, where they march with China and Tibet. They are never found at a lower elevation than 9,000 feet, unless driven down by the snow in winter, returning again to the tops of the hills as the snow recedes.

The hills in which they live are covered with dense bamboo and rhododendron jungle, and as they are extremely shy it is most difficult to obtain a shot at them; they are generally found in small herds of from four to ten.

The method adopted by the Yawyins in hunting

them is either with hunting-dogs or by sitting up over a salt-lick.

The former method is the one most often employed, as the Yawyins have no fire-arms and shoot their game with poisoned arrows shot from a powerful crossbow. The method of procedure is for three or four men with their dogs to set out from the village and climb up three to four thousand feet from the valley where the village is situated, and make their camp under an overhanging rock or cave near a ravine which the takin are known to inhabit. They then start out with their dogs, having left behind at the camp all impedimenta in the way of blankets, cooking pots and food, with which they were loaded on the way up. As soon as the dogs have picked up the scent of a takin the men scatter, taking up positions from which they can hear the dogs, which give tongue freely.

When the dogs get up to the herd the females make off, but the male, after going a short way, stands at bay; this is the opportunity the men are on the look-out for, and while the attention of the takin is taken up with the dogs they are able to approach and shoot off one of their poisoned arrows, and as long as they can get an arrow under the skin they are certain of getting the animal, as although the takin may break away from the dogs, the latter follow giving tongue the whole way, until he again turns to bay or the poison takes effect and the animal succumbs. The nearest point to civilisation where takin are to be found is near the village of Hpimaw, situated on the high dividing range between the Irrawaddy and Salween Rivers, 150 miles north of the town of Myitkyina, which is the head-quarters of the district and also the northern terminus of the Burma Railways.

Mules can be hired at Myitkyina for the journey by road to Hpimaw, along which are rest houses for the accommodation of travellers. Beyond Hpimaw coolies would have to be hired for the three or four stages from the village of Hpimaw up into the hills where the takin are to be found.

Practically no supplies of any kind can be obtained after leaving Myitkyina, except a little rice and a chicken or a few eggs, at each stage. It is most advisable to cut down all equipment and stores to the barest necessities, as coolies are hard to get as the country is very sparsely populated.

All equipment and loads should be made up into packages of not more than 60 lb. each, as this is the limit of weight a mule can carry on each side, the full load for a mule being 120 lb. The best time for an expedition to start would be to leave Myitkyina at the end of November or early in December, as at this time of year the snow covers the highest hills and the takin are found at the lower elevations; also at this season of the year it is possible to hire pack mules in Myitkyina from the Chinese traders who annually bring over merchandise from China, returning again before the monsoon breaks at the end of May.

There are no regular shikaris as the country the takin inhabit is seldom visited by white men, but a Kachin or Yawyin interpreter could be obtained either at Myitkyina or Bhamo, who would be able on arrival at Hpimaw to arrange with the headman of one of the villages near to supply the men and dogs required. It is a good plan to take up a supply of cheap knives, beads, and blankets, which could be obtained in Rangoon, as the country is so remote from civilisation that it is very often easier to obtain supplies and coolies by barter of goods of the above description than by the offer of money.

CHAPTER XV

THAR (*Hemitragus jemlaiacus*)

Native names—*Tehr*, *Jehr* (male), *Tehrni* (female), Hindi; *Jhula*, *Esbu*, Sutlej Valley; *Kurt*, Kulu, Chamba; *Kras*, Kashmir.

THAR are essentially Himalayan animals and are found on almost every mountain and range of sufficient altitude to the south of the crest-line of the Great Himalayan Range. Although they are exceedingly plentiful on almost all the southern slopes of the main axis, and even in the gorges cut through it by rivers rising further north, they are apparently never found on the northern slopes of the Great Range. If it were not for the river gorges this would be easily understandable, as thar never by any circumstances wander above the tree-line, and so they would have no inducement to explore across the snowy range. But they are plentiful in almost all the gorges through the main axis, so why should they not wander through to what seem excellent thar grounds on the northern slopes of the Great Range? It is a question I cannot answer, but I do not believe they ever do. Within a few miles of the river gorge in which I have seen and shot these animals, I have frequently seen splendid-looking thar country on the northern slopes, but no thar were ever found there, while all the local hillmen declared that none ever had been, and scouted the mere possibility of such an idea. This has always seemed to me an extraordinary interesting fact. It would be different if the subsoil was of another nature, but it is granite throughout, and in the gorges and on the southern slopes thar thrive on granite, and I can think of no explanation for their never sending outposts through the gorges on to what would be, for them, virgin pastures.

Amazing as this hard and fast boundary is, a knowledge of it may save the sportsman considerable trouble. I once read a book in which the author described some days spent in fruitless search for thar in apparently excellent-looking country. Now I happen to know this particular district well, and it lies just to the north of the main axis. If that sportsman had been better acquainted with the geography of the Himalayas and the distribution of the animal he was hunting, he would have known that he was wasting his time. His shikari was not a local man, and in that particular neighbourhood villages are scarce. Some goat-herd from the nearest village would have put him right, but he was trusting to a professional who, no doubt, was a very excellent shikari, but who unfortunately had never been in that district before, and was therefore useless.

The western limit of the thar occurs in Kashmir and roughly follows the line of the watershed between the Jhelum and the Chenab, though the species occurs on the Jhelum side of the Pir Panjal Range, and has been known on the continuation of this range west of the Jhelum. Eastwards they extend to Bhutan, and their exact boundary is unknown. The sketch map shows their distribution plainly. It will be noticed that they do not quite reach the Great Himalayan Range slightly to the east of its bifurcations with the Dhauladhar and Pir Panjal Ranges. This is merely because the two valleys formed by these bifurcations (those of Bashahr and Lahoul) are devoid of vegetation at their upper ends, and the thar refuses to wander away from the tree-line.

I do not think the thar gets fair play. By this I do not mean to say that his pursuit is not carried out fairly, as in ordinary circumstances it is difficult for a mere white man to do anything else than give this beast more than a sporting chance. But he is not given the place he deserves when trophies are considered in order of merit. This is because his horns cannot compare in size with those of some of his cousins. But is size of horns everything? I think not. I would be the last to deny the lure of a large animal with a great head, but in pursuit of such game some men seem to forget that quality is the aim of true sportsmanship and are satisfied in slaughtering small specimens of large animals. Which is the better head, a 30-inch burrhel or a 40-inch ibex? A 20-inch para or a 30-inch sambhur? Mere horn measurement is far from everything. There are other claims to be considered. It may be urged that even a good thar of 13 inches set up with mask complete is not a really imposing trophy, while without his mask his skull is hardly worth looking at. Here, again, I do not agree.

It would be foolish to maintain that a thar can ever compare, trophy for trophy, with ibex or markhor. But surely in the value to be set on a trophy obstacles overcome are an important factor, and the greater the obstacles the greater the value. The obstacles which hamper the successful pursuit of the thar are so great that I prize his trophy beyond very many others of species which are usually considered more noble game. And the memories which each head recalls are pleasanter than those conjured up by almost any other head. Perhaps that is my real reason for rating the thar so high.

Much has been written of his powers of climbing. It has been claimed by some that his only possible rival is the markhor. This I doubt. All goats can climb marvellously, and I do not think that the actual capacity for climbing possessed by thar is greater than that of the ibex, as I have more than once heard men say it is. I should say that markhor, ibex and thar can all climb equally well when put to it. The point about the thar is that he seems to climb as a sport, where the ibex climbs as a duty. No animal in the Himalayas invariably lives on such appalling ground. He revels in the steepest precipices in the district and, apparently, hates to leave them even for food. These precipices are invariably clothed in parts with thick scrub, and this is another point against the hunter. The thar likes such shade as there is, and will lie up all day in the thickest bits of jungle he can find, emerging only at evening time. Soon after 9 a.m. he is back in the thickets and impossible to find unless previously located.

It is possible to shoot many ibex without having to do any real climbing. There may be just a chance of this in certain districts with markhor. But it is never

An 11½-inch Thar shot at 10,000 feet.

so with thar, although naturally some ground is worse than others.

So far there does not seem to be much in the thar's favour beyond the hard work which his pursuit entails. But I would put forward another plea on his behalf. He is much more ubiquitous than the markhor or ibex as a study of his habitat will show, and he lives nearer to the plains. This means that an expedition after thar takes up neither so much time nor money as a trip after other Himalayan game—a great boon to the impecunious subaltern or other official whose leave is short. Within recent years thar have been shot but two marches away from Mussoorie, although it is preferable to go further afield. In planning a trip after thar adopt the principles which I have already urged in regard to other animals. Study the map, and select some river which either rises in or beyond the Great Himalayan Range and make this the main artery of your route. All these rivers have innumerable tributaries, any one of which is a sure road to thar ground provided it rises in a mountain or range which has an altitude of 12,000 feet or upwards, preferably upwards. Naturally, the further you go towards the Great Himalayan Range, the more ground you will have at your disposal; but if your leave is short do not think that you will have no chance of finding thar if you can only reach some intermediate range. I have already stated that the thar is never found above the tree-line, which is usually between 11,000 and 12,000 feet; but he likes to go as high as he can, and this little weakness should be remembered. I believe there is almost as much unexplored (from the sportsman's point of view) thar ground as there is Trans-Himalayan burrhel ground, and the chances of really good heads are excellent.

Buck thar will stand from nine to ten hands at the shoulder, and they are heavily built, weighing up to 200 lb. The hair on the head is short, and they have no beards, but the body is covered with long hair, and the old bucks have regular manes which reaches nearly to their knees. There is much variation in colour, and the males are usually dark, particularly about the back and quarters, but I once saw three good bucks which

HOW TO JUDGE THAR HEADS.

A big thar is shown on the left. In the centre is a medium head, while on the right is a small head which should not be shot.

had not a dark hair on them, being a dirty white in colour. Kinloch mentions a similar instance of colouring, but I think it is very exceptional. The females are much lighter both in build and colour than the males, and frequently inhabit more open and less precipitous ground. As a rule the old males keep in bands by themselves until September and frequent the thickest undergrowth and most precipitous cliffs.

The horns of the thar are small, and it is not easy to judge their length with very great accuracy, as it is with some other animals. Attention should be paid their

EARLY SPRING IN THE GREAT HIMALAYAN RANGE.
Photograph taken from 11,000 feet.

"*June* 4. Still in the same camp. Set off at 4 a.m. and soon saw the thar far below us. The stalk was long and the ground very difficult. We descended 2,000 feet down an almost sheer precipice, which was covered with thorns. I had to take off my hill shoes and socks so as to be able to cling on with my toes as well as my fingers, and when we got to the end of the descent both my feet and hands were torn and bleeding. We carefully peered over the ledge and looked at the spot where the thar ought to be, to find that they must have split up, as only one female and a small male remained. It was now nearly 9 a.m., so I decided to wait where I was until the evening and then have another try. I wished I had brought some tiffin with me, but we never expected to be out later than 10 a.m. We waited on a bare rock until 4 p.m. and then started up. At about 6 p.m. we saw the thar—seven in all, including two good males—right below us. It was too late to think of such a long stalk on that ground, so we had to leave them. As it was we did not get in until 8 p.m., and it took me nearly an hour to get all the thorns out of my feet, for I had been compelled to go barefooted in the ascent as well."

I spent two more very similar days after those same thar, but failed to get a shot.

One of the chief difficulties in stalking thar is dealt with in the chapter on red bear, namely the monal pheasant. In some nullahs they are a veritable curse and seem to take an especial delight in giving you away.

Gooral and black bear may frequently be obtained from a thar camp, and there is always the chance of a leopard, while if the tent is pitched on the edge of the tree-line on the Great Himalayan Range alternate days may be spent after thar and Himalayan burrhel, and I have sometimes seen red bear in the same nullah as thar. Accordingly it will be seen that the pursuit of thar gives opportunity of a variety of sport, but of all the animals which live in such close proximity none to my mind are so entirely worthy of being selected by the hunter in search of arduous sport as our friend the thar.

CHAPTER XVI

TIBETAN ANTELOPE (*Panthalops Hodgsoni*)

Native names—*Chiru, Tsōr,* Tibetan.

TIBETAN antelopes roam in herds of countless thousands all over the Chang Tang, the great desert of Northern Tibet, which has a mean altitude of 17,000 feet above the sea. Except in one locality they never seem to occur to the west or south of the Ladak Range, and the only spot in Indian territory in which they are ever found is the Chang Chen Mo Valley. This is reached by the Marsemik La (18,300 feet), a pass over the Ladak Range, and the antelope never under any circumstances cross the Shyok River. They do not come into Chang Chen Mo in any numbers until July, when considerable herds cross over from Tibet by the Lanak La, the pass at the head of the valley, but these herds are nothing to those which have been seen by various explorers in the Chang Tang. Their northern boundary is probably the Kuen Lun Range, and their eastern limits are unknown.

The only place where they cross the Ladak Range appears to be just east of the Manasarowar Lakes, and in the upper Tsangpo Valley they exist in numbers over a limited area. The late General Rawling, in describing the journey he made up the Tsangpo and down the Sutlej after the Tibet Frontier Mission in 1905, when he was accompanied by Colonels Ryder, Wood and Bailey, said of this particular bit of country: "For two days, and two days only, we passed through the Tibetan Antelope country. . . . Many thousands were passed during those two days."

The Tibetan antelope is decidedly larger than the black buck and more heavily built. The colour is a light fawn with dark legs, and the old bucks have dark faces. Their chief peculiarity is the muzzle which is enlarged and has a puffy appearance. The does are hornless.

They are not particularly difficult animals to stalk, but their inaccessibility and the beautiful symmetry of their horns make them prized trophies among all keen Himalayan shikaris.

TIBETAN GAZELLE (*Gazella picticaudata*)

Native name—*Goa*, Tibetan.

The Tibetan gazelle is about the same size as the chinkara, and similar in colour, but the short black tail on the white rump is more accentuated, and unlike the chinkara the females are hornless. The exact limits of their distribution are not known, but the sketch map gives our existing information. In Ladak they are not encountered to the north of the Indus, and in Western Tibet they do not occur to the south of the Sutlej except close to its source in the neighbourhood of the Manasarowar Lakes. They are found all along the valley of the Tsangpo, provided the elevation is above 13,000 feet, to the country east of Yamdrok Tso (lake), but

DISTRIBUTION OF TIBETAN GAZELLE

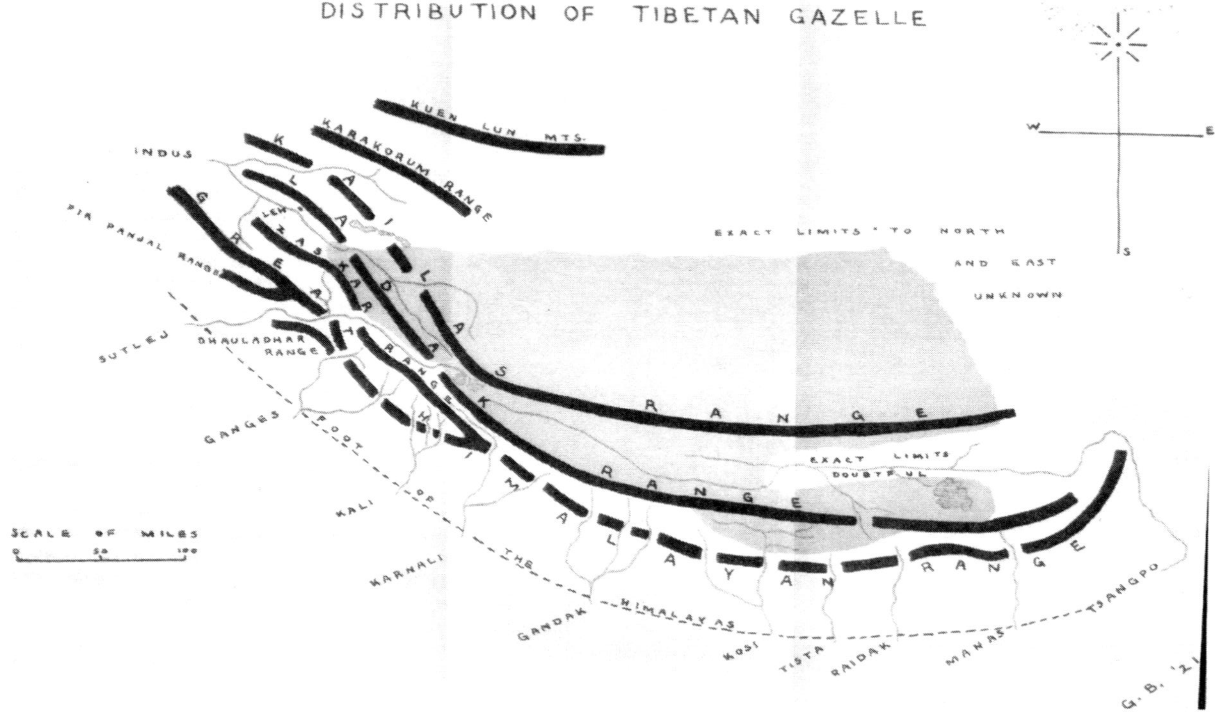

they do not cross the Ladak Range anywhere between the basins of the Karnali and Bhotia Kosi Rivers. They certainly exist to the south of this range from the basin of the Arun Kosi eastwards, and sometimes move into Sikkim, near the Tso Lhama (lake), at the source of the Tista. This is the only spot in Indian territory outside Ladak where they are ever found, and they only come here occasionally.

In Ladak they are getting more scarce every year, and their small but extraordinary beautiful little horns are among the most difficult trophies the Himalayas or the country beyond can offer. If the political restrictions are ever removed from Tibet the difficulties will not be so great, for they are undoubtedly common in many parts of Tibet, and although they are distinctly shy little beasts they are not nearly so difficult to stalk as *Ammon*.

TIBETAN LYNX (*Felis Isabellina*)

Native name—*Ee*, Tibetan.

This animal is rarely encountered and consequently the exact limits of its habitat are somewhat conjectural, but I fancy that it is almost identical with that of *Ammon*. Lynx skins are sometimes brought down to the various hill stations by native traders, and I have never handled softer or more beautiful skins. They are savage animals and do not hesitate to attack sheep and goats, sometimes working considerable havoc.

Personally I only know of one sportsman who has

ever shot a Tibetan Lynx, and he killed his specimen in Ladak comparatively near his camp. He did not know what the animal was, and thinking that it was merely a rather big wild cat, left it where it was. On return to camp he looked the animal up in Ward's *Sportsman's Guide to Kashmir and Ladak*, and realised his good fortune. He at once sent a couple of men to retrieve the body, which they fortunately succeeded in doing before it had been mauled by any birds or wolves, and he thus obtained an almost unique trophy.

TIBETAN WOLVES (*Canis lupus*)

Native names—*Chanko* (grey variety), *Chanko Nagpo* (black variety), Tibetan.

There are two varieties of wolves found in Tibet, the grey and the black, and they occur all over that country. They are not as a rule gregarious, and their habits are almost entirely nocturnal. For this reason they are seldom seen by sportsmen, but in spite of this fact I believe them to be far more common than is generally realised. They are bold and savage and sometimes do much damage to the Tibetan flocks of sheep and goats. Apart from their comparative rarity as trophies and their handsome skins, they should invariably be shot on sight whenever an opportunity occurs, as they are, I am convinced, chiefly responsible for the premature death of a very large percentage of big *Ammon* rams. This I have already explained in the chapter on *Ammon*.

An Open Plain in Western Tibet, 15,300 feet.

TIGER (*Felis tigris*)

Native names—*Sher, bagh,* Hindi.

Tiger are very seldom shot in the Himalayas proper, but they exist in the hills in not altogether inconsiderable numbers. They inhabit the thickly wooded ranges which lie to the south of the main axis, and are more numerous to east of the Bhagirathi. I believe the highest altitude at which a tiger has ever been actually killed in the Himalayas is 8,000 feet.

Hill tigers are invariably great wanderers, and never stop long in one locality, and luck must undoubtedly largely enter into success.

A friend of mine was once shooting in the hills in Kumaon, and was returning to camp after an unsuccessful morning round in search of black bear. He had given his rifle to the shikari to carry. The little party were following a narrow path in single file, the sahib leading, when a tiger suddenly walked out into the path but ten yards ahead of him and proceeded to follow it up just ahead of them. My friend stretched out his hand for his rifle, but the shikari and coolie had both vanished, and he watched the tiger walk away switching its tail from side to side until it disappeared behind a bend in the path. The moral of this story is too obvious to need emphasis, but it should be remembered that such chances usually occur about once in a generation, and the feelings of the man who missed it when it did occur through not being ready must be too awful for words.

YAK (*Bos grunniens*)

Native name—*Dong*, Tibetan.

Wild yak can be distinguished from the domesticated animals by their superior size and the fact that they are invariably all black. They live in higher and more desolate regions than any other known animal, and it is a never-ceasing wonder to me how they can find sufficient food to support their huge frames, - a big wild bull will stand from sixteen to eighteen hands. It is true that burrhel ascend to just as great altitudes, but while burrhel are sometimes found in the comparative warmth of such low levels as 13,000 feet or so, wild yak never lapse from their self-imposed Spartan existence, and I doubt if they ever descend much lower than 17,000 feet. They seem to exist all over the barren mountain ranges of Tibet wherever the altitude is sufficiently great, but their home is undoubtedly the same as that of the Tibetan antelope, namely the Chang Tang, where they roam at will in great herds. The only place in which they regularly enter Indian territory is the valley of Chang Chen Mo, and here they may not be shot, because the Maharaja of Kashmir is a Hindu, and regards them rightly as belonging to the *bos* tribe, and therefore to a Hindu sacred. They are certainly found on that part of the Ladak Range which lies between the Indus and Sutlej in Tibet, but not on any other part of this mountain system, and they exist in limited numbers on some of the higher mountains which lie between the upper part of the Sutlej in Tibet and the Zaskar Range. In fact they very occasionally cross the crest-line of the Zaskar Range into Kumaon near the Kangri Bingri Pass, in the same place where *Ammon* sometimes cross it. It is most interesting to conjecture why this particular locality should be so favoured by Tibetan game.

Kinthup, the Indian explorer to whom I have already referred in the section on the shou, reported that he saw "yak" on a mountain to the north-east of Lhasa, but when interrogated he told me he could not be certain whether these were wild or domesticated yak sent out to graze, but that he thought they were wild ones.

Rare Varieties of Tibetan Game

We now come to three rare varieties of Tibetan game which deserve mention, but about which comparative little is known. They are: takin, Thorold's deer, and the Tibetan blue bear.

The takin is found on the thickly wooded slopes of the mountains which form the boundary between Tibet and Assam in the basin of the Tsangpo. Exactly similar specimens have also been obtained in exactly similar terrain in Szechuan, so I think it is but reasonable to assume that the species occur all along the unknown ranges which fringe the southern limits of the Tibetan plateau. Takin shooting in Northern Burma has already been described by Mr. Lowis.

It is an ungainly animal with an ugly head and small horns, and its rarity is really its chief claim to value as a sporting trophy.

Thorold's deer, on the other hand, will provide a head worthy of being placed in any company. It is about the same size as a Kashmir barasingh, but the trez tine is missing, and at the point where it should be the antlers take a sudden backward bend. It is believed to inhabit the wooded mountains to the east of Lhasa at considerable elevations.

The Tibetan blue bear is a small animal, but its skin must make a very handsome trophy. Its habitat is probably the same as that of Thorold's deer.

CHAPTER XVII

GENERAL HINTS ON SHOOTING IN THE HIMALAYAS

WHEN you have decided on your route and selected the nearest hill station as your base, the next point for you to remember is that an official Chaprassie of the State in which you are shooting is almost indispensable. Such an individual is usually told off to accompany sportsmen on expeditions in order to assist them in obtaining supplies and transport. His utility varies in different States, and in Kashmir he can be dispensed with altogether, as the shikari will do all that is needful, and the ways of sportsmen are so thoroughly understood that everything is greatly simplified. In Garhwal and Kumaon it is almost impossible to travel without a State Chaprassie. An application to be provided with one should be addressed to the same individual as was the letter asking for permission to shoot in the country. These Chaprassies arrange for coolies from day to day and for food for any permanent members of the staff. They should be carefully watched or they will use their official position as a State servant and as the sahib's helper for the purpose of bullying the simple hill folk in a most abominable manner and of extorting all kinds of little perquisites for themselves of which the sahib never hears, and for which no payment is ever made. Bearers and shikaris will sometimes play similar tricks, but they have not the local government brass badge to help them and so they lack some of the authority of the Chaprassie. It should never be forgotten that no one ever oppresses the unsophisticated villagers so much as a fellow Indian who is given a little authority, and in nine cases out of ten the sahib's name is used as the authority for the carrying out of what are really petty outrages. State Chaprassies are particularly bad offenders in this respect, and they must accordingly be kept well in hand.

Before you actually march out from the base, arrangements should be made with the post office or some large shop, or better still with a personal friend, if one sufficiently accommodating can be found, for all letters and parcels to be kept until you send a dak coolie in to fetch them.

Shikaris

I have already touched on the subject of shikaris elsewhere. In Kashmir there are many really excellent shikaris who know their work well, but such men naturally add to the expense of an expedition, and I am convinced that a trip in Kashmir will always cost at least 30 per cent more than a similar trip in less sophisticated States. Outside Kashmir I do not believe in ever engaging any shikari at the starting place unless he has been personally recommended by some reliable sportsman. Undoubtedly the best plan is to march up to the grounds you have decided to explore and there to engage some local goatherd Many of them have acted as shikaris from time to time, and are really splendid *on their own particular grounds.* It is impossible to do better than engage such a man, and I have never heard of any district where at least one man of this type was not available, although in some countries, such as Spiti, the local inhabitants are not hunters by instinct, as are the majority of the real hillmen. If you do engage a shikari at the hill station from which you start you will certainly find him quite useful on the march in many little ways, but no more so than a good bearer, or orderly, and he will be quite useless in helping you to find nullahs which have been little shot in. This is where the local goatherd comes in, but you must remember that, although he will probably be as keen as mustard on finding game, and although his eyesight may be really wonderful, his ideas of stalking will be most elementary, and if you want to obtain success as well as the greatest possible pleasure out of your trip you will have to conduct every stalk entirely on your own, merely asking him if such and such a way is possible.

The worst of these local men is that they get spoiled so soon. They probably show excellent sport, and the sahib is correspondingly generous. The sudden wealth thus earned so overwhelms them that they too often waste it in drink and other forms of riotous living. One man in particular whom I knew intimately and whom I employed on several occasions was a really marvellous shikari provided you employed him first in the season. But once he had been on a trip with a sahib he was always utterly useless until the following year when he had blown all his money. During the second part of the leave season he was never, or at any rate very, very seldom, sober, provided he had been employed during the first half.

The one disadvantage of local men is that they seldom have any proper authority over the coolies, and this throws much extra work and worry on the sportsman himself. A good orderly would be invaluable in such a position.

Transport

In the Himalayas the unit of transport is the coolie, and this should never be forgotten even if you have planned to use pony transport all the way. One day you may suddenly find yourself compelled by a sudden snowfall or landslide to change from ponies to coolies, even if it be but temporarily, and if your loads are not interchangeable you will have much bother in rearranging them. The three types of transport employed by sportsmen are Coolies, Ponies or Mules and Yaks. Let us now consider the peculiarities of each separately.

Coolies

By far the commonest. They are usually engaged by the stage, arriving early in the morning and leaving when they have accomplished the day's journey. Always pay them yourself personally before they go. If you leave this job to an Indian subordinate the coolies will be mulcted almost to a certainty. Coolies engaged by the stage invariably bring your loads along very

Yak Transport in Tibet; 15,400 feet.

quickly as they are anxious to return to their homes as soon as possible. This is the great advantage of this method of hiring them. If you engage a band of coolies when you start they will accompany you throughout your trip, and you will be saved the constant worry of procuring coolies at the beginning of every march, which is the drawback of the other system. But you will find that speed is no object at all with them as they have not got to return to their homes, and you may have to wait the greater part of the day for your kit, which is a nuisance. Another point to be remembered is that in the further Himalayas the villages are very small and cannot supply a sufficient amount of food for a large band of outsiders suddenly thrust upon them. This difficulty will make both you and your coolies very unpopular with the local inhabitants, and this is always a bad thing if you want good sport. For this reason I do not recommend engaging coolies at the beginning of a trip in spite of the anxiety which you may have to suffer on account of the daily supply of coolies before your destination is reached. Once you have got to your grounds you should engage a permament staff of local coolies who will accompany you up any nullahs in their immediate neighbourhood, and when you move on they will hand you over to another lot recruited from the new hunting grounds. You will find these men far hardier and better workers all round than any taken on at a hill station.

I once thought I had struck on the ideal method of travelling. I was returning to my previous haunts and made plans for my old band of real hillmen to march in and meet me at the hill station from which I was starting. The party duly arrived, but my plan proved a most dismal failure, as these men who lived right among the snows of the Great Himalayan Range found the heat of the valleys of the lesser ranges so great that they could hardly march at all until the journey was more than half over, and frequently they did not come into the new camp until 10 p.m. This was nothing to do with laziness: it was simply that they suffered from the heat almost as much as the burrhel which lived above their villages would have done. Once we were in the cool of the true hills they went along splendidly.

On the whole I think the best plan is to engage coolies from stage to stage, and take on a permanent gang of local ruffians when the hunting grounds have been reached.

Some men forget that their coolies are human beings. I have ever regarded the overloading of coolies as a crime. Sixty pounds is, in my opinion, the maximum load which they should be expected to carry under ordinary circumstances, and all loads should be made up accordingly. Coolies dislike anything hard as a load, such as a wooden or tin box, as it is painful against the back when carrying the load. It is sometimes impossible to avoid a few loads of this sort, but this is a point to be borne in mind when sorting out kit prior to an expedition, and if one or two boxes are deemed necessary, it is not a difficult matter to arrange that three different men should take the hard load turn and turn about with soft ones. Little attentions such as this repay themselves a thousandfold. Hillmen are very human and most appreciative of kindness, and you will get the reputation of being a good sahib, which will help you enormously in the matter of getting coolies and receiving many little forms of assistance which go so far towards making the trip enjoyable. Even if a purely selfish point of view is the only one considered it will pay to study the comforts of your followers.

Over bad ground, crossing difficult passes, or when marching at altitudes over 13,000 feet, I invariably reduced my loads to 40 lb. and would advise everyone else to do the same.

Ponies or Mules

I have had very little personal experience of marching with ponies or mules, as I always avoided them on account of the expense. They make an ideal form of transport where the track is good, and there is not too much snow, as they can travel much faster than coolies, and if you mount yourself and your less mobile followers, you will be able to get along at an amazing rate. This plan is a good one to adopt when marching to Ladak over the Zoji La during the second part of the leave season, but the expense is considerable. Kashmir is the only State in which pony transport can be obtained with anything like certainty.

A pony will carry about 120 lb.

Yaks

The best of transport wherever they are obtainable, which is only in Tibet and Ladak. A yak will carry 240 lb. (3 maunds) and is a wonderfully sure-footed beast. They live entirely by grazing and feed as they go along. This means that progress is not very rapid and that continuous long marches are out of the question. If yaks are kept marching regularly at a greater average daily rate than 10 miles they will knock up and lose condition, although of course occasional long marches can be made.

In Spiti and all the Bhotia villages in the Zaskar Range to the east of that State cross-bred yaks can be obtained. They are called zhos, jhos, zhobos, jhobos, and jibboos (N.B.—Z and J are the same to the uneducated Indian) and possess all the advantages of yaks except that they are not quite so strong or hardy. They can, however, usually take a load of 200 lb. (2½ maunds), and are much more docile than the average Tibetan yak, which will bolt for miles should it get a good whiff of white man's scent, which is not at all a compliment when the appalling stench of their Tibetan herdsmen is remembered. This they endure with perfect equanimity.

Marches

The stages along all the routes in the Himalayas have been fixed by custom for generations, and such is the power of *dastur* (custom) in India, that nothing will induce coolies engaged for one stage to carry the loads on for the next stage. At times this is most maddening, especially if you happen to be in a particular hurry with two short stages immediately ahead. You may be able to effect the double march by arranging to have the fresh lot of coolies all ready waiting for

A Typical Village in the Zaskar Range, 10,000 feet.
In the foreground Bhotias may be seen ploughing with a zhobo.

you at the end of the first stage, and I have more than once managed like this, but it is a difficult matter because coolies hate starting a march in the middle of the day, and are most difficult to collect from the fields where they are working. On the whole, double marches are mostly a snare and a delusion. I have tried them again and again, sometimes with changes of coolies as described, but more often with the same lot of men. Once I had to wait until nearly midnight before all the loads were in, but this was not so bad as the experience of a friend of mine whose loads did not all arrive until the following morning.

I am quite sure that the best plan is to bow to *dastur* and allow ample time both for marching out to the hunting grounds and back again, taking things easily and not attempting double marches. You will be saved an infinity of bother and will really enjoy yourself much more; but I know you will not take my advice: in fact I doubt if I would act on it myself were I to find myself in the Himalayas once more. But I am positive we should both be wrong. There is always plenty to do in camp, such as writing up the diary, studying the map, or hunting for gooral, bear, or kakur.

If a snow-covered pass has to be crossed a very early start is essential. The snow is hard early in the morning, when it can be walked over easily and without any exertion; but once the sun rises well up the snow becomes soft and one sinks up to the knees at every step, and sometimes even up to one's waist and armpits. The difficulties of moving along under these conditions, especially at high altitudes, are almost insuperable. Coolies realise this as well as anyone else, but in spite of their knowledge, it is extraordinarily difficult to get them to start sufficiently early.

In the spring avalanches are a very real danger in some localities, and then an early start is imperative. The aim should be to reach the end of the march by 7 a.m. If by any mischance the start has been delayed the march should not be attempted at all that day. Such a wait will be most irksome, but it is not fair to risk the lives of your coolies when you are out purely for your own pleasure. I am not exaggerating the danger, and two coolies were killed by an avalanche when marching with a man just behind me on one occasion, because this point was neglected. The local villagers will know the dangerous marches perfectly well, and on such occasions will be just as keen as you to make a really early start.

Akin to avalanches is the danger from falling stones. These stones are held by accumulations of snow, which loosens them when it melts and allows them to hurtle down the mountain-sides. I was once caught in such a fall and have never forgotten it. I was doing a short march and was walking with my coolies chatting to them when we were suddenly caught by a fall of stones which consisted of rocks of all sizes from that of a sheep to a marble. They whizzed past us with terrific force. The only thing to do was to keep still. One of my loads was cut clean off a coolie's back and was carried over the khud. As bad luck would have it this load consisted of seven tins of Delhi flour, all the white flour I had. It was most annoying to see each of those 7-lb. tins hit against some rock and burst with a white cloud like a shell. Happily that was the only casualty.

These falls of stones usually occur at the same places every year, and all such spots can be passed with absolute safety before 7 a.m. when the snow is still sufficiently frozen to hold the rocks in position. In the summer when all the snow has melted the danger is over.

Snow Blindness

This is due to the intense glare of the tropical sun on snow, and it is an ever-present danger, especially early in the season. Tinted glasses are an absolute safeguard, and should always be carried in the pocket, as you never know when you may not have to cross some unexpected snowfield. Failing glasses a blue veil is sufficient protection, and all personal servants and coolies should be provided with strips of this veil even if they assure you that such a precaution is unnecessary. Your bearer and shikari will appreciate blue glasses as being rather more dignified, but the strips of veil, double for preference, are equally efficacious. A cheap and simple way of obtaining sufficient veiling for several trips is to dye an old mosquito net in indigo which can be obtained in any bazaar.

Failing glasses or veiling, smearing the bridge of the nose and the face immediately below the eyes with burnt cork is a very fair protection, as the dead black helps to reduce the glare.

Hillmen sometimes make very fairly efficient screens for the eyes out of pine needles.

The very best protection of all is obtained from glasses

made of Fieuzal No. 6. This glass does not blacken everything like ordinary blue or "smoked" glass, and is superior in every way.

Should any coolie get afflicted with snow blindness —and such a contingency is quite likely because some of them are so obstinate they will remove their veils directly your back is turned—the best cure is rest in as dim a light as possible. The pain is very considerable and can be relieved by dropping a few drops of a weak solution of zinc sulphate into the eyes every few hours.

Passage of Rivers in the Zaskar and Ladak Ranges

I gave up the study of Latin as soon as I had passed the Army entrance examination, and at once began to forget as rapidly as I could every word which had been instilled into me with the accompaniment of much anguish—mental, moral and physical. I must admit that the more I forgot the better I felt, but there was one line which always stuck in my head. It runs, *Rusticus expectat ripa dum defluat amnis*, and means, "The country bumpkin sits down on the bank and waits for the river to flow away" (in order that he may cross over dry-shod, be it understood). This line was always impressed upon me as an example of Horace's cleverness and wit at the expense of the stupidity of the country bumpkin. I could never understand why my brain insisted on retaining this single line until I had travelled through the Zaskar Range into the land beyond. Then I realised that it was Horace who was the bumpkin while the countryman, or his opposite number on the marches of Tibet, was the wise man.

Here the torrents *do* flow away in order to enable the traveller to pass over dry-shod, or at any rate with greater ease, and this is a useful fact to realise. Until the end of June the melting snows feed every stream and torrent, increasing its volume to a wonderful extent. The hotter the sun the greater the flow of water: but the intense frosts of night cut off the supplies by changing them to solid ice, and the stream dries up or decreases in size so that it becomes almost insignificant.

The first time I came across this phenomenon was when I had crossed the Zaskar Range by a fairly high pass (17,500 feet) and dropped down the other side. I had intended to camp beyond the stream I found at the bottom of the valley, but this was a raging torrent and quite unfordable. My Bhotia guide comforted me by assuring me that all would be well in the morning, and sure enough when we started off at 4 a.m. the next day there was but a gentle trickle of water, not more than a foot deep.

On another occasion I pitched my camp on the edge of a stream at an altitude of 15,100 feet. I first arrived at this spot at 2 p.m. and the stream was then of very considerable dimensions. Three hours later I would have hesitated to ford it—quite apart from the question of the cold. I set off at 3.30 a.m. the next day and was astonished to find that there was no stream at all. The valley was bone-dry: the river had, in fact, completely flowed away. I wished that my old enemy Horace could be there to take note of the fact, as I crossed the valley dry-shod. I stayed some time at that camp and noticed that a trickle of water began at about 9 a.m. and gradually increased in volume as the day wore on and the sun gained in power. This was early in June; I expect that six weeks later there would have been no stream at all, as in this particular spot it was entirely fed by the melting of winter snows.

Mountain Sickness

This is due to the insufficiency of oxygen in the air and the reduction in atmospheric pressure at high altitudes. Some men seem almost immune except for the inevitable shortness of breath and panting when anything approaching physical exertion is attempted. Others are invariably affected at such comparatively low altitudes as 14,000 feet. Personally I have never been worried by it in the least, although of course I found great difficulty in breathing when trying to do anything at all vigorous, but I never had a sign of a headache or suffered in any way from insomnia. I have had coolies with me who showed great distress, such as severe headaches, bleeding at the ears and nose, and inability to sleep. The best cure is rest, failing a return to lower altitudes, and I have given a good many great relief by bleeding them slightly on the scalp.

Chlorate of potash is recommended by some as a preventive as it gives off oxygen. My own experience of it was that it made not the slightest difference. I tried it myself and gave some to all my coolies who were in any way uncomfortable, but it seemed to have not the slightest effect one way or the other. Personally I believe that mountain sickness is of two distinct types, each of which is due to a different cause. The first is caused by reduction in atmospheric pressure, and the symptoms are nausea, headache and bleeding. This is the type which is most likely to affect sportsmen and their followers, and begins at about 14,000 feet, according to the sensitiveness of the individual. The second type is chiefly due to lack of oxygen, but is, of course, combined with reduced pressure. This is the type which bothers mountaineers at altitudes of 20,000 feet and over, and it need not be considered by ordinary sportsmen. Of course lack of oxygen is undoubtedly a partial cause of the first type, but I think the principal reason is low atmospheric pressure, and it is possible that this is why I found chlorate of potash of such little use, as its function would merely be to supply oxygen.

Medicines and Ailments

This is a subject on which no one who is not a qualified doctor can write with any authority, and Moore's *Family Medicine and Hygiene for India* is the best book for the layman. Throughout all the less-civilised parts of India, and more especially in the Himalayas, the local inhabitants regard every sahib as a heaven-born doctor and surgeon, and impose in him implicit confidence. Unhappily this confidence is not always well placed. The eagerness with which the simple hill-folk will throng to one's camp in the hopes of being cured of all the ills of the flesh is sad and pathetic, and all sportsmen will feel sick at heart at their own helplessness and lack of knowledge. One is merely asked for *dewai* (medicine) which is to cure any complaint from a stomachache onwards. Amongst other diseases, accidents, or ailments, for which I have personally been asked for *dewai*, are goitre, difficult cases of child-birth, cut throats (a man in one village got excited and cut the throats of three men, two of whom were dead by the time I managed to arrive), axe wounds (very common among woodcutters), various diseases of the eyes, and what I could only conclude were internal tumours of the largest size. The commonest complaints are of pains in the stomach, and fever. For the former, essence of Jamaica ginger is splendid. A little goes a long way and makes a strong dose, which is very warming to the inside. The patient gasps and says it is " very strong " medicine and goes away happy. Quite likely he is rendered better, for faith has a great deal to do with healing in the case of these simple savages, and it certainly will not do any harm. For fever give quinine.

It is to be feared that there are some malingerers who fain sickness in the hope of getting alcohol. Never give any.

Jamaica ginger, an ample supply of quinine, aspirin, some potent pills, a bottle of chlorodyne, iodine, Dover's powders, vaseline, permanganate of potash and perchloride of mercury tabloids (in case of any strong disinfectant being required for bad wounds) should be all the drugs required in addition to any others which I have mentioned above. A thermometer and a supply of lint, bandages, cotton-wool, waterproof silk and a syringe will complete the medicine-chest.

Personal Servants

A personal servant of sorts is indispensable. In Kashmir the matter is simple because every proper shikari has some special crony who always accompanies him on his trips to act as cook and bearer for the sahib, and they rob in unison accordingly. In all other parts of the Himalayas you will have to make your own arrangement for a bearer and cook. There are several points which you must always remember. First that, except in Kashmir, all hillmen are Hindus until the Great Himalayan Range is approached or crossed, when they are mostly Buddhists. In Kashmir alone will you find Mohammedans. Now any Plains bearer who will cook must be a Mohammedan, and if you take such a man with you into the hills he will have no co-religionist with him. He will not like always having to live to a very great extent apart, and there will always be difficulty about his food, for there will be no Mohammedan to *hallal* any animals which you may shoot and so make the flesh lawful for the consumption of a follower of the Prophet. The second point to note is that all hillmen without exception have an utter contempt for Plains men, while the latter despise the hill folk. The combination of these two facts usually means that there is a certain amount of friction in your camp as oil will not mix gracefully with water. One advantage of such differences will be that your bearer will tell you at once if your shikaris or coolies are defrauding you in any of the many ways in which the Oriental servant is so expert, while the shikari will be just as keen to tell tales of the bearer. But for my own part I hate to feel that any of my servants or followers are unhappy or bickering when I am on leave for my own pleasure, and I would sooner have pilfering in moderation by a friendly coalition.

On one long trip I took no bearer from the Plains at all but engaged a coolie who had accompanied me on previous trips and who showed great promise as a plain cook. I may here mention that hillmen are not nearly so particular about caste as Hindus of the plains, and the Brahmins at the sacred shrines in the hills will all eat meat with avidity, while all rajputs will cook food for white men. This coolie really did me remarkably well in every way, and of course he was one of the same lot as my shikari and permanent coolies, all of which were recruited from three small villages situated on the northern slopes of the Great Himalayan Range. But my fare was of the simplest, and I would not recommend the plan to anyone who was at all particular about his food or creature comforts.

I think the best plan of all is to take a well-trained Mohammedan bearer or khitmutger with you from the plains who seems really keen to accompany you. Many such servants really enjoy shikar trips, and one should do them well in the way of warm clothes, bedding, and a small tent to themselves. This is only fair. All natives of the plains feel the cold tremendously, and you cannot expect them to be happy if you take them to places where the nightly temperature drops to below zero Fahrenheit without giving them ample warm clothing. In addition to a good warm suit they should be provided with a Tommy's Coat British Warm and a sweater, as well as four or five blankets and a rezai. This may seem unnecessary, but I have always thought it is up to the sahib to look after the welfare of any servants who accompany him into the snows.

In addition to a bearer I am sure that an orderly would be most useful. He would be able to live with the bearer in a little tent, and each would be a companion for the other. This orderly would be invaluable on the march in looking after the coolies, and would thus save you the necessity and expense of engaging a professional shikari at your base. He could sometimes accompany you out shooting and *hallal* the kill, thus enabling you to feed both him and the bearer without the expense of buying sheep.

I would regard such a combination as an ideal arrangement for any part of the Himalayas except Kashmir.

Permanent Staff

In addition to a bearer and orderly a permanent staff will be necessary when the shooting grounds are reached. In Kashmir your shikari will bring his own friends, but elsewhere you will have to make your own selection. I strongly advise putting off engaging any permanent staff until you have reached your grounds and settled on some village as your advanced head-quarters. You will thus get hold of better men and save the expense of their wages during the march out and back. If you require a tiffin coolie on the march it is a simple matter to engage one extra coolie daily to act as such, and a few annas will always induce those who are first in at the new camp to collect sufficient wood for fires and fetch water should it be at all far away.

But once you have reached the neighbourhood of your goal you should engage a permanent staff. This should consist of a shikari, tiffin coolie, dak coolie, and perhaps two other coolies who will help with the camp, fetch wood and water, and make themselves generally useful, in addition to carrying any loads when on the march. These extra men are not essential, but they will be found very useful. The dak coolie's task will be to travel backwards and forwards between you and the hill station which you have made your base with letters, etc., and he will be able to bring out any additional stores should you find yourself running short.

In Kashmir your shikari will almost be sure to want you to engage a chota-shikari as well as a tiffin coolie. This is entirely unnecessary, and only adds to the expense.

Outside Kashmir I think it is a good plan to take up a few old Army blankets so as to provide each of your permanent staff with one. They will greatly appreciate this kindness and work all the better. I also think it is a good plan to provide them with a small tent in addition to the one used by your bearer and orderly. It is amazing to see the number of hillmen which can squeeze into a small *shuldari* (servants' tent), and I am sure it pays to keep them as dry and as comfortable as possible, quite apart from any feeling of humanity. The shikari will without doubt demand a suit. I do not think this necessary unless he is a really good man, but if he does you well, the price of a hill coat will not ruin you.

Selection of Camping Grounds

In all the Himalayan ranges there is frequently but little choice left for the selection of a camping ground. Along all the regular routes there are certain "paraos" which have been definitely fixed by generations of custom and experience, and as often as not there are no level places in the neighbourhood with the exception of these "paraos." Sometimes they are of considerable extent, in which case the tent should be pitched as far away as possible from any village or bunnia's shop which may be there, and sometimes they are only just large enough to accommodate two or three tents, in which case Keating's powder should be employed even more freely than usual. Villages and bunnia's shops are always centres of concentration for every known, and possibly a good many unknown, species of obnoxious insect. Flies are particularly bad in some localities, and I have at times been compelled to have all meals under mosquito curtains. For this reason these nets should always accompany the sportsman on his march through the hills.

In the Zaskar Range at certain seasons in the year all the "paraos" are covered with flocks of sheep on the way to the grazing grounds at high altitudes. In all such cases the earth on which the tent is pitched will probably be found to be a solid mass of sheep and goat droppings in which ticks abound and lice are not exactly rare. But if Keating's powder is used with sufficient vehemence I have found that all these creatures can be kept at bay. Flies are the only insects against which Keating's seems to be of no avail, and if these are really bad, mosquito netting provides the only protection. It may as well be pointed out that these nets can be hung from the fly of any tent more easily if a few rings are attached to the tent for the purpose.

Once the regular paths have been left, the risk from the attacks of insects is greatly reduced, but precautions should never be dropped, for every coolie provides free transport for many battalions of fleas, lice and bugs.

It is when the advance has been pushed towards the actual shooting grounds that more care must be exercised in the selection of a site for the camp. A slight slope is always preferable to anything approaching a hollow, even though the latter may appear more level. Sudden rainstorms are very common in the hills, and then a dry depression in the ground may be converted into a miniature lake. For the same reason the tent should never be pitched too close to any stream, which may easily rise to a perfectly astonishing extent.

Another danger to remember is that arising from avalanches and falling stones. The local Indians will probably know all risky places, but they should be carefully interrogated. The ground immediately underneath a precipice should always be avoided.

A trench should *always* be dug round the tent as soon as it is pitched. This should be made a standing order no matter what the appearance of the weather. If this is done and the site has been selected with proper caution you need have no fear of sudden storms, but if snow starts falling heavily it should be swept off the tents as often as possible; otherwise the weight may become too much for both ropes and poles.

WATER SUPPLY

In the hills the water supply is far and away cleaner and more reliable than in the plains. There is little fear of enteric, dysentery or cholera germs being harboured in a clear mountain torrent, but below villages the water should never be trusted. There is, however, another risk in the Himalayas which is common to mountainous regions all over the world, and that is goitre. The exact cause of it is unknown, but water has been proved to be the carrier, and even snow water is unsafe. Boiling and the addition of just a trace of iodine renders all water perfectly innocuous, and for this reason I would recommend all sportsmen to adopt these measures. They really give little trouble, and I am sure they are sound. Goitre is prevalent throughout the Himalayas, but it seems to be more virulent in certain localities. I know of one little village just south of the main axis in which every man, woman and child seemed to be afflicted with goitres of the largest size. It may be urged that it is only continuous drinking of hill water which causes this complaint, and that during a trip of three months there is no risk. This view may be correct: I would not like to offer an opinion, but I know of many white men who have been attacked with goitre, and precautionary measures are so simple that it would seem foolish not to take them.

Driving

Sooner or later you are bound to come across a position in which a stalk is undoubtedly a very difficult matter and when your shikari will suggest driving the game instead. Never under any circumstances give in to him. If the stalk is really hopeless, wait until the next day, when the animals may have moved into a more favourable position: but never risk a drive.

I have only once been persuaded into trying one, and the story certainly provides a lesson.

It was my maiden effort at Himalayan shikar, and I had just completed the first march out from the hill station which formed my main base. A local villager soon appeared, and having informed me that he was a shikari, asked me whether I wanted to shoot a gooral. Of course I was wild with excitement at the idea, but expressed surprise at there being any game so close to the hill station. He assured me there were gooral, and suggested that if we saw any I should pay him a rupee, while if he failed to show me game I need not give him an anna. This seemed a perfectly fair and genuine bargain, and the next morning I was off before the dawn had fully broken. We had not gone very far when we arrived at the bottom of a tall and fairly steep *khud*. Near the top were some pines, and among these pines my guide suddenly pointed out two gooral. He had earned his rupee and I was delighted. The stalk would certainly be a long and tiring one, though it did not appear to me difficult, but the shikari assured me that by the time I had reached the top they would have left their feeding grounds for the day, and that the better plan would be for him to drive them to me.

At first I demurred, but he pointed out that he could reach the same level as the gooral far more rapidly than I could, which was probably the truth although I did not like his saying so, and that he knew exactly which way the gooral would move on being disturbed. They would without doubt come downhill past that boulder yonder. If the sahib would but hide behind the boulder he would certainly shoot one, and perhaps both. All this seemed so plausible, and the manner in which he had found the gooral so impressed me as to his knowledge of their local habits, that I allowed myself to be persuaded against my own judgment. The result was of course a fiasco. The gooral certainly did move downhill, and within two hundred yards of the boulder behind which I was hiding too, but at a pace which made the chances of a successful shot too remote for me to think of risking one. They came down that *khud* like rockets, bounding from boulder to boulder, and were only visible for moments at a time. The shikari expressed his regret; I curbed my disappointment, and he got his rupee.

But there is a sequel to this story. I afterwards met an old gentleman who had settled down in India for good and who lived in the neighbourhood of that same hill station. He knew my friend, the local shikari, well, and also knew all his tricks and habits. My first suspicion that the country had been long ago shot out was absolutely correct; as far as he knew, and as far as the shikari knew, there were only those two gooral left in that particular neighbourhood, and they were to the shikari a regular source of income. Any sahib who passed his village on the way out to more distant fields would be asked if he wanted to shoot a gooral, and would be told that if they saw none not a pie need be paid, but if they did find game, which was very scarce, why, let the sahib give a rupee for his skill. On the sahib agreeing the shikari would trot him round to where his two pet gooral lived, and having surprised his employer by showing game so readily, would suggest a drive, assuring him he knew the exact habits of the animals (which was certainly true). The sahib invariably agreed, with the result that the gooral lived to provide another rupee on a future occasion!

I believe this to be absolutely true and have long ago forgiven that shikari for the trick he played on me, but I sometimes wonder whether he or his son still carries on the same trade with the descendants of the gooral which he showed me, and I must admit that I hope he never lost his capital by some such untoward accident as a sahib insisting on a stalk.

Shooting Alone

From the point of view of sport there can be but little doubt that a man should shoot by himself in the Himalayas. His movements will not be hampered by having to conform to those of a companion and he is certain to get a better chance of actual sport. It is frequently impossible to make plans beforehand even though you may know the country well. A nullah in which you enjoyed good sport one year may be empty of game the next, and a previously bad nullah may become really good. When you are alone you have no one to consider but yourself, and should occasion arise you can pack up and move thirty miles away at a moment's notice. The less the ground is disturbed in any one district the better the chance of ultimately picking up a good head, and it is obvious that two parties must disturb the country more than one. All this may sound very selfish, but it is in truth merely human nature, and the keener a man is the more anxious he becomes. There is plenty of room in the Himalayas for men to shoot by themselves, so I fail to see any reason why they should wish to join forces.

A common practice is for two men to march up to their shooting grounds together and then to separate. When shooting in new country I think that even this is a mistake. Two men want twice the number of coolies that one man does, and I have already explained the difficulty of obtaining a large body of coolies at short notice. The smaller and more self-contained any expedition is the better its chances are for unhampered travel.

In some places like Chamba where game is fairly plentiful, but where the limit of animals allowed to be shot is small, two men might work together for a whole shoot, taking alternate shots or stalks. But this has never seemed to me a very satisfactory arrangement. The fewer men actually doing a stalk the better, and there is the same difficulty about the increased number of coolies, although this point is simplified to a certain extent by both sportsmen sharing a tent and cooking outfit.

For myself I have never felt lonely, and I am unable to understand how any man can lack for companionship when surrounded by "the hills and the snow of the hills."

AMUSEMENTS

During any shooting expedition there must come certain periods when there is nothing to do and time hangs very heavily on one's hands. Some kind of amusement is essential, but the means to this end must be neither bulky nor heavy. Keeping a detailed diary is a most instructive and interesting pastime, but one cannot write throughout the whole of the inevitable periods of inaction. Reading is a stand-by, but books are both heavy and cumbersome; and consequently any books which are taken should be chosen for the solidity of their matter rather than for the excitement of their narratives. But solidity must go hand in hand with interest. It is difficult to make any recommendations as so much depends on personal taste. Darwin's *Origin of Species* and *The Descent of Man* are in my opinion almost unrivalled for shooting trips. A careful perusal of either of these books will take an ordinary man at least six months. For lighter reading nothing can be more suitable than *Kim*. It is a book which I have read and re-read again and again; a book of which I have never tired; and above all, it is a book which contains the best descriptions of Himalayan scenery which have ever been drawn by the written word.

Those who are fond of cards will probably take a

couple of Patience packs in their bedding-roll. Others may take a "pocket" chess-board. And a few really fortunate ones will find more than sufficient occupation with a paint-box and sketch-book. These are matters which each must decide for himself, but the importance of having some form of amusement should not be forgotten.

Small Game Shooting

Small game abounds in the Himalayas, but it is by no means easy to make a bag. It is impossible to combine a regular small game expedition with one after big game. The continual banging of a shot-gun will frighten all four-legged animals in the district. But a gun should certainly be taken, as good sport may frequently be met with on the march, particularly when homeward bound, as there is then not the same risk of disturbing good heads. A ·22 rifle is invaluable for shooting for the pot in the further Zaskar Range where Tibetan pigeon are sometimes extraordinarily plentiful and wonderfully confiding, far more so than any snow pigeon I have ever seen. A long-barrelled ·22 pistol would be even better than a rifle, as it is much handier and takes up less room, but a pistol is certainly not everybody's weapon—more's the pity. Looking back I think a good catapult would have been extremely useful on many an occasion.

When shooting purely for the pot the fewer cartridges fired the better, partly because but a small allowance of shot-gun ammunition can be taken on a trip in the hills, and partly because the less the country is disturbed the better the chances for sport. Bearing these facts in mind the principles of enfilade fire should be thoroughly mastered, even when shooting with a rifle or pistol.

CHAPTER XVIII

OUTFIT

THE outfit necessary for a trip into the Himalayas is not necessarily considerable, and at a pinch the usual belongings of the average Britisher in India will need but few additions. There are two great principles which underlie the selection of an outfit no matter what part of the Himalayas it is intended to make for. They are: first, that you will have to combat against extreme cold, particularly at nights, and secondly, that the amount of transport available will always be decidedly limited.

Let us take the latter point first. Villages in the Himalayas are not to be found in anything like the same number as the Plains. This means that coolies must be recruited from a small number of villages for any particular march or period. The size of hill villages, particularly beyond the Great Himalayan Range, is very small, and consequently few coolies are actually available in any one village. It is comparatively easy to collect a dozen good coolies, but every additional one adds to the difficulty in remote regions, and if twenty to thirty are suddenly required at short notice a delay is almost inevitable. It is not that the men will not come, it is simply that they are not there, and a large area of country must be drawn upon in order to collect the necessary number. Marching with but a dozen coolies is invariably a simple matter, free from worries and anxieties; but a team of thirty is always a nuisance and difficult to collect.

It may be urged that this difficulty would be surmounted by engaging the requisite number at the beginning of the trip, but, as has already been pointed out, this plan is not to be recommended owing to the insufficiency of food supply in the small villages of the further ranges. To swoop down on one of these remote hamlets with a gang of thirty coolies, not to mention shikari, bearer, and other members of a permanent staff, would present the local inhabitants with a quite impossible task in the matter of providing food, and the sahib would inevitably be regarded as a most unwelcome visitor, which would be decidedly detrimental to chances of good sport, to look at the question from the most selfish point of view.

If animal transport is used, the same thing applies to a very great extent. It is true that ponies can live chiefly by grazing, but a certain amount of grain should be given if long marches are contemplated. Yaks or zhos can seldom be obtained in large numbers, and the grazing grounds in the bleak valleys of the Zaskar and Ladak Ranges are not very extensive.

To return to the question of the cold. This is really intense even in the height of summer. At one camp I was once in, at an elevation of 15,100 feet, the thermometer used to drop to just below zero Fahrenheit every night. This in itself may not be regarded as anything out of the ordinary, in comparison with temperatures which prevail in Canada for instance, but it must be remembered that in the Himalayas the day temperatures are really warm, and it is this contrast which makes the cold of the nights appear even more bitter than it really is. Consequently tents, clothing, bedding and food must all be selected with a view to their cold-resisting properties, and at the same time lightness and portability must be an equally important governing factor.

I will give my own views on an absolutely ideal outfit for a trip into the further Himalayas, and these can be adapted according to circumstances and personal taste.

Bedding

(1) Kapok camp mattress.

(2) Reindeer-skin sleeping-bag. I obtained one of these through Messrs. Lumley & Dowell, St. James' Street, London, in the autumn of 1915, and found it perfectly invaluable in France. The hair is on the inside, and makes such a soft bedding that I frequently slept in luxurious comfort on a stone-flagged floor. I never found any additional bedding necessary, but I would like to have something extra if I were starting for Chang Chen Mo. These bags are made to cover up the head if necessary and are very roomy. In spite of this they are marvellously light, only weighing 12 lb. The one drawback they possess is the high cost, viz., 12 guineas, but I am sure that this would be money well laid out.

They should be turned inside out and hung in the

sun to air for an hour or so every day if possible, but otherwise need no attention.

(3) Jaeger three-fold sleeping-bag. This is for use during the march up when the reindeer-skin bag would be too warm. It can be used with either two layers on top and one underneath, or vice versa. The reindeer bag would make an additional mattress. When the latter comes into use the Jaeger bag should be placed underneath it and on top of the kapok mattress.

(4) A good warm rug or blanket, preferably " double-bed size," so that it can be used folded double. In intense cold this should be thrown over the reindeer bag.

(5) A small, but good, down pillow. This adds very greatly to one's comfort, weighs very little, and occupies but a small space. I think it is well worth while. I once slept for over a month with a bag of atta as my pillow, but never again! I had no conception that flour could be so hard. An air pillow might be excellent, but I rather doubt the rubber standing the Indian climate for long.

These five items are all that is necessary, and they should be kept in a really good Willesden canvas valise of sorts. Before the war there was not much scope for a selection, but now the different patterns are legion, and choice is entirely a matter of personal taste or inability to withstand the blandishments of some particular salesman.

I always used to keep my washing materials in a small enamelled iron leather-topped basin inside my valise, and this is as convenient an arrangement as any.

Laden Coolies crossing a hastily constructed Bridge in the Great Himalayan Range. Altitude 7,000 feet.

Clothes

(1) Warm knickerbocker shikar suit. My own experience is that the best wearing material is some finely woven kind of gaberdine lined with flannel. Puttoo or other loosely woven cloths do not last nearly so long, nor do they keep out a slight shower in the same way. There should be plenty of pockets, and two "hare" or "poacher" pockets will be found most useful on occasions. The knickerbockers should be very loose and baggy at the knee, and I would strongly advise having the elbows, knees, and seat of knickerbockers reinforced with an extra thickness of material.

The colour should be some fairly light neutral tint.

(2) Three woollen vests of medium thickness.

(3) Three khaki twill shirts.

(4) Three pairs of pants. Personally I have never found anything to better the Tommy's "drawers cotton," and have worn nothing else since I was a cadet at Woolwich.

(5) Leather vest with sleeves.

(6) Sweater.

(7) One pair of old flannel trousers.

(8) An old shooting-jacket.

(9) One suit of pyjamas.

(10) Coat British Warm lined with camel fleece and with an additional and detachable lining of leather or sheepskin. This will stand the wet much better than a poshteen and is superior in every way.

(11) One pair Gilgit boots.

(12) Puttees.

(13) One dozen pairs of thick socks and the same number of thin ones. This may seem excessive, but nothing is more important.

(14) One pair of khaki shorts.

(15) Four pairs of stockings.

The last two items are very useful for wearing during the march up, which is frequently along some very hot and steamy valley. They are light, cool, and easy to put on in a hurry.

(16) Two dozen handkerchiefs.

(17) One bath towel and four face towels.

(18) Warm scarf.

(19) Balaclava helmet.

(20) A light waterproof. This is a most difficult problem, as anything which will stand the climate is quite ineffective against Himalayan downpours. I have tried all kinds of different materials and have come to the conclusion that nothing can equal a long waterproof cape made of mackintosh as made for syces or jampanis in hill stations. This is really effective, only costs a few rupees, and can be thrown away at the end of a trip, as it would never last for another year.

The Coat British Warm, leather waistcoat, sweater, pyjamas, scarf, Balaclava helmet and Gilgit boots should be carried in the bedding roll, and some spare handkerchiefs should always be kept in a pocket of the valise. This should make up one good load of about 60 lb. The remainder of the clothing which is not being worn is most conveniently carried in a Tommy's waterproof kit-bag, which in its turn should be placed in a Willesden canvas holdall. Dirty clothes should be carried in a small dirty-linen bag, for which room should also be found in the holdall.

Footgear

So far I have made no allusion to boots or shoes. These present a most serious problem, and the best plan to adopt is to wear as far as possible the footgear of the country in which you happen to be shooting. Where grass shoes are understood nothing is better, but do not forget to get the special socks made with a separate division for the big toe, in order to be able to fasten a grass shoe on. In Kashmir, Chamba and some parts of Garhwal your shikari should be able to make your grass shoes, and a load of grass should be carried for this purpose, but in other parts of the Himalayas grass shoes are not understood, and a kind of raw hide shoe with woollen uppers is in vogue. These are excellent in every respect, although not so good as the grass shoe for climbing over bad ground. There is no harm in taking a pair of good stout shooting-boots, but they are a considerable weight, and once they are at all worn they become useless, for no hill *mochi* will be able to repair them.

On the march *chaplies* are very comfortable and I can thoroughly recommend them, but take care not to pull the back strap too tight at first, otherwise a blister is inevitable. The best *chaplies* that I have seen came from Cockburn's agency, Srinagar. The *chaplies* which are frequently for sale at various railway stations near the Himalayan termini are utterly useless. I have found that one good pair of *chaplies* will do for a hundred miles over ordinary Himalayan tracks.

In Ladak or Tibet rope-soled boots are good, but they soon get badly cut about on the sharp shales. The long Tibetan boots are quite satisfactory and can be repaired by almost any nomad.

When after thar in a country in which grass shoes were not available I always wore my socks outside my puttees, so as to be able to take them off in a moment and go bare-footed over any particular bad places.

I have always imagined that moccasins would be particularly suitable for Himalayan climbing, but of course they would wear out very quickly and an ample supply of hide would be essential, but I see no reason why the sportsman should not make them for himself out of the hides of animals which he shoots. These could be easily dried, and the manufacture would help to pass the hours which are frequently spent in waiting on a hill side and watching favourite feeding grounds, etc. I think this experiment is decidedly worth trying.

Tents

In Kashmir tents are usually hired at Srinagar before actually starting on an expedition. This is cheaper on the whole than taking your own up with you owing to the enormous freight charges between Rawal Pindi and Srinagar. But if a bullock cart is hired a couple of months before the actual start, tents and all the rest of one's personal kit could be sent on ahead to Srinagar at a comparatively low cost, and this arrangement would probably be cheaper than hiring. The same means of transport would have to be employed on the homeward journey. Everywhere in the Himalayas outside Kashmir the sportsman must take tents with him, so I will assume that he wishes to fit himself out accordingly.

Let us first consider the servants. As I have already pointed out, I think, two small *shuldaris* are advisable; they should weigh about 25 lb. each and will together make up one load during the march up, but if very bad ground has to be negotiated later on they can be separated, each forming the nucleus of another load.

And now for the sportsman himself.

The tents most generally used in the Himalayas are the ordinary double fly 80-lb. Kabul tent, a smaller edition of this which nominally weighs 40 lb. (both of these tents being fitted with bathrooms), and a single fly tent which weighs 40 lb. I do not consider any of these patterns really suitable for camping at high altitudes in the further Himalayas and beyond. One of the greatest difficulties against which any tent will have to contend in these regions is the wind, and in the case of any tent where the outer fly does not reach right down to the ground there is every chance of a really strong gale getting right under the outer fly and lifting it up. In all cases the outer fly should come right down to the ground.

Similarly the wind has a horrid way of whistling right underneath the bottom edge of the inner fly even though this part of the tent is pegged to the ground along its entire length. The cold and draught is then intense. This may be prevented by sewing canvas flaps about 2 feet in width along the bottom edges of the inner fly and weighting them down on the inside of the tent with one's bedding, kit, stones, etc.; but even this plan is not ideal. The only method of making the inside of the tent really snug against wind is to have the whole floor covered with a canvas carpet, which is in one single piece with the inner fly. The only joint will then be at the door, and the tent can nearly always be placed so that it is facing down wind. A canvas carpet can certainly be attached to any of the tents which have already been mentioned as being in general use, but the additional weight would be very considerable, and it is a better plan to purchase a specially designed and constructed tent.

Such a tent is made by Messrs. Silver & Edgington, King William House, Eastcheap, London, E.C.3. It is known as the "Double Fly Whymper Tent with rounded end." It is made throughout of Willesden canvas, and the carpet and inner fly are in one piece. The outer fly reaches right down to the ground. The end is rounded so as to withstand the force of a gale. The whole tent complete with poles and tent pegs fits into a Willesden canvas bag and weighs but 60 lb. There are no unnecessary ropes, and there is ample room for a tall man, while at a pinch two can use the tent without undue discomfort. This tent is to my mind ideal. The Willesden canvas, of which it is made, does not absorb water as do the cotton tents prevalent in India, and there is consequently no increase in weight when the tent has been subjected to a night's heavy rain, and the tent itself can be put up with less bother.

There are two other patterns of "Whymper" tents sold by the same firm, but neither are so satisfactory for the sportsman as the one I have described. One is similar in all respects with the exception of the outer fly, which is lacking. A double fly is the greatest boon in the Himalayas and Tibet, as it affords protection from the sun as well as from the cold, and is well worth the extra cost. The other pattern has a double fly, but the back is square with the sides instead of rounded. As has been pointed out, a rounded back gives a great advantage in the matter of wind resistance and the increase in weight is negligible for all practical purposes.

The tent pegs for the guy ropes had best be made of iron and they should be both long and strong. Aluminium is the best material for all other tent pegs. They are rather expensive in the first place, but are far stronger and more satisfactory in every way than wooden ones, and their extreme lightness, which at the same time is combined with compactness, greatly facilitates matters of transport. It should be remembered, however, that in the further Himalayas and Tibet, where wood is scarce and metal almost unknown, both iron and aluminium pegs will be stolen to a certainty unless they are made with rings or eyes and all kept together strung on an iron chain, which is fastened with a padlock. Pegs should always be kept thus when the tents are not actually pitched, and it is a very bad system to distribute the pegs among the various loads, as is sometimes done. All the pegs, both those of the sportsman's tent and those belonging to the servants' tents, should be kept on one chain and given into the personal charge of the shikari, orderly, bearer or some trustworthy coolie, who should be made personally responsible that the full number of pegs is collected whenever the tents are struck. If this plan is adhered to rigidly and strictly enforced there should be no losses from theft, and breakages with metal pegs are of rare occurrence; even so it is as well to have a few spare pegs in case of accidents.

If the sportsman is unable to afford the outlay necessary for the purchase of a "Whymper" tent such as I have described he had best use either an 80-lb. or 40-lb. pattern double fly tent as supplied by any of the Cawnpore mills, but let me assure him that money spent in a good tent is well laid out, and that in the long run he will be amply repaid by incurring the extra expense.

Whatever tent or tents are used all the poles should be jointed, as unjointed poles are very awkward for purposes of transport. If jointed poles have not been obtained the best plan is to give one single pole to as many coolies as there are poles; the men will probably use them as khudsticks, but you must take the risk of any damage being done.

Sometimes the sportsman may want to make a flying dash to the head of a nullah or some other remote spot to which it would be most difficult and inconvenient to move the whole camp. He will probably only be away for a night or two at most, and under these circumstances a small valise tent is very useful. I had one from the Elgin Mills, Cawnpore, known as "Colonel Young's Valise Tent." It weighed but 12 lb. and was excellent in every way. On many occasions it has been the only tent I have taken for an exploratory trip up some nullah lasting four or five days, and on one occasion it was all I had with me for over a fortnight, when I was never camped much below 15,000 feet, and usually well above this altitude.

Food and Stores

It is the greatest possible mistake to try and subsist on poor or indifferent food when shooting in the Himalayas (or anywhere else for that matter), and it is in addition the worst form of economy imaginable. There is a great difference between plain wholesome food and luxuries—the former is a necessity while the latter are superfluous.

Bread is the most important item to be considered, and it is essential that the cook should be able to make this well. Unfortunately when shooting in and beyond the Zaskar Range it is often extremely hard to obtain a sufficiency of fuel for baking, and on such occasions chappaties only can be made. These should be thin and crisp, and then they are really excellent and wholesome, but on no account should local hill atta be used, as this is warranted to upset the stomach of any ordinary white man in less than twelve hours. White flour does not make quite such digestible chappaties as atta, and if any sojourn in barren regions is anticipated some good atta should be taken with the rest of the stores from the Plains. Some men always take Paisley flour; this is really only a substitute for ordinary baking powder. It undoubtedly gives an excellent flavour to the bread, but it is expensive and much more of it is required than of ordinary baking powder, and consequently it takes up more room. My own view is that it is unnecessary, and in saying this I may add that I have used it very considerably.

An allowance of 5 lb. of flour per week is a fairly good estimate, and the total amount should consist half of good quality Plains atta, and half of white flour, or all atta if so preferred. A proportion of atta should certainly be taken for making chappaties, and for bread a mixture of atta and white flour is excellent. Those who do not like the idea of chappaties can take tins of biscuits instead, but this will add very considerably to the initial cost of the stores.

Before starting, a clear understanding with the bearer and orderly (if one is taken) is essential on the subject of the local atta. They should be warned of its inferior quality and high cost and should be offered the chance of taking a fairly ample supply with them from their homes. The extra coolie load will be well worth while as it will keep the servants in a better humour and to a great extent stop them from pilfering from the sportsman's private supply.

An ample supply of jam is most important because in all cold climates men are seized with a craving for sweets and fats which they never have under ordinary circumstances. Butter should be taken for a similar reason. This really adds but little to the weight of stores, half a pound a week being all that is necessary. Chocolate is supposed to be sustaining, but I have never found it so; perhaps I did not get the right kind, but I have tried a good many different sorts. Cocoa is a matter of taste. I always used to have a good big mug of cocoa before starting out in the morning.

I regard condensed milk as bordering on a luxury, but perhaps on the whole some should be taken. Milk can sometimes be obtained in the hills in most unexpected quarters, but generally it is difficult to get much. One small tin per week is a fairly generous allowance, and these should never be opened except in times of stress or emergency.

Eggs can never be obtained outside Kashmir, and if they are greatly fancied some "Cooks' eggs" might be taken, but I do class these as a luxury.

Potted meats are not very satisfactory as a tin lasts no time, but anchovy and bloater pastes are very different. With these a little goes a long way and they make excellent appetisers.

Potatoes can usually be obtained locally, but no other vegetables are grown. Garlic grows wild in great profusion beyond the Great Himalayan Range, as does wild rhubarb. Both are perfectly wholesome, but a little of either will go a long way with most men. Greens of sorts can sometimes be purchased, but this is not often. Dhal is not grown in the hills, and a good supply of this excellent food should be taken. The rice which is purchased locally in the further Himalayas is frequently very bad in quality and exceedingly gritty. It is better to take a supply up.

Tea is a perfect standby and a great pick-me-up at high altitudes. A good supply should be taken, as the coolies all love it and few things please them more than having a small daily ration of tea issued when in camp. This ration should of course only be given to a staff of coolies who have been engaged for some little time to carry loads up some remote nullah.

The following list of stores will provide a fair guide

as to what should be taken for a month's trip. For two or three months the amounts can be doubled or trebled.

Tins of Delhi flour (7 lb. each)		2
Atta (country flour)	lb.	7
Rice	lb.	6
Dhal (Lentils)	lb.	3
Tins of jam (1 lb. each)		10
Tins of condensed milk (small size)		4
Tea	lb.	2
Cocoa	lb.	2
Butter	lb.	2
Bottles of Bovril (large size)		2
Tins of anchovy and bloater pastes (small)		8
„ „ Cerebos salt		1
„ „ Baking-powder		4
„ „ Curry powder		1
„ „ Keating's insect powder		4
Bottles of Lea & Perrins' Worcester Sauce		1
„ „ Tabloid "Saxin" (in place of sugar)		1
Soup tablets		12
Tins of mustard (small)		1
Bottles of pepper (red or white)		1
Dozens of candles		3
Packets of Bromo		1
„ „ Lux (for washing clothes)		2
Tablets of soap		2
Boxes of matches		12

Total weight of stores above is as near as possible 60 lb.

Cooking utensils should comprise a good strong kettle with a folding handle if possible, a small nest of aluminium deckchies, a frying pan (also with a folding handle), a round tin for baking bread and a couple of baking-tins for bread, and last but not least, a Wellbank's "Boilerette." This is really a kind of large double saucepan. The space between the two walls is partially filled with water and the food is "steamed" rather than boiled. Steaming is a simple process and always results in tender meat. There are doubtless other excellent patterns of steamers on the market, but I have found " Boilerettes " so simple and so satisfactory that I would always regard one as an essential article of camp equipment. These invaluable utensils can be obtained from the Army and Navy Stores.

Among the etceteras should be a good supply of strong jharrons and some muslin, which is most useful for covering meat as a protection from flies.

Some knives, spoons, forks and enamelled iron plates and mugs complete the list as far as crockery is concerned.

Your bearer is sure to insist on taking at least one empty kerosine oil tin, and it will really be very useful for boiling your bath water, and as a receptacle for water in general.

I have omitted any reference to wines or spirits as I regard them as an unnecessary luxury in the hills, but one bottle of good brandy should be taken in case of emergencies, and this should be kept under lock and key in the same box which contains the cash.

Tiffin-Basket and Waterbottles

A tiffin-basket is not a necessity, but it will prove a great convenience. A haversack will answer the purpose, but a small-sized basket (of the size usually sold for two persons) will add very materially to one's comfort when on the march or on the actual shooting-grounds. The tiffin coolie will easily carry such a basket on his back and will suffer no inconvenience. The two small provision-tins which invariably comprise a part of the fittings of a proper tiffin-basket are most useful receptacles for meat, biscuits, chappaties, bread, or even *dhal bat* (lentil and rice curry), while a tin of jam or potted meat can always be carried in the basket.

Before the war waterbottles were rather a problem. The ordinary Army enamelled iron waterbottle is excellent until the enamel begins to chip. Apart from the fact that chips of enamel are somewhat unpleasing to swallow, the iron which is exposed has an injurious effect on tea, lime-juice or alcohol, and as cold tea was my favourite drink this was a serious disadvantage. Glass bottles were excellent until they broke. I then tried vulcanite and thought that I had found the ideal bottle. This material was light and strong, and it had no effect on tea or lime-juice. But one day I poured the tea into my bottles when it was still hot instead of letting it cool first. The result was astonishing, for the effect of the heat was to warp the vulcanite, and the bottles so changed their shape that instead of holding a quart each they would scarcely hold a pint. I have mentioned these early experiences in order that they may put others on their guard.

But during the war various firms made most excellent metal waterbottles which were silver or nickel plated inside. This plating was absolutely durable and the bottles were both light and strong. I bought one early in 1915 from Messrs. Hill, Haymarket. It holds 2½ pints, and after ten years' constant use, first of all in France, and later on fishing in England, it is still as good as new. It is fitted with a bayonet-jointed stopper, but if I were going on a long expedition away from the amenities of civilisation I would take a few spare corks of the right size in case of accidents.

I would advise two such bottles being included in any Himalayan outfit.

Presents for Indians

It will be as well to take up a small collection of cheap trifles to give away as presents to the lumbardars of distant villages, shikaris, tiffin coolies, or any other Indians who make themselves especially helpful. Tommy's clasp knives are invariably highly prized, while I have found magnifying glasses gave great pleasure when the use of a burning glass had been explained. The Indians all thought it was an excellent plan to make fire with the help of the sun, and they always carry tinder on them. Cheap tobacco is always welcome.

Money

All the money which is taken on a trip must be in hard cash, and at least Rs.100 must be in small change, i.e., in four-anna and two-anna bits. Annas are not so useful and take up more room. Notes are quite useless. At first it is difficult to know how much money to take. A good plan is to make a very liberal estimate of every expense which you think you will possibly incur and then to double this amount!

All money should be kept locked up in a tin box.

Camp Furniture and General Kit

In addition to the enamelled iron basin to which I have already referred the only camp furniture which I consider necessary for the Himalayas is a folding bath, a stout waterproof sheet and a couple of folding candle lanterns. A bed is quite superfluous. It is always warmer to sleep on the ground, and the weight of even the lightest of camp beds is considerable. A tin suit case about 22 inches long is essential for the safe storing of money, brandy, maps, diary, note-paper, etc., and this will make an excellent table. Nothing can be more comfortable than the reindeer-skin sleeping-bag for sitting on, and there you are. No chairs, table, or anything else is required. Although the cost of the reindeer bag may seem very high in the first instance it will save this sum over and over again on account of its lightness and extreme portability, which enables one to dispense with other heavier articles that require two or more coolies to carry them.

Candles certainly do not give a very good light, but oil is a nuisance and has a knack of oozing everywhere. Personally I always tried to have my light out for the night by 7 or 8 p.m. and was invariably up by 3 a.m. This gave me just on eight hours sleep, which I found a very necessary amount when marching or climbing hard at high altitudes.

A good axe is most necessary.

A couple of canvas buckets will be found invaluable, for often one's camp may be situated some distance above water. I took a small *mussuck* with me on one trip and found it very useful, but I always feel rather dubious as to the cleanliness of the inside of a *mussuck*!

A methylated spirit stove which burns solid spirits (refills for a "Tommy's Cooker") should certainly be included in the outfit. It may never be required, but it takes up but little room, and might come in very handy on occasions. If one is not taken it will be wanted to a certainty.

It has been suggested by a good many sportsmen that "Primus" stoves would be peculiarly suitable for Himalayan work, particularly in districts in and beyond the Zaskar Range where fuel is so scarce. My own opinion is against them, partly because of my objection to oil when one is continually on the march, and partly because of the extra weight entailed by both oil and stove with all its accessories, such as methylated spirits. When shooting in the Plains of India I always took a "Primus" stove with me, but there the difficulty of transport is not so acute, nor is there the same danger of leakages caused by constant shipping and unshipping of loads. But if anyone has a very strong partiality for a "Primus" let him take one by all means, not forgetting that they do not give out the same heat at high altitudes as they will near sea level, and that they will not function at all above 20,000 feet. After all this latter point is more likely to affect mountaineering expeditions than sportsmen, as the latter will seldom find it necessary to camp over 17,000 feet. If a "Primus" stove does form part of the kit it should on no account be a "folding" model. These always leak, no matter how tight the nuts are screwed up.

Field-Glasses

A pair of good field-glasses are as important and essential a part of one's outfit as a rifle. The modern prismatic glasses are so infinitely superior to the old Galilean type that a comparison is superfluous. The usual power, or magnification, is one of six or eight diameters, and I do not think there is any material difference between the two. Personally, I have always used an eight-power Zeiss glass. It is slightly inferior in both luminosity and field of view to a similar six-power glass, but the difference is so trifling as to be negligible—at any rate in the clear atmosphere of the Himalayas. In mist, of course, all glasses are equally useless. A higher power than eight is a mistake. Quite apart from the loss in both field of view and luminosity one cannot hold such a powerful glass absolutely steady without a rest: the greater the magnification of a glass the more apparent becomes any unsteadiness in holding.

In choosing a glass the chief points to be considered are: (1) power, (2) luminosity, (3) field of view, and (4) weight.

As I have already said, there is little to choose between a six or an eight, but glasses vary much in the other three points. It may be taken as an axiom that, power for power, the luminosity varies with the size of the object glasses; and so large object glasses should be preferred provided the whole field-glass is not rendered too heavy or bulky.

The field of view can easily be tested. On the whole

I think that a field of view of six degrees is the minimum which should be allowed.

Weight is a very important factor and should not be forgotten. There are various excellent models of glasses now on the market which possess phenomenal optical qualities, and marvellous luminosity and field of view. But they are so bulky, and their weight is so excessive, that they must be debarred for practical purposes of sport. It should be remembered that a field-glass, to be of any real use, should be small enough to be carried comfortably in the pocket.

Some men prefer a monocular to a binocular, arguing that a glass of greatly superior optical qualities can thus be used without undue bulk. This argument is undoubtedly true, but personally I prefer the binocular type: they are much more restful to the eyes when in use for long periods of time on end, day after day.

If you happen to have a spare pair of glasses you will find them very useful for your shikari, although any local goatherd will probably be unable to use them with advantage. But he will be pleased by the occasional loan, chiefly because it will make him appear clever and important to his fellow-villagers. There are very few shikaris who can use a high-powered telescope.

There is one point which should not be forgotten when lending your glasses to Indians, and that is that ophthalmic diseases are very common in the Himalayas, and that such can be communicated by the eye-pieces of field-glasses or telescopes. Consequently, if any shikari or local villager has very bloodshot eyes, or in any way seems sore about the eyes, on no account let him touch your glasses. If such a man should use them before you can stop him, wash the eye-pieces well with a strong solution of permanganate of potash before using them again yourself.

Telescope

In the Himalayas a really good telescope is a necessity. I would never recommend one for use in the Plains of India, but the clear air of the Himalayas gives wonderful visibility, and high-powered glasses can be used with advantage. They are useless for spotting game, but will save endless time and bother by enabling one to judge heads when still at a considerable distance. I first used one which magnified 20 diameters, but this was not really sufficiently powerful, and then I took to a glass by Cook, which had a pancratic eye-piece giving magnifications of 25, 30, 40 and 50 diameters. This was ideal, and I usually used the 40-power, as the 50-power was just too powerful for perfect vision.

Aneroid Barometer

An aneroid barometer which enables one to read altitudes is a most interesting and delightful instrument to have when travelling or shooting in the Himalayas. It is a mistake to get too small a one, and the watch type are of little practical use. A barometer which has a diameter of about 3 inches is the smallest practical size. Such a glass can best be carried in a leather case with a shoulder-strap and can be given either to the shikari or tiffin coolie.

It should be remembered that a barometer really only indicates the actual atmospheric pressure, and that this is dependent on the weather as well as on the altitude. During a storm the barometer may easily show variations in altitude of over a 1,000 feet without ever being moved from the tent. Whenever opportunities occur the barometer should be checked and re-set by altitudes marked on the map. Provided there is no very marked change in the weather, a barometer will generally show with fair accuracy the *differences* in any altitudes which may be reached in a single day. During a march the barometer should be read carefully every evening and morning, and if there is no variation in the reading, the *relative* altitude of the camp may be taken as being correct in comparison with that of the previous camp. This will not, however, mean that the reading gives the *actual* altitude, unless the altitude of the previous camp had been fixed by some reading marked on the map. If a certain camping-ground is visited on different occasions the mean of the readings taken may be assumed to give a fairly accurate approximation to the true altitude.

Camera

I regard a good camera as indispensable as a good rifle. Few pleasures can be greater than turning over the pages of one's diary which are illustrated by one's own photographs; but the photographs must be good. I have no strong views on the actual type of camera chosen, but personally I prefer something which is not too bulky, and for this reason pin my faith to roll films, rather than plates, and a folding type of camera rather than a reflex. If the sportsman is an enthusiastic photographer before all else by all means let him take his reflex and plates, but he will find the difficulties of changing plates considerable, while the additional weight to his baggage will not be slight. I have tried all sizes of cameras from half-plate down to the vest-pocket size and have come to the conclusion that the 2¼ inch by 3¼ inch size is the best. It is not too small for contact prints, lantern slides may be made without any bother of reducing, and it will provide enlargements up to any size provided the lens is really first class. Lenses working at very large apertures are seldom necessary although they may prove very useful on occasions when a record of some camp is wanted late in the evening or for photographing an animal which has been killed far from camp when the sun has almost set. But on the whole I have found a stop of F 22 the most generally useful.

The usual focal length for a lens for a 2¼-inch by 3¼-inch camera is 4½ inches. I prefer one of 3½ inches focal length as this greatly eliminates the difficulty of judging distances of comparatively near objects. The shorter the focal length the nearer the point when everything is in focus. The disadvantage of such a short focal length lens is that it may fail to cover the plate or film with perfect definition when used at full aperture. But, as I have pointed out above, one seldom uses a full aperture, and any good 3½-inch lens will cover a plate of 3¼ inches by 2¼ inches when used at F 22. The same difficulty may be found when using the rising front, but it can be overcome in the same way, that is by stopping down. On the whole the advantages of the short focal length outweigh the disadvantages. It must be remembered, however, that distorted proportions will occur when photographing objects within a very few feet, and so this practice should be avoided. It is easy to take the photograph from 3 yards and enlarge, and a far better result will be obtained than if it had been taken from 3 feet.

The camera should be provided with a really strong case, and a tripod is useful. A telescopic tripod of aluminium weighs but a few ounces and can always be carried by the tiffin coolie as well as the camera.

I have found the Burroughs and Wellcome's *Photographic Exposure Meter and Record* a most interesting and lucid little brochure, not only on exposure in general, but also on the whole science of photography. I have followed the instructions given therein for many years in many different latitudes and altitudes and they have never let me down.

I make no mention of the question of photographing wild animals because, I am sorry to say, I have no experience. As a sport it must far outrival shooting. To be successful the equipment must be both heavy and expensive, and those who are likely to wish to use the camera in place of the rifle should seek advice from some firm which specialises in the manufacture of apparatus for the photography and cinematography of wild life.

Rifles

I have dealt with the important question of the best rifle for the Himalayas so fully elsewhere[1] that I have no intention of repeating myself here. It must, however, be remembered that the greatest difficulty which the sportsman has to overcome in the Himalayas is that of judging distance, and consequently a rifle with a flat trajectory is essential. There are now a good many modern rifles which have trajectories so flat that scarcely any allowance has to be made for any distance up to 300 yards, but some of these only attain this result by sacrificing bullet weight. The game of the Himalayas is tough and a good bullet is necessary if it is to be killed outright—the desire of every true sportsman. On this account I would not recommend the use of any bullet of less than 140 grains in weight, no matter what the velocity. I have had personal experience with the following rifles, all of which might be considered suitable for Himalayan game: ·400, ·375 Magnum, ·375, ·360, ·350 Magnum, ·350, ·303, ·280, ·275 and ·256. Of these the ·375 Magnum is, in my opinion, the best. It fires a bullet of 235 grains at a muzzle velocity of between 2,800 and 2,900 f.s. with the result that the trajectory is so flat that the bullet drop at 300 yards is only 9 inches, while up to 250 yards scarcely any change need be made in aim. The ·350 Magnum is very similar but the trajectory is not quite so flat. After these two I would select a ·280. There are now other rifles of

[1] *Notes on Sporting Rifles*, by Major Gerald Burrard. London: Edward Arnold, Ltd. Price 4*s*. 6*d*. net.

very similar ballistics to the ones I have mentioned which would doubtless prove equally satisfactory.

The question of double or single must be a matter of individual taste and purse, but personally I prefer a double.

For every hundred sportsmen who use a rifle I doubt whether more than one cleans his properly! I do not think this is in any way an exaggeration, and so trust that the following hints may not be altogether out of place. As soon as possible after firing pull the rifle through so as to remove any superfluous residue. On return to camp pour about half a pint of hot water through the barrel and dry out carefully with rags. Then scrub the bore well with B.S.A. "Cunirid" paste spread on a flannel patch wrapped round the jag of the cleaning rod. After this swab out with some thin oil such as B.S.A. "Kleenwell" oil or Young's ·303 oil, both of which are excellent. If the rifle is to be put away for any length of time a thicker oil should be used for preserving the bore and ordinary mineral jelly is hard to beat. I do not believe in B.S.A. "Safetipaste," especially in a damp atmosphere such as that of the Himalayas in the rains.

All oil should be removed from the barrel and chamber before firing and a little petrol or paraffin will greatly help this work, as both will dissolve oil, when the barrel can be wiped out dry almost immediately.

Preservation of Trophies

Most hillmen can skin an animal moderately well, but few can skin really well. This is an art which can only be learnt by long practice, and I would strongly advise all embryo hunters of big game to study Rowland Ward's *Sportsman's Manual*. It is a most informative little book, excellently illustrated, full of details, and costs but 4*s*. 6*d*. I will assume that the sportsman is in possession of this book and will add but a few hints.

When the skin of any animal has been removed, any blood which may be on the hair should be washed off and the hair dried as much as possible before pegging the skin out on the ground. This last operation should always be done in the shade whenever possible, but in the Zaskar and Ladak Ranges and beyond there is usually no shade. In these regions, therefore, the skin must be dried in the sun, and this can be accomplished without any danger, provided the utmost care is used. At least two coolies should be in constant and continual attendance on the skin until it is thoroughly dried; and they should be employed in rubbing wood ashes well into the skin with smooth stones. The constant fresh supply of wood ash will combine chemically with the fat which is drawn out by the sun. If the skin were merely sprinkled with wood ashes the fat would be drawn out by the heat of the sun too rapidly to be changed chemically and would decompose. Once any decomposition has set in, the hair on the other side is almost bound to slip.

Once a skin is thoroughly dry it may be rolled up with the hair inside, and tied round with a bit of cord, the legs being turned in so as not to make too awkward a bundle. A skin in this condition will keep for months provided it does not get damp, but before it is put away it is advisable to rub plenty of "Taxidermine" round the nose, ears, eyes and claws (in the case of bears or leopards) on *both sides* of the skin. The hair should be liberally sprinkled with insect powder.

Masks should be treated in exactly the same way. In skinning a mask, see that a very long neck is left: it is far easier to cut some of this off than to add any on, and a long neck is essential if a mounted head is to look its best.

All flesh, etc., which can possibly be removed from a skull with a knife should be scraped off, and then the skull should be boiled until the horns come off the cores. If too much flesh is left on the bone before the boiling process is begun the skull is liable to become discoloured. In the case of trophies in which the mask is mounted this discoloration is immaterial, but it detracts considerably from the appearance of a skull mounted on a shield. When the horns have been detached, they and the skull should be thoroughly dried in the sun, the jaws being tied on so as to avoid loss.

Every single step in the skinning and subsequent preservation of the trophies in the field requires constant and thorough personal supervision. If the work is left entirely to the shikari or some coolie there will be considerable risk of the trophy being spoiled.

Do not, I beg of you, send your heads to be set up with the masks on to some Indian in the bazaar. It is lamentable to see the number of fine trophies which are ruined every year in India in the setting up. If a head is worth setting up at all it is worth setting up properly, and deserves to be sent to a good taxidermist.

To my mind nothing looks more horrible or tragic than some of the caricatures of noble beasts which one sees in many Indian bungalows—the ghastly work of various bazaar *moochis*. It is far better to have a bare skull mounted on a good shield than some hideous and distorted mask.

CHAPTER XIX

PARTICULARS OF THE PRINCIPAL HIMALAYAN STATES

BARA BANGAHAL. The peculiar cauldron formed by the approach of the Dhauladhar Range towards the Pir Panjal Range at the source of the Ravi which has already been described in the section on Himalayan Geography. This little country is only approached by passes from Chamba, Chota Bangahal and Kulu. The game consists of ibex, red bear and musk deer. For permission to shoot apply to the Deputy Commissioner of Kangra.

Bashahr. Bounded on the north by the Sutlej and contains portions of the Dhauladhar, Great Himalayan and Zaskar Ranges. The Baspa is the principal river. Bashahr is most easily reached by means of the Hindustan–Tibet road from Simla, or by passes from the valleys of the Tons and Pabar, the Borendo being one of the best known. Yet another way is over the Nela Pass from the valley of the Bhagirathi in Tehri-Garhwal. Game includes burrhel (both Himalayan and Trans-Himalayan), thar, red and black bear, musk deer. For permission to shoot apply to the Deputy Commissioner, Simla Hill States.

Bhutan. An independent State to the east of Sikkim. The game probably consists of burrhel (Himalayan and

Trans-Himalayan), thar, black bear, gooral, takin, musk deer.

British Garhwal. Formed by the basins of the Alaknanda and its various tributaries, and reaches from the foothills to Tibet. Contains the holy shrines of Kedarnath and Badrinath to which there are good pilgrim roads. Game consists of burrhel (Himalayan and Trans-Himalayan), thar, gooral, musk deer, black bear. Permission to shoot can be obtained from the Commissioner of Garhwal. The country is best reached from Raniket or Naini Tal.

Chamba. A protected State, ruled by a Rajah, which is formed by the basin of the lower Ravi and that of the middle Chenab. It reaches from the Dhauladhar Range to the Great Himalayan Range. Game includes ibex (small), thar, red and black bear, musk deer, gooral. There are strict game laws. For permission apply to the Private Secretary to H.H. the Rajah. Chamba is reached by two long marches from Dalhousie.

Chitral. A small district near the North-West Frontier, including the valley of the Chitral River, which is a tributary of the Indus. As a rule the only individuals who are allowed to shoot in Chitral are the political officers and officers of the military garrison of Chitral. The game includes ibex, markhor, shapu, red bear (very rare), black bear.

Chota Bangahal. A very small State just to the south of Bara Bangahal. Best reached from Dharmsala. Game consists of thar, gooral and black bear. For permission to shoot apply to the Deputy Commissioner of Kangra.

A Snow Bridge in the Great Himalayan Range, 9,500 feet.

Dehra Dun. A considerable part of the Dehra Dun district lies in the Himalayas and is sandwiched between the River Tons and the Indian State of Tehri-Garhwal. The lower part of the Jumna flows through Dehra Dun territory. Game includes thar, gooral, black bear. This district is best reached from Mussoorie or Chakrata. For permission to shoot apply to the Collector of Dehra Dun.

Hunza Nagar. A wild State on the extreme northern frontier of India. It can only be reached through Kashmir and Gilgit, and permission to enter and shoot must be obtained from the Political Officer at Gilgit, or the Government of India. The game consists of ibex and markhor. As a rule this district is never entered except in travelling to the Pamirs.

Kangra. A little State in the foothills. The game consists of black bear, kakur and gooral. It is reached from Dharmsala or Kangra, which is situated on the way to Dharmsala. For permission to shoot apply to the Deputy Commissioner of Kangra.

Kashmir. The largest of Himalayan States, with the exception of the independent States of Nepal and Bhutan. Every species of game which inhabits the Himalayas is met with in Kashmir territory. It is divided into many smaller districts, the principal of which are: Punch, Jummu, Kishtwar, Suru, Zaskar, Ladak, Baltistan, Astor and the Gilgit Agency. There are strict game laws, and a permit to shoot and licence can be obtained from either the Secretary, the Game Preservation Department, or else through Cockburn's Agency, both in Srinagar. Kashmir is best reached from Murree. Before going, one of the many good handbooks which are published should be obtained. The sportsman is thoroughly well catered for, but a shoot in Kashmir will always cost considerably more than a similar shoot in other parts of the Himalayas.

Kulu. The basin of the Beas. The game includes ibex (small), thar, Himalayan burrhel, red and black bear, gooral, musk deer. Kulu is best reached from Dharmsala. For permission to shoot apply to the Assistant Commissioner of Kulu.

Kumaon. The basin of the Kali and its two main tributaries. Situated between British Garhwal and Nepal it stretches from the foothills to Tibet. The game includes *Ovis Ammon*, yak (both very occasionally), burrhel (Himalayan and Trans-Himalayan), thar, gooral, black bear. For permission to shoot apply to the Commissioner of Kumaon. The State is best reached from Almora.

Kunawar. Bounded on the south by the Sutlej and the north by Spiti. This district is best reached by the Hindustan–Tibet road from Simla. The game includes ibex, burrhel (Himalayan and Trans-Himalayan), thar, red and black bear. For permission to shoot apply to the Deputy Commissioner, Simla Hill States.

Lahoul. The basin of the Chandra and Bhaga Rivers which form the Chenab. The game consists of ibex and red bear. The country is reached either up the valley of the Chenab through Chamba, or by passes from Kulu. For permission to shoot apply to the Deputy Commissioner of Kangra.

Mandi. A small State in the foothills near Dharm-

MAP SHOWING HIMALAYAN STATES

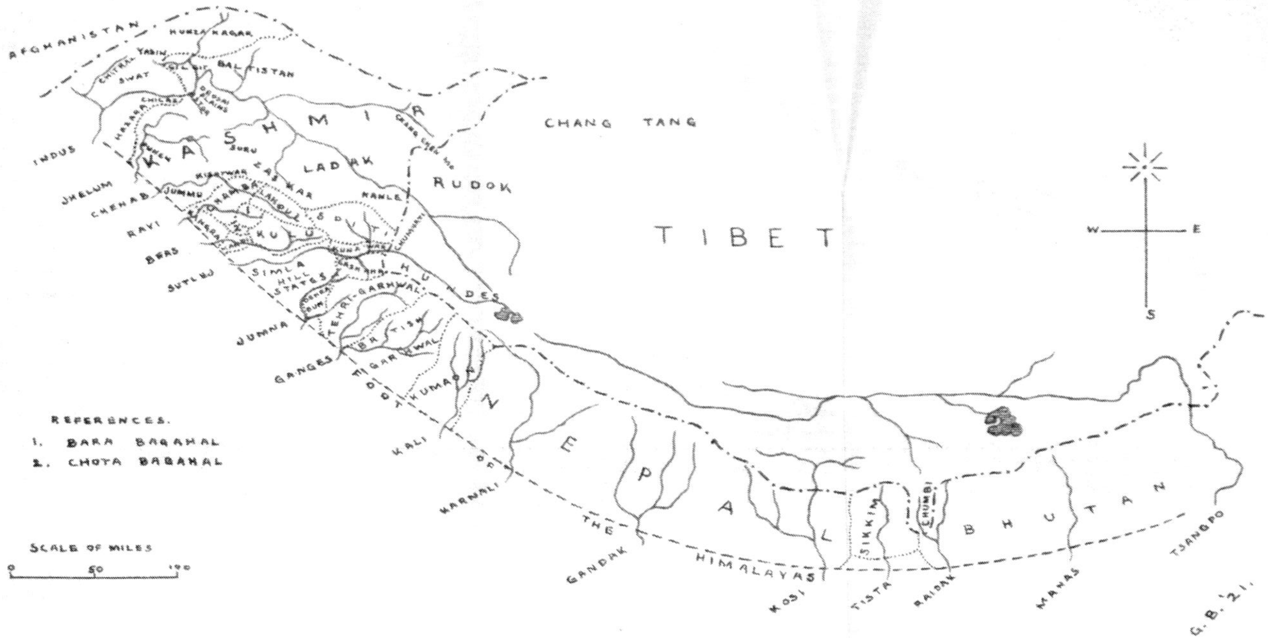

sala. It holds black bear, gooral and kakur. Permission to shoot is obtained from the Deputy Commissioner of Kangra.

Nepal. Independent and the largest of all the Himalayan States. It forms the basins of the Karnali, Gandak and Kosi Rivers together with all their tributaries; is bounded by Kumaon on the west and Sikkim on the east, while it stretches from the Plains of India to Tibet. The game consists of burrhel (Himalayan and Trans-Himalayan), thar, gooral, black bear. No Europeans are allowed into Nepal without special permission from the King.

Sikkim. The basin of the Tista. It is reached through Darjeeling, but permission to shoot must be obtained from the Political Officer at Gangtok. The game includes *Ovis Ammon* and Tibetan gazelle (both animals sometimes enter Sikkim territory), burrhel (Himalayan and Trans-Himalayan), thar, gooral, black bear.

Simla Hill States. The various States which lie in the valley of the Sutlej, but this district also includes the country down to the River Tons. The game includes thar, gooral, red and black bear. Permission to shoot must be obtained from the Deputy Commissioner, Simla Hill States. The country can be best reached from Simla, but some of it can be shot over equally well from Chakrata.

Spiti. The basin of the Spiti River. Game consists of ibex and Trans-Himalayan burrhel, and very occasionally *Ovis Ammon.* Spiti is best reached by the Hindustan–Tibet road from Simla, and then over the Babeh Pass to the north of Wangtu Bridge, but a good alternative way is through Kulu. For permission to shoot apply to the Assistant Commissioner of Kulu.

Tehri-Garhwal. The basin of the Bhagirathi and its tributaries and the upper part of the Jumna. This State holds the holy shrines of Jumnotri and Gangotri, to which places there are good pilgrim roads. The game includes burrhel (Himalayan and Trans-Himalayan), thar, gooral, red and black bear. It is best reached from Mussoorie. For permission to shoot apply to the Private Secretary to H.H. the Maharajah of Tehri-Garhwal, for it is a protected Indian State.

NOTE.—Those animals which are encountered more often by chance than design, such as leopard, serow, sambhur and tiger, have not been mentioned in the foregoing lists of game, but they are to be found in any State which contains a part of those mountain systems which form their habitat.

INDEX